Handbook of
Reporting Methods

Maxwell McCombs
Syracuse University

Donald Lewis Shaw
University of North Carolina

David Grey
San Jose State University

Houghton Mifflin Company

Boston   Atlanta   Dallas

Geneva, Illinois

Hopewell, New Jersey

Palo Alto   London

Cover photograph Tim Eagan/Woodfin Camp & Assoc.

Photographs
Chapters 1, 2, 3: Elizabeth Hamlin, Stock/Boston
Chapters 4, 5, 6, 7, 8, 9, 10 and title page: Rocky Weldon/DeWys, Inc.
Chapters 11, 12, 13: © Jan Lucas/Rapho/ Photo Researchers, Inc.

Printed in the U.S.A.

Library of Congress Number: 75-31009

ISBN: 0-395-18958-6

Contributors

Steven Chaffee
University of Wisconsin

Richard Cole
University of North Carolina

David Grey
San Jose State University

Peter Johansen
Carleton University

Maxwell McCombs
Syracuse University

Donald Lewis Shaw
University of North Carolina

Keith R. Stamm
University of Washington

James W. Tankard, Jr.
University of Texas

G. Cleveland Wilhoit
Indiana University

Contents

Preface

There is a common assumption in journalism that good writing is the equivalent of good reporting. That is a misunderstanding. Even Bob Woodward, whose superb reporting along with that of Carl Bernstein caused the Watergate episode eventually to preoccupy many front pages and news programs, has joked that around the *Washington Post* newsroom English was not regarded as his "native language."

But digging in—reporting—was scarcely foreign to him or to Bernstein. A journalist is both writer *and* reporter and, as Bernstein has shown us, if one characteristic has to dominate, let it be the reporter. This distinction is not arbitrary. It is essential to both broadcast and print journalism.

Most people become journalists because they have a flair for writing or a desire to pursue a writing-oriented career. While writing certainly is important, sound reporting remains the greatest challenge and is becoming even more difficult as our communities become increasingly complex. Often, the title appearing under a by-line is "staff writer" rather than "reporter."

We live in an age in which politicians regularly employ polling to determine what issues people favor and what kinds of people favor them. Computers turn out results for Democrats and Republicans alike, and politicians rely heavily on all sorts of experts to tell them the districts in which they should concentrate their campaigning and the issues they should stress. Political advisers have always done this, of course, but the situation is different now. Somehow *horse sense* has been elevated to a *science*. Will Rogers would have been astonished! Whether right or wrong, the world regularly reported by the print and broadcast media is peopled by experts.

The ability of the old journalistic standby, the interview, is being pressed to the limit to explain trends in our communities. We must remember that even the skillful interviewing of Woodward and Bernstein, which resulted in a Pulitzer Prize, did not answer the many *whys* raised by a Watergate or how such a thing could have happened.

More and more journalists are realizing the common ground they share with behavioral scientists. Both groups seek accurate descriptions and explanations of people's behavior in the local community. Some journalists are beginning to explore and use the techniques of behavioral science to report about their communities in depth, especially to explore the *whys*. The techniques of the behavioral scientist—field surveys, experiments, and content analysis—are becoming as much a part of the better journalist's skills as the art of interviewing.

Such publications as *Psychology Today* attest to the success of solid, up-to-date writing about science, while journalists are beginning to absorb some of the systematic approaches of such behavioral science disciplines as sociology and psychology. Schools and departments of journalism have always stressed the importance of traditional reporting as well as news writing. But more recently, many of these schools and departments have established reporting courses that rely heavily on the observational methods of behavioral science in order to equip journalists with a wider range of reportorial skills.

This book is designed for these schools and journalists as a map of the common ground of behavioral science and journalism. While the journalist is usually more constrained by limited time and by the need to explain *particular* events, both the journalist and the behavioral scientist have one overriding professional need if they are to do their jobs well. They must be acute observers and reporters.

However, if journalism is considered in terms of mass communication, then good reporting is the necessary prerequisite to good writing. If the goal of journalism is to communicate the daily happenings and situations to a general audience, then developing skill in reporting that yields solid information must precede skill in writing style. One can write beautifully with little substantive content, but for the journalist, content that relates to the needs and desires of the audience is absolutely necessary. The novelist can create content simultaneously with the very act of writing; the journalist cannot. Observation of the real world must precede the writing. In short, the journalist is, above all other professional writers, a professional observer. *Reporting is observation.* This book is about systematic techniques of observation.

Journalists have seldom been very self-conscious or systematic about their role as observers. Criticism of techniques of observation and assessment of their strong points and their weak points has remained largely implicit in our professional dialogues. In contrast, behavioral scientists have been quite explicit about their techniques of observation and the variety of techniques used to glean information about the individuals and communities around us. Behavioral science methodology has a contribution to make to the reporter, and journalists must be more self-conscious about their sources (methods of obtaining information).

The purpose of this book is to spell out the contribution that behavioral science methodology—techniques of observation—can make to journalism. This is far from an exhaustive treatment of behavioral science methodology. Each chapter examines an area of methodology with an extensive literature and accumulation of knowledge that two, or even three, college courses would not begin to exhaust. Nor is this a "cookbook" outlining the essentials of an observation technique in a manner that should be blindly followed by the faithful. It is an introduction to behavioral science methodology for both prospective and professional journalists, a translation of reporting goals and tasks into the framework of behavioral science methodology.

Our central premise is that this translation will enhance the quality of news reporting in two ways. First, behavioral science methodology makes possible a whole realm of description that is simply not feasible using the traditional interview or paper-and-pencil techniques of reporting. Particularly, it is now possible to report about people as well as leaders and about situations as well as events. As a part of mass communication, journalism has traditionally described the elite few for the many. The spirit of our times demands—and behavioral science methods makes possible—a journalism that also explains the people to themselves and to their leaders.

Second, news reporting is also enhanced by behavioral science methods that lead the reporter beyond description to explanation. Even the best reporting, based on traditional techniques, can fall short in answering the *why*. For behavioral science, explanation is essential. Description is often of interest only as the first step toward explanation. While reporters may continue to concentrate on description most of the time, behavioral science methods open the way to explanation for those occasions that demand it.

In the long range, this book seeks to widen the goals and priorities of journalists by introducing techniques of reporting and modes of thought leading to the kind of systematic investigation that will improve the quality of journalism. Our immediate task is to demonstrate to students, editors, and reporters some of the ways that behavioral science can enhance the quality of news reporting and to outline the methodological roads the enterprising, creative journalist can explore.

These are not isolated, scattered techniques of observation for the journalist to use as occasional options. The various methodologies discussed here form an integrated set of techniques for exploring the local community. Therefore, readers will find some deliberate redundancy among the various chapters of the book. This repetition is especially intended to emphasize the multioperational nature of good reporting. Good reporters don't rely on a single source or mode of observation. They triangulate on the topic under investigation, using a variety of observation techniques.

Like many books, this one is a team effort, and as the title page and table of contents indicate, it is a large team. But it is even larger than the nine names listed there. Working steadily behind the scenes of Syracuse University were other key individuals: Ruby Leah Agnir, who typed and corrected numerous drafts of each chapter; John Mitchell, who provided an invaluable page-by-page critique of an earlier draft; Cathy Covert and Richard Turner, who also provided key critiques; and research assistants Jackie Powell, Wayne Towers, Gerald Stone, and Richard Lindeborg, who read and reread numerous drafts and performed the myriad tasks necessary to prepare a manuscript. Prior to publication this manuscript was also previewed by three colleagues at other universities: Robert Murphy, University of Kentucky; Paul Peterson, Ohio State University; and Guido Stempel, Ohio University. The editors express their deep appreciation to each of these individuals and to the S. I. Newhouse School of Public Communications for its extensive support of this contribution to the field of journalism.

Maxwell McCombs
Donald Shaw
David Grey

Handbook of
Reporting Methods

Part 1

Strategies for Reporting

Chapter 1

All the News . . .

Maxwell McCombs

To the naive observer the world can be a "buzzing, blooming confusion." Although psychologist William James originally applied that description to infants who had not learned to organize their perceptions, the description is not limited to infants. The sociologist who sets out to study everything about a particular community or the journalist who sets out to report everything about a particular community would be in the same predicament if their professional traditions had not taught them to ignore vast amounts of information and to organize the remainder in rather specific ways.

A key bit of jargon explains why journalists do not have a sense of a buzzing, blooming confusion as they face the complexity of the local community. *News events.* That's what the journalist is after. A long tradition of journalism says that the reporter should focus on discrete events, happenings with a distinct location in time and space. Continuous, on-going situations generally fall outside the journalistic jurisdiction defined by news events. Furthermore, definition of this jurisdiction is further sharpened by the adjective "news." Not all events qualify. They must be newsworthy—that is, timely, proximate, prominent, or dramatic, to name a few of the traditional criteria.

So journalists do not attempt to report everything going on in the community. They seek out the news events. This *event orientation* of the press has dominated the style of reporting for generations. Journalists report on city council meetings or county commissioners meetings because they are deemed newsworthy. But here we encounter some problems with this purely event orientation; it assumes that readers are interested in these events, *as events*. Actually, one can argue strongly that the two events just mentioned, meetings of government bodies, are not really interesting per se to most people in the news audience. What the readers or viewers are really interested in are the implications of what takes place in these meetings. But strict, narrow interpretation of the event orientation frequently leaves these implications unstated. What is most often reported is simply the event itself. For instance, the city council passed a resolution and approved an expenditure—but the real meaning of the council meeting for the community audience is left unsaid.

This orientation of the press has also given rise to the *pseudo-event,* the contrived or staged happening produced by the campaign managers or public relations committees to gain attention for their clients in the mass media.[1] Because the media respond primarily to events, such happenings—press conferences, staged public appearances, rallies, marathons, and so on—are almost always covered by the news media.

When a local hamburger-king-turned-politician called a press conference in Charlotte, North Carolina, in early 1972, every major news medium in the state attended because each guessed that the hamburger king was going to announce a second try at the Republican nomination for governor. He had been the party's nominee during the previous election. Such an event—an announcement of candidacy—would be a news event. Actually, the hamburger king made a few bland pronouncements amounting to personal publicity and nothing more. But, because the press had ballyhooed this pseudo-event in advance stories, a follow-up story was necessary, and the king got his free publicity.

The pseudo-event is the logical, albeit sometimes absurd, outcome of the intensive event orientation of the press. Certainly, this orientation simplifies the task of the journalist. Neat, well-defined boundaries are drawn around each set of observations. "Events" have clear beginnings and endings. But there is a real

---

[1] Daniel Boorstin, *The Image,* Harper & Row, New York, 1961.

question of whether all these bits and pieces, no matter how skillfully and faithfully handled, ever come together to form the full mosaic of our contemporary history. "History is made up both of the accretion of small happenings that add up to a transformation as well as of major events that produce crashing discontinuities with the past." [2]

The press is quite adept at handling major misfortunes such as assassinations of political leaders, outbreaks of war, and economic catastrophes. The press can respond rapidly to such events, more rapidly than most public or quasi-public institutions. Political scientist Bernard Cohen reports that in times of international crisis the White House and State Department follow the news wires of AP and UPI closely, not the cables and reports of their own agents, because the press is usually more up to the minute.[3] But when it comes to reporting the broad secular sweep of history, the major trends and thrusts of the times, then the press often lags significantly behind other public institutions. It is not in the press that one often enough learns of deeply embedded social problems, significant social realignments, and proposed solutions to the problems of the day.

For example, journalist Norma Jean Langford searched one local newspaper for reports on creative ideas for solving community problems.[4] She defined "idea" stories as those that concerned plans and proposals for the future, alternative solutions to problems, suggested goals, or novel adaptations to new situations. Her content analysis located 463 news stories about seven types of local problems during a one-month period. But the average proportion of space devoted to "idea" stories in each category was only 6.2 percent. The highest proportion was 15.9 percent of the space devoted to legal and criminal problems and the lowest, 0.9 percent of the column inches, described welfare, poverty, and civil rights problems. Are the news media performing their leadership role fully?

---

[2] Leo Bogart, *Silent Politics: Polls and the Awareness of Public Opinion*, Wiley-Interscience, New York, 1972, p. 83.

[3] Bernard Cohen, *Press and Foreign Policy*, Princeton University Press, Princeton, 1963, chap. 7.

[4] Norma Jean Langford, "Creative Thinking in Newspapers," *Journalism Quarterly* 46 (1969): 814–817.

Things seem to have changed little from the time Walter Lipp-mann observed, "As social truth is organized today, the press is not constituted to furnish from one edition to the next the amount of knowledge which the democratic theory of public opinion de-mands . . . ." [5] When Lippmann made this evaluation fifty years ago, news reporting was almost entirely event oriented, and be-havioral science research methods were rather primitive. Today, behavioral science research methods offer some powerful tools for observing the local community in depth [6] and, as we shall see, en-terprising reporters are beginning to take advantage of them.

Iceberg Theory

The traditional focus of the press on social conditions might be called the *iceberg theory*. Just as radar scans sea lanes for the tips of icebergs portending danger, the news media daily scan the local community and the nation for signs of imminent disruption and danger. That, of course, is part of the job of the press, but the unaided human observer unfortu-nately can describe only the tip of the iceberg. The major portion of this polar phenomenon remains invisible and undescribed be-neath the surface.

The analogue holds. Public affairs reporting, with its emphasis on discrete news events, typically describes only the tips of our social icebergs, and usually only when they are close to being major disruptive forces in our communities. This function alone is a valuable community service and justifies journalism as a useful profession. But the capability is available for the profession to render much more valuable service. The appearance of social ice-bergs can often be anticipated, and more than their tips can be de-scribed. For communities as well as for ships, what lies beneath the surface is far more important than the clearly visible tip of the problem. Gradually, the press has become aware of the fallacies of iceberg-theory reporting.[7]

---

[5] Walter Lippmann, *Public Opinion,* Macmillan, New York, 1922, p. 361.
[6] Philip Meyer, *Precision Journalism,* Indiana University Press, Bloomington, 1973.
[7] See, for example, Lester Markel, *What You Don't Know Can Hurt You,* Public Affairs Press, Washington, 1972, especially chap. 17.

A major criticism is that the iceberg theory leads to incomplete, invalid reporting even though the traditional journalistic ethic of objectivity is usually adhered to. A classic example was the press coverage of Senator Joseph McCarthy in the 1950s. When McCarthy announced during a speech at Wheeling, West Virginia, that he had in his pocket a list of 200 known Communists in the State Department, the press faithfully reported that assertion—with, we might add, very careful attribution. Even though no one ever saw the list, and the number of names allegedly on it changed from time to time, the press continued to parrot what McCarthy said. The news reports were objective in that they faithfully reflected the essence of McCarthy's public behavior. But these reports were quite incomplete in their assessment of the Communist situation in the federal government. Here, a narrow view of objectivity and a narrow event orientation made the press an unwitting accomplice to one of the most sordid periods in American history.[8]

Let us examine more recent examples. When Watts, Detroit, Newark, and other cities exploded into flames and riots during the 1960s, the press responded to these major events in a more responsible way than it had fifteen years earlier to Senator McCarthy. Statements made at the time of riots were not always accepted at face value. Some hard, analytical digging into the causes of these riots was done by many members of the press. For example, the *Detroit Free Press* conducted an extensive scientific survey among blacks in the riot area to identify the grievances and other reasons that led to participation in the riot.[9] The reporting of these events was far more systematic than the reporting on McCarthy, but it was still constrained by the event orientation. Until half a dozen cities exploded and created major events, there was nothing in the press to indicate the gravity of the social and racial situation in metropolitan areas. In this larger sense, the press was still unsystematic in its reporting of the local community.

This criticism of press performance can be juxtaposed with another one of more recent vintage: The press reports only "bad"

---

[8] For additional discussion on the press and the McCarthy era see Elmer Davis, *But We Were Born Free*, Bobbs-Merrill, Indianapolis, 1952.

[9] "The People Beyond 12th Street: A survey of attitudes of Detroit Negroes after the riot of 1967," *Detroit Free Press*, 1967.

news. Why don't we hear some good news instead of just all the news about what's wrong? As the press becomes more systematic in its reporting about the local community and social conditions, this criticism of excess attention to the aberrant should disappear. When we begin systematically to assess our communities and their situations, we typically are going to obtain a mixture of the good and bad, of bright areas and problem areas. There will be just as many optimistic reports as pessimistic reports when we begin to look more systematically about us. But this approach will mean shifting away from a strict event orientation toward more concern with *trends* and *overviews*. From the audience's perspective it will mean receiving more than simple factual descriptions. It will mean receiving the facts—what the city council did, what the mayor's report said—in a larger community context so that the facts become information that readers and viewers can really use. Reporters communicate a lot of facts. How much information do they communicate? Accurate descriptions do not automatically yield understandable explanations.

Reporting Social Mosaics

In one area of public affairs reporting the press already has moved away from a narrow event orientation. Probably the best examples of systematic reporting of social trends occur in the area of economics. This may be because of the vividness of the Great Depression of the 1930s that persists in the minds of a generation of news executives who grew up during that time. The depression produced scores of events that could be reported—plants shut down, banks failed, the federal government spawned dozens of new agencies and programs. Each of these events was important and could be reported. But only by taking the larger picture, by examining the larger mosaic of which these events were parts, could one fully understand what all this meant. So, in the area of economics the press has become more systematic in its reporting. It takes the larger view and it does report the good and the bad.

A handful of economic indicators are routine grist for news. There are monthly reports on the percentage of the unemployed in the labor force, changes in the wholesale price index, and changes in the consumer price index. In human terms, these indicators reveal how many people are receiving a regular paycheck and how much less that paycheck will buy because of inflation. The overall economic situation in the United States is further reflected by quarterly and annual reports on the Gross National Product, the total value of all goods and services produced in the country. Yet even in handling these systematic national aggregate indicators of the economic situation, the press often continues to reflect its basic event orientation to news. There is a tendency to regard the indicator per se—that is, the actual document and the comments made by government officials at the time of its release—as the news rather than the broader meaning of the economic indicator.

We can illustrate this in several ways. The first example comes from the Nixon Administration. Most economic indicators are presented to the press by middle-level federal executives, career men who have some degree of expertise in the particular economic area involved. These men are concerned primarily with the technical subject under consideration, and so their remarks tend to be apolitical. They do not extract the maximum political mileage from the indicators or use them as propaganda devices for furthering the goals and glory of the incumbent administration. So the Nixon people decided to change the spokesmen at these meetings and install more "politically responsive" men.

The press was outraged that politics was being inserted into what it regarded as a technical data area. In one sense, the outrage was justified. But if the press was not so dependent on the comments of federal officials to give the economic facts some meaning, if it did not limit itself to reporting an event created by the issuance of a federal report by some government actors, then it need not be outraged at having the content of its stories almost totally at the whim of a political appointee. If the press had some expertise of its own, or even sought some out among non-government economists, then it would matter little who the federal spokesman was, so long as the economic figures themselves remained technically pure and untampered with.[10]

---

[10] Every reporter who uses any economic statistics should carefully examine Oskar Morgenstern, *On the Accuracy of Economic Observations,* Princeton University Press, Princeton, 1963. He discusses both the general nature of economic data and seven specific types of economic data often reported in the press.

Statistics—A Waiting Bulldog

Douglas Southall Freeman, for many years editor of the *Richmond News Leader,* once was asked about the training of prospective reporters. What would he have them study?

Dr. Freeman might have responded by ticking off a familiar list—history, literature, languages, law. His oversimplified answer, instead, was: statistics. He looked upon any given set of statistics with a combination of respect and suspicion, as one regards a waiting. bulldog. The years had taught him that statistics can be handled obediently if one deals with them firmly; but the fellow who tries to get too friendly with statistics is likely to lose the seat of his pants.

These recollections are prompted in part by the publication a few weeks ago of four essays by Geoffrey H. Moore, former director of the Bureau of Labor Statistics. . . . Let me come back to these in a moment.

The whole business of statistics, especially federal statistics, has been much on our minds in recent months.

Until a few years ago—let us face it, until the Nixon administration came into office—federal statistics were accepted, if not uncritically, at least confidently. Professionals generally regarded the data from U.S. agencies as the best such data in the world. . . .

An uneasy feeling has developed that federal statistics, especially in the economic area, demand closer scrutiny these days than they have in the past. . . .

We of the press—because most of us are not trained in statistics—have a special need for expert, non-partisan interpretation of the statistics that swamp us every day. Dr. Moore provides an example of such interpretation in his recent essays on unemployment data.

The second example is typical reporting on the Gross National Product. The quarterly and annual reports on GNP are traditionally reported like box scores from a track meet. By how much was the old record exceeded? And when Nikita Khrushchev predicted that the U.S.S.R. would bury the U.S. economically, the track meet took on a deadly serious tone. Each quarter the rate of growth in GNP was intensely noted and compared with the Russian growth rate. In part, this kind of reporting is an extension of the progress ethic, which holds out as the national goal "progress," defined almost exclusively in terms of sheer growth. Numerous social commentators have noted the American fascination

Except for the cost of living index, no federal figures command greater attention than statistics that deal with unemployment. They are constantly cited to prove how poorly Nixon is doing; they carry great weight in legislation affecting blacks, teenagers, and women.

Yet as Dr. Moore makes clear, some of the figures, notably those on black unemployment, have to be treated as cautiously as bulldogs. The problem of jobless blacks is undeniably serious, but because of the margin of error in a small statistical sample, month-by-month fluctuations may be much less significant than they seem.

Dr. Moore suggests a new and more revealing index on unemployment that would reflect (a) the number of jobless persons and (b) how long they had been out of work.

On this "severity index," the record of the Nixon administration looks not so bad. The rate of unemployment is relatively high, but people seem to find new jobs. The Johnson Administration had a still better record, to be sure, but in grappling with the stubborn and intractable problems of unemployment, Nixon merits more credit than his foes have been willing to give him.

One often hears that there are "lies, damned lies, and statistics." It is a foolish saying. Every advocate, of course, will try to turn statistics to his own best advantage, but if raw figures are reliable, and if they are honestly interpreted by non-partisan professionals, the public is not quite so likely to be deceived.

It is something for this administration to keep constantly in mind.

SOURCE: Columnist James J. Kilpatrick, *Washington Star Syndicate*, September 2, 1973.

with growth and bigness per se. The stereotype of the Texan is really a caricature of most Americans. So economic progress has come to mean an annual growth rate of about 8 percent in GNP. Each quarter the press reports the latest box scores in the international and national race.

Social Indicators

But more does not necessarily mean better. With increasing concern in recent years about the quality of our environment, this fact is becoming very clear. A fifty-percent increase in automobile production would skyrocket the Gross National Product and rate of economic growth. But the

U.S. Happiness Scale

Washington—The United States has a Gross National Product to measure its output.

There's a consumer price index to watch the cost of living.

Do we need a national happiness scale to check on our general well-being, to gauge the good life, to take the pleasure pulse of the nation? . . .

The idea of determining a "net national welfare" is not new. The Lyndon B. Johnson Administration toyed with it. An international panel in Paris has been over the groundwork. And the Japanese are after something like it.

But can such a scale be established? Should it be? And is the new OMB [Office of Management and Budget] publication, *Social Indicators 1973*, a start? . . .

There were problems about what areas will be covered by such a report. OMB chose eight: Population, health, public safety, education, employment, income, housing, and leisure and recreation.

What about energy and environment, clearly two urgent fields of social concern?

OMB project director Daniel B. Tunstall said the number of subjects to be covered had shifted throughout the five years the book was in preparation. There had been as few as five, as many as fifteen at different times.

On the lack of environmental data, Tunstall said the federal Council on Environmental Quality (CEQ) felt so shaky about its own figures, there was no use including them in OMB's report.

---

effects on air pollution and traffic congestion would be close to disastrous.

Unfortunately, most of our systematic reporting about social conditions emphasizes quantity rather than quality.

> We find that the major indicators deal not with how good but how much, not with the quality of our lives but rather with the quantity of goods and dollars. This continuation of "economic Philistinism" is exacerbated by the increasing emphasis upon "cost-benefit" analysis . . . , operating on the premise that any meaningful benefits from government programs can be expressed in dollars and cents.[11]

---

[11] Raymond A. Bauer, ed., *Social Indicators*, M.I.T. Press, Cambridge, Mass.; 1966, p. xiii.

But, a questioner asked, why reject CEQ data, then base the public safety section almost entirely on FBI crime reports which have been attacked as unreliable?

It was just a question of judgment, Tunstall said, admitting that "the book can be faulted to some extent. . . ."

The project director for the 1969 book, Manour Olsen, Jr., will be on the panel to review the new publication. When he worked on the previous book, Olsen was a deputy secretary of Health, Education and Welfare. He is now an economics professor at the University of Maryland.

Olsen finds the OMB book "useful, a more than negligible step along a path that is going to be increasingly traveled."

But he readily concedes the problems in establishing a national happiness index, or whatever such a scale might be called.

Economic indicators are based on the dollar, Olsen—and almost everyone else interviewed, including the OMB specialists—pointed out.

There is no such common currency in social values. A value scale developed by one person "is acceptable to only those who share your social views," Olsen says.

Those views change from one individual to another and would certainly vary from one presidential administration to another—and those differences would bear directly on a government-established national welfare scale.

But, Olsen says, "I think we at least need to think in some overall conception of well-being. . . ."

SOURCE: *Houston Chronicle*, February 17, 1974.

We need not only a measure of the Gross National Product but also a measure of the Gross National Good, an indicator of the quality of life. And, in fact, this idea is already taking hold. In addition to the usual economic statistics on conditions in the nation, the Japanese government recently undertook a measure of the Gross National Good. This is the real frontier in social reporting that journalists should be actively exploring.[12]

People in the federal government, the universities, and some

---

[12] For an attempt at measuring that other GNP, "Gross National Psychology," see William Watts and Lloyd Free, eds., *State of the Nation*, Universe Books, New York, 1973. Also see Gene Gregory, "Measuring Japan's Happiness," *Western Economic Journal* 6 (1971): 31–32.

major newspapers and television stations have already begun this exploration. The general strategy guiding these explorations of the quality of life in our communities is called *social indicators*. Social indicators are "statistics, statistical series, and all other forms of evidence that enable us to assess where we stand and are going with respect to our values and goals, and to evaluate specific programs and determine their impact." [13] Social indicators can yield a comprehensive, systematic view of the community and the conditions in it. Such news sources yield not just the abnormal and the aberrant. From social indicators a total picture can be obtained, including both the normal and the abnormal, the bad news and the good news.

At the present time, the social indicators approach to community reporting means using statistics in a systematic fashion. But social indicators are not limited to statistics. All kinds of indicators are being devised. Social scientists at the University of California at Berkeley, at the University of Michigan, and elsewhere, are devising new measures of community life from existing statistics and from new techniques of observation. Creative journalists will also derive numerous additional social indicators. But those most easily tapped immediately are the reams of statistics that abound in the offices of government agencies.

As President Kennedy remarked in a state of the economy address to the Congress:

> I know that statistics and details of the economy may sometimes seem dry, but the economy and economic statistics are really a story of all of us as a country. And these statistics tell whether we are going forward or standing still or going backwards; they tell whether an unemployed man can get a job, or whether a man who has a job can get an increase in salary or own a home, or whether he can retire in security or send his children to college. These are the people and the things behind statistics.[14]

Used in the way President Kennedy suggested, statistics become more than dull digits. The job of the journalist is to link these statistics and other systematic information about social conditions to the people and the life of the community. The journalist's job is to convert facts into useful information that readers can relate to their daily needs and desires.

---

[13] Bauer, *Social Indicators*, p. 1.
[14] Quoted in Bauer, *Social Indicators*, p. 90.

Probing a Decade

Ten years ago Birmingham was living through a series of events that would stamp themselves indelibly on the city's memory.

Firehoses, snarling dogs, demonstrators, bombings, and a tense populace were the marks of that era.

The subject, of course, was civil rights.

Now, ten years later, a team of *Birmingham News* reporters has taken an inquisitive look at the ten years between 1963 and today. They've researched statistics, talked to people who found themselves on each side of the conflict, and pulled together the story of Birmingham's movement over the last decade.

Writers Ralph Wright and Ingrid Kindred went on a search for the personalities of 1963. In trying to pinpoint where they are now, and what they have done over the last decade, the search sometimes ranged far from Alabama. Carol Nunnelley used her experience as an urban affairs reporter to probe economic progress among the races in Birmingham. Education reporter Garland Reeves wandered over the rocky terrain of school desegregation.

Peggy Robertson's probing of progress in law enforcement and politics brought her into contact with many of the leaders of 1963 on both sides. The series was edited by Wallace Henely.

SOURCE: *Birmingham News/Dimension,* June 25, 1973.

A few newspapers have taken on this task and have begun to apply a social indicators strategy to the reporting on their community. The *Louisville Courier-Journal & Times* took a comprehensive look at its city, examining housing, employment, education, health, technological innovation, race relations, and political participation. Their series told the complete story, both the bad news and the good news.

Two characteristics of the "Lessons for Louisville" series should be emphasized. The assessments were *systematic,* and they focused on the *quality of life* in the city. The good reporter is thorough and systematic. He collects all the evidence, and he collects it in depth.

The Louisville series was able to report not just where Louis-

Schools Ten Years Later

Now, in 1973, West End High School looks not much different from the way it did ten years ago. It stands stately on Pearson Avenue on a tree-shaded campus. Cool breezes rustle leaves, and only an occasional squealing tire tears the silence. Inside, the chatter of students and the clatter of lockers being opened and slammed shut echo down the dim, wide, long halls.

But West End is different—perhaps in ways that are indicative of what has happened to the Birmingham school system during the past decade.

One of the first to undergo change, the school is now about 65 percent black. In 1963, two black students were enough to send 1,000 students raging through the streets. Now, the white students shrug, accept the situation matter-of-factly and say the important thing is that black and white students mostly get along.

"I don't guess it makes much difference as far as I can tell," said sixteen-year-old Stephanie Latham, a tall, slim majorette. "After quite a few years in grammar school I guess you get used to it." Stephanie is white. Sitting next to her in the girls' advisor's office—where they act as aides—was an attractive black girl. Her name was Patricia Dees. "We get along nicely," said Pat. "In fact I like some of them better than some blacks. . . ."

SOURCE: *Birmingham News/Dimension*, June 25, 1973.

---

ville stood, but how it stood in comparison to similar cities. A frequent bonus of the social indicators approach is that comparable statistics exist for other communities.

For news audiences, the *quality* of social conditions has more immediate and personal meaning than sheer quantity. Our concern is typically not with how much or how little, but rather with how good or how bad, with how it affects those who live in our communities. Making that assessment systematically is the function of journalists using community social indicators. It is a valuable strategy for the working reporter. And it places him on the social frontier, developing new forms of *social accounting*.[15] So-

---

[15] John Lear, "Where is Society Going? The Search for Landmarks," *Saturday Review*, April 15, 1972, pp. 34–39.

Ten Years Later: Jobs

Nurses, shop clerks, policemen, insurance salesmen, bureaucrats, reporters, telephone operators, bank tellers, accountants.

Ten years ago the people in these jobs in Birmingham were almost sure to be white.

Today, the hand that takes a bank deposit, writes a speeding ticket, or holds a thermometer may be black.

"Discriminatory attitudes of employers are no longer a barrier to equal opportunity for blacks. The question now is the ability of people to fill the jobs available," says Cecil Bauer, president of South-Central Bell, the five-state communications conglomerate that put its headquarters in Birmingham in 1970.

Birmingham blacks, who are making seventy to eighty-five official racial discrimination complaints against local employers each week, apparently do not believe the city's overall hiring is as color-blind as Bauer sees it.

Nevertheless, Bauer and his company's statistics offer a significant look at employment in the city in recent years.

South-Central's Birmingham operation increased its total black employment from 5 percent in 1966 to 16 percent by the end of 1972 when 607 blacks and 3,345 whites had jobs there.

Operators, the category in which South-Central hires the largest number of blacks, has increased from 14 percent black in 1966 to 45 percent at the end of 1972.

South-Central has found progress in black employment slower in its higher skilled jobs.

In 1972, 14 percent of the company's craft employees in Alabama were black. Currently, sixty-six of Alabama's 860 installer-repairmen are black. In another higher-skilled job, switchman, seven of 225 workmen are black.

South-Central's report showing progress mixed with persistent problems for black workers is a one-company indicator reflecting the general picture in Birmingham. Birmingham, in turn, is a local version of the nationwide black-white job pattern. . . .

SOURCE: *Birmingham News/Dimension,* June 25, 1973.

---

cial indicators are an application of behavioral science to journalism, an application that seeks to make journalism more humanistic, to shift its concern more from things and isolated events to the people and the quality of their lives.

The foundations for social indicators reporting already exist. Every journalist could profitably spend several hours browsing *The Human Meaning of Social Change.*[16] This book reviews the social trends and available indicators in such diverse areas as leisure and recreation, changes in the use of time, the quality of criminal justice, social psychological change in the black population, and political change. Any creative reporter could pursue one of these topics for weeks at the local level, producing a top quality series of articles.[17]

The Press and Social Accounting

The proper role of the press in regard to social indicators is not that of a passive carrier, of simply passing along the information developed and interpreted by other public and quasi-public agencies. The press has an active role to play in the *actual development* of social indicators as well as in the *interpretation* of these indicators. The press should be involved in the collection of basic data, and it should play a central role in the transformation of this data into meaningful information for local communities. Social indicators are powerful *tactical tools* for carrying out the traditional public responsibilities of the press.

The concept of the watchdog function of the press, or the designation of the press as a fourth estate, implies an active social role. In contemporary terms these concepts mean that social accounting, systematically collecting and evaluating precise information on conditions in the community, is a prime activity and responsibility of the local press.

Setting social priorities involves three elements:

1. A real set of problems or objective needs on the part of the constituency. Many of these may be unarticulated or even unper-

---

[16] Angus Campbell and Philip Converse, eds., Russell Sage Foundation, New York, 1972.

[17] For an earlier volume dealing with a similar variety of topics, see Eleanor Bernert Sheldon and William E. Moore, eds., *Indicators of Social Change*, Russell Sage Foundation, New York, 1968.

ceived. Many of them may be the special needs of particular segments or subgroups. They may contradict, compete, or conflict with each other.

2. A leadership that imposes its own judgment, assumptions, or biases to organize these needs into a program or agenda.

3. A communication system through which the needs may be expressed, considered, debated, and eventually ranked and handled by the constituency or its representatives.[18]

The press is obviously this third element. Traditionally, the press has emphasized the second element, the leadership and its expressed priorities. Social indicators include this element; but more importantly, social indicators begin to map systematically the first element, the public of your community and its needs. In our political system this is the most important. The public and its needs are the keystone and should be reported in greater depth.

---

[18] Bogart, *Silent Politics*, p. 59.

Chapter 2

Social Indicators for Local Communities

Maxwell McCombs

 Concern about the quality of life in our communities—concern ranging from air pollution and the availability of parks to housing standards, health conditions, and the quality of education—has led to consideration of social indicators by government officials, behavioral scientists, and journalists. How, they are asking, do we measure the quality of life experienced by an individual, a neighborhood, or an entire metropolitan area?

To translate this general concern with *social accounting* and *social indicators* into specific reporting assignments, let's look at four broad areas. Each includes traditional journalistic concerns and roles. What is added here is a systematic look at these roles and the tools—social indicators—available for carrying out the role.

Using Social Indicators

While the emphasis is on quantitative analysis of aggregate data, remember that social indicators are by no means limited to such data. Social indicators include all forms of evidence "that enable us to assess where we stand and are going with respect to our values and goals, and to evaluate specific programs and determine their impact." [1] Numerous other forms of systematic evidence that the journalist can use are reviewed in subsequent chapters on surveys and polls (individual quantitative data) and on content analysis (qualitative data).

MEASURING SOCIAL ILLS

Most of the topics that can be listed here are traditional concerns in journalism: crime, divorce, school dropouts, pollution. But the emphasis in social indicators reporting is presenting these social ills as part of the overall social condition of the community, not as some isolated facet. Of the four examples listed, only crime news regularly appears in the press. And it is typically covered from an event orientation. Individual crimes are reported. Seldom is there any comprehensive discussion of crime as a social problem. Who is affected by crime? What parts of the city are involved? What kinds of crimes are committed? Who are the criminals?

When police reports are regarded as sources of social indicators, these are the kinds of questions journalists begin to ask. The other three topics cited as examples appear in the press less often because they do not surface typically as discrete, newsworthy events. Yet these social ills demand better coverage than an annual isolated Sunday feature. The divorce records at the courthouse, attendance and transfer reports at the board of education, and pollution measures available from the Environmental Protection Agency can all be analyzed, for example, to show in-depth trends over time. Precise knowledge of just what the problem is must precede any meaningful public debate on proposed alternative solutions.

MEASURING SOCIAL ASSETS/OPPORTUNITIES

Communities have assets as well as problems. A community's housing, supply of jobs, schools, sewers, and streets are its *physical capital*. The people are its *social capital*. Their level of education, state of health, spirit, and crea-

---

[1] Raymond A. Bauer, ed., *Social Indicators*, M.I.T. Press, Cambridge, Mass., 1966, p. 1.

tivity are important social assets. Yet the press does little to monitor these assets of the local community on a regular basis.[2] Occasionally, it focuses on their shortcomings. But civic awareness and planning for the future is more than a matter of patching up the deficiencies in the present situation. The public in each community—the audience of the local press—should set the priorities for future development of the community—their community. But unless the local press reports the current situation, there is little likelihood of any real community dialogue on priorities for the future.

Concern about social indicators of community assets has already led to an awareness of the need for two new kinds of information. The first might be called *personnel accounting*, or *population accounting*. The idea is to include the value of our social capital on the community balance sheet. Education, health, and creativity have a real value in the marketplace even though it is difficult to measure their value in dollars and cents. Work is proceeding, however, along these lines, creating a new area for journalistic exploration.[3]

A second need is for information on the *consumption of public goods*, such as education, recreation, and transportation. Traditional economic measures show the *inputs*, how our tax dollars are allocated. But they do not really measure the value of the *outputs*. Let's take the unusual example of the 1973 North Carolina legislature, which had a $100 million tax surplus to distribute. Would the public be better served by spending the money for kindergartens, mental hospitals, a state zoo, or public recreation programs? Just citing the amount of money allocated to any of these functions is a poor and very indirect social indicator of how well the public good is served. Some indicators of the real value of these public goods, the extent to which the public actually benefits, are needed. This is a form of monitoring the government, an aspect of the watchdog function of the press, that merits intensive exploration.

These first two areas of reporting—measuring social ills and as-

---

[2] For examples of social indicators measuring community assets see Jeffrey K. Hadden and Edgar F. Borgatta, *American Cities: Their Social Characteristics*, Rand McNally, Chicago, 1965 and E. L. Thorndike, *Your City*, Harcourt, Brace, New York, 1939.

[3] *Toward a Social Report*, U.S. Department of Health, Education and Welfare, January 1969.

sets—can also be considered in *systems theory* terms. Two aspects of the local community as a system can be examined: the *structure* of the system and the *performance* of the system. Let's take some basic elements of a community and briefly consider the kinds of structural and performance descriptions that can be made the basis of in-depth news stories. This is another way of regarding the social indicators that specify the social ills and social assets of the local community.[4]

As part of the community *structure*, people can be described in terms of their social status, occupations, geographical distribution in the community, and similar characteristics. In *performance* terms, however, we can describe their productivity, creativity, political participation, awareness and civic pride, and personal pride and happiness.

Similar descriptions and comparisons can be made of the physical capital in each town and city. The size of the bank deposits, the manufacturing capacity, the condition of its street and sewer system, for example, are key aspects of any community's *structure*. In *performance* terms, however, what is this money and industrial capacity creating? Is the town "progressing"? What about the output of public goods? Is public investment in streets and sewers adequate? Are the people of the town well served by their physical capital? Is it yielding social dividends? Beyond description lies *explanation*—why and how the community structure and performance reached its present state.

ASSESSING SOCIAL PROGRAMS

Governments at all levels now undertake a broad variety of programs aimed at insuring social progress and improving the lot of their citizens. Public health programs seek to better people's physical condition. Vocational programs strive for financial success. Legal aid and police community relations programs work to improve the functioning of the judicial system. There are music festivals, lecture series, and recreational programs for all ages, designed to bring happiness and enlightenment. The list of organized social efforts supported with tax dol-

---

[4] For an extended discussion of social structure and social performance see Bauer, *Social Indicators*, pp. 185–255.

Finding Out the Urban Doctor
Was a Quack

No phrase is thrown at the public more than "the urban crisis." Everybody with an angle uses it, the politicians, the city planners, the social workers, the foundations, the think tanks, even the aerospace industry uses it to cut in for some government money to solve it. . . .

The most galling thing is that the public has done what the politicians, businessmen, and experts said had to be done. We went to the urban doctor and found out he was a fake.

Well, now a group of people have come along and have documented that he was not only wrong, but in fact was hastening and feeding the very processes he was supposed to be reversing. . . . They teamed up to see if they could find out what the real sequelae have been to their following the best advice, that is, to build up the city's economic base by building up the downtown with huge, flashy buildings. Everywhere we're told that's how the city will save itself, will generate tax revenues, create jobs.

They checked it out and the result is a surprising book, *The Ultimate Highrise,* edited by Bruce Brugmann and Greggar Slettleand, The San Francisco Bay Guardian, 1070 Bryant St., San Francisco, 94103, $2.95.

It was difficult, tedious work, requring weeks of going through government budgets, tax rolls, and the rest of the numerical flow that spouts out of the computers of modern administration. What they found was that San

lars is extensive. A simple list of municipal, county, state, and federal programs operating in any town or city would provide a reporter with several dozen potential news stories.

But the reporting job is more than describing the existence of these programs. If the press is to function as a fourth estate, as a watchdog over government, then part of the reporting job is to assess the performance of these programs. And not just government programs. It is also part of the reporter's job to assess the performance of non-governmental programs like United Appeal and other civic endeavors. The citizens who are paying for them are entitled to detailed information on whether the goals of these organizations are being met.

Francisco's skyscrapers—and it has more than any other city but New York and Chicago—are destroying the economy.

Far from adding to the tax base, they cost the city $5 million more a year to service than they bring in. Nor does San Francisco profit indirectly. The suburbanites who work in the new highrises don't shop in the city but where they live, so there's no sales tax revenue. Moreover, the enormous concentration of people doesn't afford an opportunity for economies of scale. As the book points out, the per capita cost of operating a city of under half a million is $144 while the cost of doing the same in a city of over a million is $444.

A booming downtown does raise property values, however. Not that this is a blessing because it means the taxes go up and fewer home-owning families can afford to stay. But it's factories, too. They can't afford to hang around either, and with them go the jobs, especially the low-skilled jobs which keep people off the welfare rolls.

That happened in San Francisco, as *The Ultimate Highrise* demonstrates. In the last decade, the city got more than 60,000 new jobs, but only 1 percent of them, 600 measly jobs, went to San Franciscans. . . .

Pretty soon the shiny new buildings begin to destroy their own economic base. The book's authors say that the congestion and the destruction of what was uniquely San Francisco is already eroding the tourist industry, the city's biggest source of revenue. . . .

The Ultimate Highrise . . . a way of finding out, not what the urban crisis does, but what it is.

SOURCE: *Washington Post*, Nicholas von Hoffman, February 7, 1972.

Henry David Thoreau remarked, "If I knew for a certainty that a man was coming to my house with the conscious design of doing me good, I should run for my life. . . ." While our skepticism toward social programs may not be as deep-seated as Thoreau's, objective examination of what our tax and charity dollars are buying is certainly in order. Extensive information of this sort is increasingly available just by asking because more and more demands are being made for a systematic evaluation of the performance of social programs. Does vocational training help individuals break the poverty cycle? What do children learn from "Sesame Street"? Do neighborhood recreation programs reduce delinquency? *Evaluation research* is a rapidly growing segment of the behavioral sciences.[5] Journalism can draw on this research for its reporting, and it can conduct some evaluation rssearch of its own.

Social indicators are routinely collected and compiled for many news events and social conditions. The volume of statistical information available in government offices is staggering. But there are some very newsworthy conditions and events for which no existing social indicators are compiled. These social indicators fail to exist primarily because these events and conditions are not ongoing situations, nor can they be routinely anticipated. For unexpected, but newsworthy, events and social conditions *standby research capabilities* are needed to insure that systematic social indicators are collected. Just as the fire department stands by for those infrequent, but vital, occasions on which it is needed, there must be trained social observers standing by. For many kinds of events, this means having the ability to conduct public-opinion polls on short notice. But social indicators are not limited to polls and surveys. Other forms of observation are needed for other kinds of situations.

The press is the ideal locus for this "fire-house research," [6] for this rapid production of social indicators at the very time situations are developing. Too often our social indicators for such traumatic occurrences as the assassination of a president are based on retrospective reports. People tell us what they recall they did and felt at the time. The pitfalls of retrospective recall are well documented.

The press is especially suited for fire-house research because timeliness and rapid reaction to situations are the hallmarks of American journalism. An emphasis on deadlines, stated in hours or at most days, not in weeks and months, is the *modus operandi*

---

[5] Francis G. Caro, ed., *Readings in Evaluation Research*, Russell Sage Foundation, New York, 1971; Peter Henry Rossi and Walter Williams, eds., *Evaluating Social Problems: Theory, Practice, and Politics*, Seminar Press, New York, 1972.

[6] For examples of both journalistic and behavioral science fire-house research see Edwin Parker and Bradley Greenberg, eds., *The Kennedy Assassination and the American Public: Social Communication in Crisis*, Stanford University Press, Stanford, Calif., 1965; Sidney Kraus, ed., *The Great Debates*, Indiana University Press, Bloomington, 1962.

of the newsroom. Furthermore, journalists are trained observers, trained collectors of facts, who are accustomed to planning their observations in advance. While assassinations and world wars cannot be anticipated, many non-routine events can be. For example, natural disasters and political crises can be anticipated. While their exact dates cannot be posted on the assignment sheets, the probability of these occurring sooner or later is quite high. Preparation for them will pay off.[7]

Most social indicators reporting draws upon information collected by others. Usually the role of the press will be limited to collating and interpreting this data. But for those non-routine, non-scheduled kinds of situations where social indicators are not routinely collected, the press can make a valuable original contribution.[8]

Expanding the News Beat

Newsmen do not try to keep an eye on all mankind. Rather they post themselves at certain key locations such as the police station, courthouse, city hall, and legislature. At this comparatively small number of locations, on these news beats, it sooner or later becomes known when the life of anyone departs from the ordinary. A small number of observers can monitor vast segments of the community from such vantage points. Put another way, the news beat is a highly economical allocation of reporters. Productivity per observer is generally high.

The traditional use of the news beat is steeped in the event orientation of the press. The result is that ". . . the news is not a mirror of social conditions, but the report of an aspect that has obtruded itself." [9] However, in the fifty years since Walter Lippmann wrote that description about the nature of news, jour-

---

[7] Bauer, *Social Indicators*, p. 53, suggests that a content analysis of the *New York Times* or other major news source would reveal "the relative frequency of occurrence of major social events of an unpredictable nature." One could further sort out these unpredictable events along a continuum ranging from totally unexpected to the problematical.

[8] Philip Meyer, *Precision Journalism*, Indiana University Press, Bloomington, 1973, pp. 14–15.

[9] Walter Lippmann, *Public Opinion*, Macmillan, New York, 1922, p. 341.

nalists have become increasingly aware of the shortcomings of reporting that limits itself to obtruding events. In the realms of economics, race relations, and a myriad of urban problems, journalists now see the necessity for anticipatory reporting, not reporting guesses, but reporting estimates and projections based on hard information. This is precisely the goal of social indicators reporting: reporting the broad outlines of current situations so that the future can be rationally anticipated.

The traditional news beats, or the more contemporary news beats organized around social functions, can yield most of the social indicators that journalists need. But there must be a new point of view on the part of the observers stationed on the news beats. This new viewpoint calls for a broader, more systematic look at the data compiled by public agencies. It looks beyond the single obtruding event to see the mosaic, to see how all the pieces fit together.

Social indicators reporting is not a radically new approach to reporting. As we have seen, the goals to which social indicators can be applied are traditional journalism goals in reporting. What is different is the systematic, comprehensive approach to reporting introduced by social indicators. In other words, social indicators add the *scientific method* to the reporter's repertoire. The fundamental values of social indicators reporting are those of traditional journalism. What is introduced is a new *strategy* for implementing the traditional goals and values. And, of necessity, a new strategy introduces new *tactics*. That is what this book is about: the new tactics of reporting and the techniques of behavioral science observation that can be applied in journalism.

The details of the scientific method, the thread that ties all these techniques together, are discussed in the next chapter. One key element of the scientific method, the *hypothesis*, is especially important for social indicators reporting. A hypothesis is a point of view, a vantage point, a focus on some specific set of elements in a situation; it is not some bias or opinion stubbornly retained. Hypotheses are frequently rejected and constantly modified as our experience in the real world of fact dictates.

But why employ a hypothesis? Actually, all observers and journalists use hypotheses to guide their reporting. Sometimes they call them story lines. What differs from observer to observer is the explicitness of their hypotheses. How well do they specify what

Delving into Suburbia

It was well into the third and final day of her unusual assignment and reporter Lynn Rosellini was becoming more distressed by the hour. Her instincts told her that she was on to a good story, but her subjects weren't telling her one.

Now, as time ran out, Ms. Rosellini launched into still another attempt to unearth the essence of the Lewis family's experience. Seated alongside Myrtie Lewis as she peeled potatoes in the kitchen of her sumptuous home, the reporter reiterated what Myrtie's husband, John, had said from the outset. "He says," Ms. Rosellini repeated, "that he's been given as much respect here as any place he's ever lived."

This time, instead of simply nodding in acknowledgement, Myrtie Lewis swung around to face the reporter. "No matter what anyone says," she said heatedly, "the situation here is not normal." And for the next hour or so, she angrily and succinctly pointed out why it wasn't.

When it appeared in *LI, Newsday's* Sunday magazine, Ms. Rosellini's story ran under the headline: A Family with Almost Everything.

> John and Myrtie Lewis have college educations, well-paying jobs, two bright children, and active roles in community affairs. But John and Myrtie Lewis have no friends on their block.
>
> The Lewises have a color TV, a 1972 Cadillac, a 1973 Cougar, a spacious home, expensive furniture, and a landscaped yard. But they cannot find a maid.
>
> John Lewis wears fine dark suits and expensive shirts. Myrtie Lewis occasionally wears a mink coat over her tailored dresses, and was named "Best Dressed Woman" by a national magazine. But a dentist's receptionist once asked her: "Are you on Medicaid?"
>
> John and Myrtie Lewis are black. East Hills, the Nassau north shore community in which they live, is predominantly white. And so is the rest of the upper-middle-class world in which the Lewises function.

The article also ran under a logo identifying it as part of "The Real Suburbia," a book-length series that took a year to prepare and appeared periodically in the magazine and daily paper from April into July.

"The Real Suburbia" was the first product of *Newsday's* projects department, which was formed to examine broad social trends and problems by utilizing sociological and other non-journalistic techniques in addition to traditional reporting practices. . . ."

SOURCE: *The Quill* (February 1974), published by The Society of Professional Journalists, Sigma Delta Chi.

they are seeking? An *explicit* hypothesis is a navigational aid through the buzzing, blooming confusion of the real world. Observers who set out to look at everything in general and nothing in particular seldom find anything in particular.

Any reporter who sets out to work the gold mine of statistics (social indicators) on the news beat will quickly appreciate the value of explicit hypotheses. Reading page after page of statistics with nothing in mind except that they are somehow newsworthy is an exhaustive, and usually, unproductive task. Sets of statistics, budgets, and similar lists of facts are too often approached in terms of an event orientation. "Give me 2,000 words on the new city budget," says the city editor. "See what you can get from this Agriculture Department bulletin," says the news director. The end result is often something like a casual rewrite of the world almanac. The story may make a good filler, but it is not good news copy. Don't rush in to write up all the social indicators at hand. Set up hypotheses. Ask useful questions. Use social indicators to tell a story. Statistics are interesting news copy only when they are translated into human terms.

The news is more than today's events. It includes systematic reports of today's situations, which are likely to produce the obtruding events of tomorrow. The news beat can be used to report both. Creativity and imagination are the principal elements of social indicators reporting and its use of the scientific method in expanding the utility of the news beat. They have always been the hallmarks of good journalism.

New Sources of News

Government files contain more facts on social conditions in our local communities than any enterprising social indicators reporter could ever use. Spend five minutes sometime compiling a simple catalog of the statistics routinely collected at the city hall, county courthouse, police station, fire department, and board of education. This will just begin to cover the government offices and the files there. The same procedure can be repeated at the state level, listing statistics on *local* finances, health conditions, unemployment, and many other public concerns. Plus there are such state-wide concerns as prisons, men-

Meet Our Newest
Reporting Team

Reporter Clarence Jones. A *Herald* computer. Together they cracked the information barrier on Dade County's rising crime rate and what happens after an arrest is made. The answers could be found among individual court records, but sorting them out was too vast a project for one reporter. The *Herald* employed twelve law students for two months, compiling data that would have taken a reporter two years. Information on 3,400 defendants, covering a twelve-month period, was processed by our computer. Printouts not only provided complete statistics on arrests, charges, court action, and final dispensation, but showed what combinations of lawyers and judges resulted in light sentences or acquittals and which in stiff penalties. The data is the basis for a series of probing articles, detailing a breakdown of the county's law enforcement machinery. Is there a need for this kind of record keeping? The sheriff's office calls us for information . . . referring to our "library" as the most complete source on law enforcement in the county.

SOURCE: Advertisement for the *Miami Herald*, in *Editor & Publisher*, November 23, 1968.

---

tal hospitals, and highways. Then on to the federal government and its vast bureaucracy. The routine statistical gathering operations of the federal government are so numerous that a 156-page paperback, *Statistical Services of the United States Government,* is required to describe the major sets of publicly available information. Since many of these statistics are reported for each county, even the national government is a key source of local social indicators.

Armed with their hypotheses, enterprising reporters can locate a broad spectrum of factual information, a vast array of social indicators, on which to base their reporting. With the increasing emphasis on social indicators in government planning, the job of the reporter in locating and collating all these facts is becoming easier. The social indicators viewpoint, coupled with technological changes in government record-keeping, is revolutionizing the news beat.

**Crime in New York City's
71 Precincts**

For the first time, crime rates in each of the city's seventy-one police precincts have been compared in a statistical study with the racial composition, economic levels, and age groupings of the people in those precincts.

The study, prepared by *The New York Times* and the New York City-Rand Institute, ranks precincts in terms of numbers and rates of homicides, robberies, and burglaries recorded by the police in 1972 and such 1970 census data as race, income (median, low, or high), and percentages of young men both out of school and unemployed.

"We've never had this kind of detailed information by precinct," Police Commissioner Donald F. Cawley said in a recent interview after being informed of the study. He added:

"It will be a tremendous assistance to us in the complicated and continuing process of deciding how many men should be assigned to each precinct."

The Rand Institute, headed by Dr. Bernard F. Gifford, is a non-profit group that conducts research on a variety of urban problems, customarily for the city and federal governments.

Dr. Gifford, a physicist who grew up in Brooklyn, said the institute hoped to use the study to predict where crimes were most likely to occur before they were committed, and thus enable the police to redeploy men to prevent more crime than they now do.

Patrick V. Murphy, the former Police Commissioner who now heads

---

The traditional forms of records that reporters are accustomed to are disappearing. Filing cabinets and dusty shelves of tomes are being replaced by computers and reels of tape. While the disappearance of this information to inside the computer creates some potential problems of access,[10] it also tremendously enhances the reporter's ability to use his or her beat for some real depth reporting. Computers are basically clerks, but clerks with no common sense or imagination. They don't think; they do literally what they

---

[10] Van Pritchartt, Jr., "Computerized City Records Pose Problems in Reporting," *Editor & Publisher*, February 7, 1970, pp. 9–10.

the Police Foundation, a Washington-based group that finances experimental police projects, said the analysis "certainly describes the crime problem in New York City in a way that has never been seen before."

Among the findings that have emerged from the study—in which 864 items of information concerning 2,159 census tracts in New York were broken down for the appropriate police precinct and then tallied—were the following:

> In the ten precincts with the highest homicide rates, the populations were, on the average, 54 percent black, 28 percent Hispanic, and 18 percent white or other. The median income in these precincts ranged from $4,950 to $10,966. For every 1,000 residents, there were 0.74 homicides, 26.20 robberies, and 34.66 burglaries reported to the police.

> In the ten precincts with the lowest homicide rates, the populations were, on the average, 2 percent black, 6 percent Hispanic, and 92 percent white or other. The median incomes ranged from $10,003 to $20,865. There were 0.02 homicides, 5.8 robberies, and 10.60 burglaries for every 1,000 residents.

Similar stark disparities were found when the precincts were examined in terms of relative wealth. . . .

SOURCE: *New York Times,* July 30, 1973. © 1973–74 by The New York Times Company. Reprinted by permission.

are told, and they do it fantastically fast. Not only can they locate a specific file or fact speedily, they can also sort files and create new files. By collating the various facts in a file or set of files, the computer can create "new" information.

Charlotte, North Carolina, is developing a model record system that will contain all the public records of both the city and county governments. New Haven, Connecticut, and a half-dozen other cities are building similar record systems. The potential of these systems for reporting public affairs is tremendous. Using a computer, a reporter could collate a dozen different social indicators for each neighborhood in the city. Bringing together the police reports, property tax records, building permits, fire inspection reports, and school enrollment/dropout figures would begin to paint an in-depth portrait of each neighborhood in the city. With these new computerized record systems this is a feasible job for one reporter over a relatively short period of time.

Even in pre-computer days, one behavioral scientist mapped the San Francisco Bay Area using simple clusters of census-type data.[11] The *behaviorally defined* neighborhoods were based on three clusters of related characteristics measuring family life, assimilation, and socioeconomic status. This kind of *behavioral mapping*[12] tells a great deal about life in the city. Political reporters, for example, will be interested to learn that there were substantial correlations between these neighborhood characteristics and voting patterns. The advent of the computer makes such reporting a relatively simple task for any journalist.

Nor is the reporter limited to statistical records as sources. Our earlier definition of social indicators specifically included non-quantitative information. Of course, much of this qualitative information—for example, written reports and judicial decisions—can be converted to quantitative indices or quantitatively summarized through the use of *content analysis*. The entire area of court reporting, for example, is a rich lode of social indicators that can be mined with content analysis.

Although our discussion has centered on the use of public records that the reporter will find on the news beat, there are many other record sets that can be used for social indicators. Private individuals, corporations, and trade associations have voluminous records that can contribute to social indicators. In fact, the pages of the newspaper itself, news items, letters to the editor, and advertisements, can yield social indicators.

Multiple Operationism

This mixture of quantitative and qualitative information from archived records exemplifies the strategy of *multiple operationism*, the use of several observation techniques to gather data for a news story. All observation tech-

---

[11] R. C. Tryon, "Identification of Social Areas by Cluster Analysis: A General Method with an Application to the San Francisco Bay Area," *University of California Publications in Psychology*, 8 (1955). Also R. C. Tryon, "Biosocial Constancy of Urban Social Areas." Paper read to American Psychological Association, 1955.

[12] David M. Smith, *The Geography of Social Well-Being in the United States: An Introduction to Territorial Social Indicators*, McGraw-Hill, New York, 1973.

Help-Wanted Ads

New York, Oct. 1 (AP)—The Conference Board said today its help-wanted advertising index leveled off at thirty-five in August, four points below its level of one year ago.

The independent business research organization said want-ad volume declined in the East North Central, West North Central, South Atlantic, and Pacific regions, rose in the New England, Middle Atlantic, East South Central, and Mountain regions and was unchanged in the West South Central region.

The index measures volume of classified advertising in fifty-two major newspapers across the country, with 100 representing 1967 levels. At the end of a recession, a gain in the index often precedes a decline in the unemployment rate. Declines have generally been followed by increases in unemployment.

SOURCE: *Washington Post*, October 2, 1971, and *AP Newsfeatures.*

---

niques lack perfect *validity.* Each has some source of error or bias. And where the observer (and his or her expectations) are a major element in the observation technique, for example, the interview, then the validity of the information may be seriously compromised. Behavioral scientists have become acutely aware of the problem of *obtrusive measurement* in recent years. In many cases the attempt to measure the situation itself obtrudes into the situation; that is, the observation or measurement technique itself influences and changes what is being observed. The strategy of multiple operationism is one response to this problem. While each technique of observation has its flaws, their nature and kind vary across techniques. So, if observations are based on a wide variety of techniques, it is likely that the errors will offset each other. If a variety of observation techniques yield approximately the same answer, one can have substantial confidence in the results.[13]

---

[13] Eugene Webb, *et al., Unobtrusive Measures: Nonreactive Research in the Social Sciences,* Rand McNally, Chicago, 1966, especially Chapter 1. Robert Rosenthal and Ralph Rosnow, *Artifact in Behavioral Research,* Academic Press, New York, 1969.

Another way of approaching this strategy of multiple operationism is to think of each observation or each news source as one
outcropping of the phenomenon to be reported. The mark of creativity is to locate as many of these as possible. Individuals'
recollections probed with an interview aren't the only outcropping
of a news story. There are many others, often far more unobtrusive,
to be examined.

Public and private records that can be used to construct social
indicators are often better lodes of information, better outcroppings, because of their unobtrusive nature. Typically, the persons
who compiled the records did not have journalists or their interests in mind. This is not to claim super-validity for records. They
are subject to such errors and biases as *selective deposit* and *selective survival;* and statistical records are often based on technical
definitions and categories that must be mastered by the user. But
the errors likely to be encountered in records are quite different
from those found in the personal interview.

Sherlock Holmes was a master in the use of physical traces to
reconstruct events. Every reporter should read and reread Holmes
and analyze his "reporting" technique. Liquor consumption can
be measured by the number of beer cans in ditches, or bottles and
cans in the garbage, as well as by sales records, interviews, and arrests for drunk driving. Jack Anderson used to dispatch an assistant periodically to rummage through the trash of the late J. Edgar
Hoover for glimpses into the personal life of the FBI director. On
a larger scale, the volume of the trash collected from the streets of
New Orleans is an excellent unobtrusive measure of the size and
festivity of the Mardi Gras crowd. These can, of course, raise
ethical issues—to be discussed in later chapters.

Nor is the reporter dependent on artifacts deposited by others.
Simple observation techniques designed by the reporter are valuable complements to more formal sources of information. Systematic eavesdropping on conversations in restaurants, buses, and
other public places can determine public interest and concern
about topics of the day. During World War II the Mass Observation project in Great Britain employed precisely this technique to
gauge public opinion.[14] In Nazi Germany, observers (eavesdrop-

---

[14] Leo Bogart, *Silent Politics: Polls and the Awareness of Public Opinion*, Wiley-
Interscience, New York, 1972, p. 160.

**Hot, Humid Weather Ignites
Air Conditioner Sales Boom**

At least the air conditioner salesmen were happy. "Fantastic" and "marvelous" is how they happily reported sales this week as Milwaukee's temperatures scorched past the ninety-degree mark since Monday.

The hot, humid weather virtually emptied department stores and their warehouses of the air conditioners and, in some cases, customers had to settle for a poor second choice—a window fan.

Predictably, both the Wisconsin Electric Company and the Water Department reached consumption peaks during the summer's first heat wave.

The Electric Company recorded its high for the year at 2 P.M. Wednesday, when it sent out 2,077,000 kilowatts of power. By comparison, seventy-degree weather requires 1,700,000 kilowatts and eighty-degree temperature requires 1,760,000 kilowatts, according to a company spokesman.

Tuesday's power consumption of 2,067,000 exceeded last summer's record of 1,988,000 kilowatts, the spokesman added. . . .

SOURCE: *Milwaukee Sentinel*, July 2, 1970. Copyright 1970, The Milwaukee Sentinel. Reprinted by permission.

pers) were systematically posted to determine public reaction to the war and to government policies.[15] Obviously, there are ethical constraints on the extent to which such techniques can be used.

Techniques of observation abound. But tactics need an encompassing strategy if they are to really pay off. Social indicators are one such grand strategy. Intermediate between this broad viewpoint and the specifics of the reporting job comes research (reporting and observation) design. A research design is a map translating your grand strategy and hypotheses into an integrated set of specific observations.

[15] Arthur L. Smith, Jr., "Life in Wartime Germany: Colonel Ohlendorf's Opinion Service," *Public Opinion Quarterly* 36 (1972): 1–7.

Nixon Taxes Stir
Little Comment

Most visitors to tax offices in larger cities around the country are not commenting about President Nixon's tax problems.

That was the observation yesterday of *New York Times* correspondents who went to the offices in a dozen cities, listened to the conversations of people who had come to the Internal Revenue Service with their own tax problems and asked I.R.S. officials for their experience.

Not a single reference to Mr. Nixon's tax controversy was heard by a visitor to the I.R.S. district offices in Manhattan and Brooklyn.

In Philadelphia as in other cities, I.R.S. aides recalled earlier comments. Mrs. Lillian Pelosi, a taxpayer assistance representative, said one person had "asked for Nixon's tax preparer so he could pay $100 less," and Rudy Thompson, a blind tax examiner, said that several phone callers had asked, "Is this the Watergate tax bureau?". . .

SOURCE: *The New York Times*, April 5, 1974. © 1973–74 by The New York Times Company. Reprinted by permission.

Secondary Analysis of
Public Records

As journalists set out to expand their reporting, to mine the wealth of information stored in news beat files and create informative social indicators, they must consider a number of tactical questions. Fundamental is the question of *original research* versus *secondary analysis* of existing data. For the most part, newspapers and television news operations do not undertake original social research. Not that they cannot or never will. Where gaps exist, especially gaps in qualitative indicators measuring public opinion, beliefs, evaluations, and states of mind, journalists should undertake original research.

More often, however, reporters will rely on the polls and surveys of others or on statistics compiled by public agencies. For these sources, the important point is to organize the data so that it is a valid social indicator with some real meaning for the audience. This is crucial because such information was often collected for purposes quite different from those which the reporter has in mind.

In the case of *secondary analysis* of polls and surveys, this means, first of all, careful attention to the guidelines in Chapter 4 for assessing a poll and what it really measures. In the case of secondary analysis of public records, this means attention to what kinds of data exist, what kinds of potential social indicators can be constructed, the advantages and limitations of these data sets, and the problems in actually constructing information about social conditions from these data sets.

Sociologist Herbert Hyman[16] devotes considerable attention to the problems of merging numerous data sources into a single, new, secondary analysis design. For example, by linking a series of surveys already done, the enterprising analyst can create new information on the overall *trend over time.* McCombs combined the national surveys of the Michigan Survey Research Center taken from 1952 to 1964 to determine the changes in media use among blacks during presidential campaigns in that era of major social change and civil rights activity.[17] Significant increases in media use by blacks were found, especially in the use of television for political news and information.

An even simpler trend design analyzing the effects of the famous 1960 Kennedy-Nixon debates is reported in *The Great Debates.*[18] Any reporter could have clipped the necessary Gallup Polls from the newspaper and created the striking political analysis reported in Table 1. The major question about those debates, of course, was their impact on the election. Popular political lore (and some research) holds that Kennedy won the opening debate and went on to win the election.

What evidence is there for this belief? If we look at the underlined figures in Table 1, we see that Kennedy/Johnson did gain three percentage points from before to after the first debate. One point came from the Republicans and two points from the undecideds. If one relied solely on the simple before-after design,

---

[16] Herbert Hyman, *Secondary Analysis of Sample Surveys,* John Wiley and Sons, New York, 1972.

[17] Maxwell McCombs, "Negro Use of Television and Newspapers for Political Information, 1952–1964," *Journal of Broadcasting* 12 (1968): 261–66.

[18] Sidney Kraus, *The Great Debates,* p. 211.

TABLE 1 *Effects of the Great Debates*

"If the election were held today, which ticket would you vote for—Nixon and Lodge or Kennedy and Johnson?" Results reported below include those registered and intending to vote who were more or less certain of their choice. Note the further adjustment of November 4.

Gallup Poll Release Date	Kennedy Johnson %	Nixon Lodge %	Undecided %
August 17	44	50	6
August 31	47	47	6
September 14	48	47	5
September 25	46	47	7
October 12	49	46	5
October 26	48	48	4
November 4 (adjusted for probable voters)	51	45	4
November 7	49	48	3
Actual vote	50.1	49.9	

SOURCE: Reprinted from *The Great Debates,* Sidney Kraus, ed. Copyright © 1962 by Indiana University Press, Bloomington. Reprinted by permission of the publisher.

one might conclude that the popular belief is correct: Kennedy did win the debate and take the lead in the race for the Presidency.

However, examine the full trend in Table 1. The overall trend from August 17 on for Kennedy/Johnson is upward. But there is a slight decline just prior to the debate. Did the debate itself enable the Democrats to recoup this loss and continue to move ahead? Or, would the general upward trend have continued without any great debate? Perhaps the best conclusion to be drawn from the overall trend analysis is that the evidence for any effect of the debate on the election results is equivocal. As intellectually unsatisfying as that is, it is quite a different story from the popular version of the debate.

Another enterprising secondary analysis design is the merger of new and old data into a trend design. An existing survey acts as the baseline, or first point in time. The analyst then conducts another survey on the same topic among the same population in order to determine the trend over time. While this is more costly than the usual secondary analysis because it means an entire new survey, the payoff can be significantly greater than that of a single new survey in isolation.

The pairing of surveys need not always involve the same populations. A local reporter could repeat the same questionnaire used in a national or state-wide survey. Here the purpose would not be to measure a trend over time; rather the purpose would be *replication,* determining if the same relationships and distribution of responses exist in a community as they do nationally or state-wide. The major advantages of this design would be the ability to place the local findings in a larger context and the opportunity to use the research expertise of others in designing a questionnaire. Here, experience in secondary analysis is leading the reporter to create his or her own social indicators, to undertake original survey research.

Social indicators are a grand strategy offering a broad orientation toward community reporting. The best tactics available for translating this orientation into quality journalism are those techniques of observation developed by behavioral scientists. As the reporter grasps the essential meaning of social indicators, the perceived utility of survey research, content analysis, research design, and all the methodological concerns of behavioral science will soar. The use of social indicators is not the only way journalism can draw upon behavioral science methodology. The reporter who is a skilled methodologist will find applications in sports reporting equal to those in public affairs reporting. The social indicators approach is a useful introduction because everything discussed in this book fits this orientation. But it is just one frontier for the enterprising reporter to explore.

Chapter 3

Reporting and Scientific Method

James W. Tankard, Jr.

". . . despite its limitations, scientific method, more than any other procedure known to man, can minimize misinformation."

Claire Selltiz, Marie Jahoda, Morton Deutsch, and Stuart W. Cook

". . . scientific method is simply the way in which we test impressions, opinions, or surmises by examining the best available evidence for and against them."

Morris Cohen and Ernest Nagel

The journalist and the scientist perform different roles for society, but there are similarities in the goals, subject matter, techniques, and attitudes of the two professions. One of the central arguments of this book is that journalists can improve traditional reporting skills by drawing upon techniques of gathering information developed in the sciences, particularly the behavioral sciences.

This is not an argument for doing away with the standard journalistic techniques of interviewing news sources, observing news events, and studying records and documents. Rather, it is an argument for refining and supplementing these techniques, when possible and appropriate, with techniques and strategies based on the *scientific method.* The scientist has developed techniques to describe reality as accurately as it is possible. Reporters, who have a similar goal of describing reality accurately, can borrow these techniques to improve the truthfulness of their own accounts, to answer questions that could not be answered before, and to draw more valid conclusions when performing the interpretative function of the journalist.

The Journalist and the Scientist

The role of the journalist has traditionally been to give a timely report of recent events that are either important, interesting, or both. The determination of which events are important or interesting enough to report is a matter for the journalist's judgment. By necessity, some events are selected by the mass media and some are not. Thus, CBS newsman Bruce Morton's comment "That's some of what's been happening lately" may be a more accurate description of a television newscast than Walter Cronkite's "And that's the way it is."

Journalists also sometimes try to go beyond the simple account of an event and attempt to put that event in a perspective that gives it meaning. The best newspapers attempt to do this through news analyses, investigative reporting, editorials, and columns.

The role of the scientist, by contrast, is to discover *new* scientific knowledge. Ideally, this scientific knowledge takes the form of laws or general statements that hold up, to some considerable degree, *universally*.

Philosopher Henryk Mehlberg has compared science with the news media in his book *The Reach of Science:*

> . . . the main difference between science and other news agencies resides neither in the higher reliability of scientific information, nor in the particular techniques of spreading such information. It is rather connected with the scope of scientific information and the uses to which it is capable of being put. The ordinary news agencies are concerned exclusively with single, particular, contemporary, and local facts, with the here and now. The scientist reaches out for the remote regions of space and time and is most anxious to find out laws governing all the facts irrespective of where and when they happen. Indeed, it is his knowledge of universal laws which enables him to get hold of remote facts.[1]

---

[1] Henryk Mehlberg, *The Reach of Science*, University of Toronto Press, Toronto, 1958, p. 14.

The basic goal of science is to build *theory*. By theory we mean simply an explanation with some generality. The scientist looks at a number of particular events and attempts to find a general explanatory principle. The journalist, in contrast, attempts to describe one particular event as accurately and fully as possible. Communication researcher Leo Bogart makes this distinction: "Mass media create interest by focusing on individuals; the social sciences deal with individuals only as cases." [2]

The differences in approach of the journalist and the scientist may be illustrated by showing how the two deal with the same topic. Let us take as an example the way the two professions deal with criminal violence. The journalist deals with criminal violence primarily by examining a single case of violence at a time, as it comes to his or her attention. This single case is described in little or great detail, depending upon its importance, its interest, or both. The press describes a presidential assassination in enormous detail because of the significance of the event. A case of assault or a mugging, however, may receive only a sentence or two in a newspaper. The journalist's approach is essentially to look upon an incident of criminal violence as a unique event, happening only once in a particular time and place, and to give as much detail as possible, depending on comparative newsworthiness and available space.

Behavioral scientists, in contrast, are more interested in making some kind of general statement about violence. They would like to find a general explanation of violence that would apply to many cases and would allow prediction and control through better understanding. One of the primary forms that the search for general statements about violence has taken is the attempt to determine the causes of violent behavior. In brief, behavioral scientists approach the task of finding general statements about violence by suggesting possible explanations of violence (*developing theory*), deriving testable consequences of these possible explanations (*formulating hypotheses*), and testing the hypotheses to see if they correspond to reality (*making observations*).

One of the general explanations that has been suggested for

---

[2] Leo Bogart, "Social Sciences in the Mass Media," in Frederick T. C. Yu, ed., *Behavioral Sciences and the Mass Media*, Russell Sage Foundation, New York, 1968, p. 159.

violent behavior, to continue with our example, is that portrayals of violence in the mass media, such as television, may cause or stimulate violent behavior in real life. Much of the recent work on violence by behavioral scientists has attempted to derive hypotheses from this explanation and to test them.[3]

In general, then, the journalist deals with a single incident of violence at a time, trying to describe each as fully as possible, while the scientist deals with the general phenomenon of violence, abstracting it from a number of cases.

Journalists do not always restrict themselves to dealing with isolated cases of violence, however. There are clearly instances in which they are also interested in generalizing about a number of cases of violence. One way they do this is to report the frequency of daily crime. For instance, the *Philadelphia Bulletin* runs on its front page a daily item called "The Crime Count," which is a box score summary of major crimes that occurred in the city in the previous twenty-four hours. The *Bulletin* is forced to report crime this way because of the large number of crimes that happen daily in Philadelphia. It is interesting that in doing so, however, the *Bulletin* has constructed an *index* of daily crime—a concept that a behavioral scientist might develop in attempting to arrive at some generalizations about crime.

Journalists also occasionally generalize about violence in a second way—by reporting summaries of crime statistics. Examples of these are a year-end report by the Department of Justice on the number of homicides or a report by the Secretary of Transportation on the number of airplane hijackings for the year. This kind of crime summary does not often originate with the journalist, however. Typically, it is a description of the release of a report by a public official—another *event*.

A third way that journalists sometimes try to make general statements about criminal violence is through columns and editorials that perform the interpretative function. The purpose of in-

---

[3] For accounts of this research, see Robert K. Baker and Sandra J. Ball, *Violence and the Media, A Report to the National Commission on Causes and Prevention of Violence*, U.S. Government Printing Office, Washington, 1969, and George A. Comstock, Eli A. Rubinstein, and John P. Murray, eds., *Television and Social Behavior, Reports and Papers, Vol. V: Television's Effects: Further Explorations*, National Institute of Mental Health, Rockville, Md., 1972.

Philadelphia Crime Count

There were 109 major crimes reported to Philadelphia police yesterday: 69 burglaries, 28 robberies, 10 weapon offenses, and 2 homicides. On the corresponding day last year, there were 52: 26 burglaries, 19 robberies, 4 weapon offenses, 2 rapes, and 1 homicide.

SOURCE: *Philadelphia Bulletin*, September 18, 1971.

terpretative reporting is to give the meaning of the news, often by exploring its causes and effects. This may be the point at which journalists sometimes venture on dangerous ground, because they are attempting to do the same job as the scientist (explaining a complex phenomenon) without using the tools and techniques of the scientist. The columnist who has approximately one day to write a column analyzing the causes of a series of recent political assassinations is forced to rely mainly on speculation. The speculations may be interesting, but there is no guarantee at all that they correspond to reality. Checking *causal explanations* against reality is the difficult task that science takes on.

Similarities of Journalism and Science

The basic similarity between journalism and science is that both disciplines are trying to describe reality. Philosopher Abraham Kaplan said: "Science is governed fundamentally by the reality principle, its thought checked and controlled by the characteristics of the things it talks about." [4] This statement also applies to honest journalism. According to Kaplan, the basic scientific question is, "What the devil is going on around here?" [5] The same question might also be a good choice for the basic journalism question.

---

[4] Abraham Kaplan, *The Conduct of Inquiry*, Chandler Publishing Co., San Francisco, 1964, p. 312.
[5] *Ibid.*, p. 85.

Essentially what science and journalism share is an *empirical* base; that is, both rely on verification as the approach to truth-gathering. Both rely fundamentally on finding evidence for statements before statements are made. This evidence can vary from the reporter's first-hand observation of an event (such as a murder trial) to the elaborate testing of a hypothesis about aggression in a psychological laboratory. In both cases, the base is ultimately empirical; that is, the statements rest fundamentally on observation.

Journalism and science also share an attitude of *objectivity.* In science, objectivity refers primarily to *inter-observer agreement.* When two or more observers agree on a description or measurement, it is said to be "objective." As speech researcher Wendell Johnson has pointed out, "Precisely because an observation is the act of an individual, there is no way of knowing whether it is true—dependable, that is—until at least one other individual has made it, too. This is the sort of thing scientific workers refer to when they speak about the *reliability* of their data. They are talking about the limits within which two or more observers, with comparable opportunities for seeing the same thing, agree in what they see." [6]

For the journalist, objectivity means making only those statements that are capable of verification. Semanticist S. I. Hayakawa has described such statements as *reports*, and has shown how they differ from two other common kinds of statements—judgments and inferences.[7] In brief, a *judgment* is an expression of approval or disapproval, and an *inference* is a statement about the unknown made on the basis of the known.

By restricting themselves as much as possible to reports or statements capable of verification, journalists (or, for that matter, any communicator) assure that they are talking about something that another person could also observe. A communicator who relies on reports can still fail to be objective, primarily through *slanting,* or selecting those details that create a particular impression. But adhering to reports will eliminate much of what people object to when they criticize the press for not being objective. Much of the lack of objectivity often charged against *Time* maga-

---

[6] Wendell Johnson *Your Most Enchanted Listener,* Harper and Brothers, New York, 1956, p. 52.

[7] S. I. Hayakawa, *Language in Thought and Action,* 2d ed., Harcourt, Brace and World, New York, 1964, p. 38.

zine, for instance, is due to the heavy use of inferences and judgments.

A number of journalists have taken the position recently that objectivity is impossible. But the success of science shows that a high degree of objectivity is achievable, for science could not exist without it. Communication theorist William Stephenson has made a similar point. He has criticized the following comment by Bill Moyers, President Johnson's former press secretary: "Of all the great myths of American journalism, objectivity is the greatest. Each of us sees what his own experience leads him to see."

Stephenson wrote, "This is a *non sequitor par excellence*. It is nonsense. . . . Each of us may indeed see what his own experience leads him to see, but fortunately large numbers of us have much the same experience and see much the same things. One hopes that when Moyers looks at a donkey he doesn't mistake it for an elephant." [8]

Behavioral Science
and Journalism

Sometimes the behavioral scientist and the journalist do essentially the same job. Leo Bogart has suggested there is little difference in scholarship between Theodore White's *The Making of a President 1960* and Arthur Schlesinger's *A Thousand Days,* although one is considered to be the work of a journalist and the other the work of a historian.[9]

Investigative reporters and behavioral scientists sometimes appear to be growing closer together in mission as both try to find out and report things about society that are important and relevant. The following examples are among the many that could be cited to show the preoccupation of journalists and behavioral scientists with the same subject matter and, to some extent, their reliance on similar techniques.

Social psychologist Philip Zimbardo conducted experiments

---

[8] William Stephenson, "Science: Science in Society," mimeographed report, Mid-American Science Communication Program, School of Journalism, University of Missouri, April 1973, p. 20.
[9] Bogart, "Social Sciences in the Mass Media," p. 162.

Prison Brutality

Social psychologist Philip Zimbardo was involved in a social science study in 1971 which ranked with much of journalism in its timeliness. Haney, Banks, and Zimbardo conducted a prison simulation study in the basement of the Stanford psychology department which involved randomly assigning male volunteers to the roles of either prisoners or guards.

The experiment was terminated prematurely after six days because of the "unexpectedly intense reactions" of subjects and the "pathological and anti-social" behavior of both guards and prisoners. The authors state that the pathological behavior resulted primarily from the prison *situation* and not from any pre-existing personality traits of the people themselves.

Shortly after this study was completed, the Attica prison revolt took place. Zimbardo testified before a U.S. House of Representatives committee studying prison reform, and *Life* magazine ran a photo-story on his project.

SOURCE: N. Faber, "Unusual Experiment at Stanford Dramatizes the Brutality of Prison Life," *Life*, October 15, 1971.

---

on vandalism several years ago in which he left automobiles on streets in various cities and observed the rate of destruction of the automobiles, as well as who participated in the vandalism.[10] A car in New York City was rendered a "battered, useless hunk of metal" in less than three days, while a similar vehicle in Palo Alto, California was left untouched in the same period of time. A few years later, Harry Reasoner presented an ABC-TV documentary on vandalism in which he showed time-lapse photography of the destruction of a car on a New York street.[11]

Conditions in public institutions have been the object of study by both journalists and scientists. In 1971, the *Chicago Tribune* conducted an investigation of state-licensed nursing homes that led to an inquiry by the state legislature. The *Tribune* reporting

---

[10] Philip G. Zimbardo, "The Human Choice: Individuation, Reason, and Order Versus Deindividuation, Impulse, and Chaos," *Nebraska Symposium on Motivation*, 17 (1969): 237–307.

[11] "The Vandals," ABC-TV, Dec. 4, 1972. Narrator, Harry Reasoner.

team, working with investigators of the Better Government Association, used *participant observation* as a principal technique. Reporters worked as janitors, medical aides, and kitchen help, and also had themselves admitted as patients in order to observe conditions in the homes.[12]

Stanford psychology and law professor D. L. Rosenhan conducted a similar participant observation study of mental institutions in 1973. His article, "On Being Sane in Insane Places," received national attention.[13]

Such magazines as *Psychology Today* and *Transaction* (now *Society*) also show that there is an area of convergence of behavioral science and journalism. Irving Louis Horowitz, the founder and editor of *Transaction*, has described the magazine as behavioral or social science journalism.[14] Horowitz said that in the second year of publication, the editors began to realize that *Harper's*, *Atlantic*, and the *Bulletin of the Atomic Scientists* could be just as useful as models for their publication as the *American Sociological Review*. The magazine began to use a more journalistic approach, with emphasis on timeliness and field reporting. He describes one example:

> At the end of the 1967 summer of violence in the ghettos, we had a special issue on the subject, something unheard of among social scientists who were always years late on an issue. This was in part made possible by new techniques of social science investigation, using journalistic modes of field research and rapid reporting.[15]

If Horowitz admits attempting to make sociology more relevant and timely by using the techniques of the journalist, it should not be too surprising. Sociologist Daniel Lerner suggests that American sociology "really grew out of the womb of journalism." [16]

---

[12] "Abuses in Nursing Homes," *Chicago Tribune*, Feb. 28, 1971; William Jones, "As 'Patients,' Probers Learn Ordeal of Nursing Home Life," *Chicago Tribune*, March 4, 1971.

[13] D. L. Rosenhan, "On Being Sane in Insane Places," *Science*, 179 (1973): 250–258.

[14] Irving Louis Horowitz, "On Entering the Tenth Year of Transaction: The Relationship of Social Science and Critical Journalism," *Society* 10 (November/December 1972): 57.

[15] *Ibid.*, p. 57.

[16] Daniel Lerner, "Summary and Conclusions," in Yu, *Behavioral Sciences and the Mass Media*, p. 251.

Early American sociology, he argues, was preoccupied with problems that are journalistic staples—street-corner society, white collar crime, the ghetto, the gang, and so on.

Newsday, the Long Island newspaper, recently formed a sociological investigative team in order to use sociological and other non-journalistic techniques as well as more traditional reporting practices to examine broad social trends and problems.[17] The first product of the team was "The Real Suburbia," a book-length series that took a year to prepare. The team used public-opinion survey techniques, but supplemented them by having reporters actually live with ten Long Island families for three days. Among their findings were these: the decision to move to the suburbs is shaped more by the "pull" of the suburbs than by the "push" of the city, and suburban housewives say overwhelmingly that they are happy and prefer their new environment to that of the city.

Journalistic Fallacies

Journalists occasionally present evidence or reasoning that the scientist would regard as fallacious. One of the benefits of a study of scientific method by journalists should be to eliminate some of these fallacies from news reporting. Here are five of the more common journalistic fallacies.

1. *Generalizing from an unrepresentative sample.* The problem often takes the form of a general statement about the opinions of a population that is not based on a survey conducted with a random sample. (The random sample is explained in detail in Chapter 6.)

For instance, the day after the Senate Watergate Committee began its televised hearings, one newspaper ran this headline: "Viewers Want Soap Operas, Not Watergate." The lead of the wire-service story stated:

> The nationally televised Watergate hearings spent more than five hours Thursday angering game show fans and those who find more drama in soap opera than in the thrill of the hunt for truth in the packed Senate Caucus Room in Washington.

[17] Bernie Bookbinder, "Delving into Suburbia," *The Quill*, February 1974, pp. 14–17.

The impression created by such a story, and particularly such a headline, with no qualification, was that the majority of the public was opposed to televising the hearings. The problem with this kind of story is that the sample it is generalizing from is self-selected. The people who called television stations and complained about the hearings were fans of soap operas who were unhappy about missing their programs. For every one of them, there might have been five viewers who were pleased to watch the hearings.

Another self-selected sample on the same subject indicated that the public *approved* of the Watergate hearings. A television correspondent reported that mail to the Ervin Committee (as of June 5, 1973) was running ten to one in favor of the hearings. These two examples taken together show very well the weakness of the self-selected sample: one indicates the hearings were overwhelmingly unpopular; the other indicates the same hearings were overwhelmingly popular.

A better way to determine the public's attitudes toward the hearings would be the survey based on a random sample. The Gallup Poll of June 14, 1973, reported such a survey, which indicated that 44 percent of the public thought the mass media had provided "too much" coverage of Watergate, compared to 11 percent who said "too little," and 39 percent who thought the coverage was about right. In other words, the "true" public opinion came closer to a draw.

2. *Misusing the word "random."* The word *random* is frequently misused in the mass media, apparently by people who do not understand what a random sample really is.

A wire-service report on whether consumers were following President Nixon's advice on how to save electricity contained the following sentence: "The random check of area residents showed that some are following the advice and some aren't, but that most were becoming aware of the need for some action."

It is unlikely that this story described a survey based on a genuine random sample. The story is made up of quotes from citizens and contains no information about the population being studied or the size of the sample. Apparently *random* was used as a substitute for *spot*. But this is misleading since a genuine random sample would be representative of the public, but a spot check would not.

Finding the Poor

A post-Watergate editorial in one newspaper was trying to make the point that "there is not really all that much wrong with this country."

Discussing the problems of inflation and poverty, the editorial commented: "Look around. One doesn't really find many people who are suffering greatly one way or another because of these alleged crises. They may gripe about the price of meat, but there is no lack of picnickers on the beach, drinking soft drinks or beer."

This editorial contains the fallacy of generalizing from an inadequate sample. Poor people probably do not go to the beach and drink soft drinks and beer. It is fallacious to conclude that because poor people are not there, they do not exist. If one really wanted to answer the question of whether or not poverty exists in this country, one would have to look other places besides at the beach.

The word *random* appears to have been similarly misused in another wire-service story:

> A number of city and state officials and party leaders applauded President Nixon's stand on the Watergate scandal, but others said public confidence would be restored only if a separate agency or prosecutor were named to investigate the case.
> Several persons contacted in a random survey said President Nixon's speech Monday night left many questions unanswered.

This story states that it deals with "several persons contacted in a random survey," and yet what it contains are interview comments from governors, party chairmen, mayors, and so forth—hardly a random sample of persons.

One last example of the misuse of the word random comes not from journalism, but from advertising, and is probably deliberate. A radio commercial for a soup company contained this sentence: "The preceding conversation was selected from random telephone calls." The catch here is that a conversation *selected* from random telephone calls is not itself *randomly* selected. Fifty calls should have been made with only five favorable responses, and these five could have been "selected."

3. *Conducting "man-in-the-street" polls.* The fallacy of conducting "man-in-the-street" polls is a special case of the problem

of generalizing from an unrepresentative sample, yet it is common enough to deserve separate discussion. The "man-in-the-street" poll is often labeled as such in the newspaper headline, as these examples show: "Poll on Street: Most Indicate Nixon Knew" and "Michigan Residents Favor Primary 2 to 1, Man-in-the-Street Polls Show."

The article with the first headline reported no quantitative data at all (not even how many people were talked to), and yet the lead sentence presented this conclusion: "The man or woman on the street of downtown Pensacola Saturday felt that President Nixon was aware of the Watergate coverup from the very beginning and most favored his resignation rather than impeachment." The only description of the sample is contained in this sentence: "Shoppers and merchants alike were asked in a *News-Journal* street poll if they felt President Nixon had prior knowledge of the Watergate coverup and whether he should resign or be impeached."

The article with the second headline did report a sample size (141 residents), and gave percentages in favor, opposed, and stating no opinion. But it also had the defect of not being based on a random sample. Any conclusions drawn from the survey, then, must be extremely doubtful.

Another newspaper story started out as if it might be reporting a valid poll: "South Oakland residents view the May 16 Presidential primary with mixed reactions. But most polled by the *Daily Tribune* say they will vote." The second paragraph revealed, however, that the story was based on a poll of *nine* residents!

4. *Making invalid causal inferences.* Making causal statements is a difficult matter, and is one that scientists approach with caution. Non-scientists are often much more willing to make statements about causal relationships, apparently because they are not aware of the extreme difficulty of proving that one thing causes another. The journalist should approach causal statements with caution—both those he or she is tempted to make and those that are made by others.

The press runs into some of its greatest difficulty with causal statements when reporting the remarks of others. This is particularly true in controversial areas, where people may have strong beliefs and do not want to accept scientific evidence that a causal relationship may or may not exist. The problem for the press is to put such remarks by a speaker into a proper perspective. Often this cannot be done unless the reporter has some understanding of scientific method himself.

Obscenity and pornography are examples of controversial areas in which many people have strong beliefs about causality. These beliefs are often proclaimed in spite of scientific evidence to the contrary, particularly during "anti-smut" drives that become tied to political campaigns. A newspaper account in Madison, Wisconsin of a speech by County Judge Russell Mittelstadt reported [18]:

> Mittelstadt told the gathering that he was convinced of the positive correlation between the viewing of pornography and a long list of problems, including drug use, crime, divorce, premarital sex, and venereal disease.

A later section of the story stated:

> When Dr. Peter Weiss, a Madison psychoanalyst, asked the judge what his evidence was to support the assertion, Mittelstadt replied, "That's a dumb question."
> "Anybody who's alive and breathing has to know that (there is such a correlation)," the judge continued.

Mittelstadt was taking a position that was contrary to the only scientific evidence at the time. He was basing his observations on his own experience—valuable, but limited. The report of the Presidential Commission on Obscenity and Pornography had stated just four months before Mittelstadt spoke that "empirical research designed to clarify the question has found no evidence to date that exposure to explicit sexual materials plays a significant role in the causation of delinquent or criminal behavior among youths or adults. The Commission cannot conclude that exposure to erotic materials is a factor in the causation of sex crimes or sex delinquency." [19]

That kind of news—in which a public figure makes statements contrary to the best known scientific evidence—poses a difficult problem for the press. Probably the best way to handle it is to bring out in the story covering the speech the scientific evidence that contradicts or balances the speaker's position. This could

---

[18] Dave Wagner, "Mittelstadt Claims Smut Causes Society's Ills," *Madison Capital Times*, Feb. 2, 1971.

[19] *The Report of the Commission on Obscenity and Pornography*, Bantam, Toronto, 1970, p. 32.

have been done in the Mittelstadt story by mentioning the Commission's report in a paragraph or two.

A similar disregard for scientific evidence is sometimes shown by advocates of capital punishment, who often cite statistics to show that the death penalty acts as a deterrent to crime.

For instance, in 1971, Theodore L. Sendak, Attorney General of Indiana, presented these kinds of statistics in a speech and argued:

> The movement in these figures, with murders increasing as the deterrence of the death penalty diminished, confirms the verdict of ordinary logic: That a relaxation in the severity and certainty of punishment leads only to an increase in crime.[20]

Sendak's conclusion, like Judge Mittelstadt's, is not supported by the best scientific evidence. A reporter who took the time to look up "Capital Punishment" in the *Encyclopaedia Britannica* would read that statistical studies indicate capital punishment does not have an influence on the amount or trend of the kind of crime it is supposed to deter people from committing.[21]

5. *Assuming that because something precedes an event, it is a cause of the event.* In trying to find the causes of crime, school dropouts, poverty, and a dozen other serious problems, the behavioral scientist, as well as the journalist, is tempted to commit the fallacy of *post hoc, ergo propter hoc* (after this, therefore because of this)—assuming that because something precedes an event, it is a cause of the event. The appendices of the Report of the Commission on Obscenity and Pornography contain a number of examples of *post hoc, ergo propter hoc* reasoning about the effects of pornography.

A former Detroit police inspector, Herbert W. Case, is quoted as saying, "There has not been a sex murder in the history of our department in which the killer was not an avid reader of lewd magazines." [22] When this is used as an argument that pornography leads to crime, as it was, it is an example of *post hoc, ergo propter hoc.*

In the same report, former FBI Director J. Edgar Hoover was

---

[20] Theodore L. Sendak, "Criminal Violence: How About the Victim?" *Vital Speeches of the Day*, 37 (July 1, 1971): 574–576.

[21] *Encyclopaedia Britannica*, 1967, Vol. 4, pp. 848–849.

[22] *The Report of the Commission on Obscenity and Pornography*, p. 637.

Corrupted by a Book?

The following paragraphs taken from an Associated Press news story illustrate *post hoc, ergo propter hoc* reasoning and a critical response to that reasoning. The story carried the headline "Sex Text Linked to Corll."

A California assemblyman says a controversial sex education textbook to be used in the state's classrooms was found in the home of Dean Allen Corll, the man linked to twenty-seven homosexual-torture murders of young men in Texas.

"I'm trying to make the point that all this type of stuff leads to warped minds and a warped sense of values in these young people," Wakefield said Wednesday in an interview. "I think it's high time we paid attention to what's happening to youth in this respect."

Wakefield "doesn't know what he's talking about," said James L. McCary, the Houston psychologist who wrote the text.

Although investigators say a copy of the college edition of *Human Sexuality* was found in Corll's residence, so was the Bible, "about twenty copies of *Popular Mechanics,* and copies of the *Reader's Digest,*" McCary added.

SOURCE: *Austin Statesman,* August 23, 1973.

---

quoted as saying, "I believe pornography is a major cause of sex violence." Part of the evidence Hoover cited was that "a 42-year-old scientist, arrested in the Midwest on charges of taking indecent liberties with a 9-year-old girl, was found to have an impressive collection of pornography in his home. . . ."

What this kind of reasoning overlooks is that even if reading pornography and sexual crimes were strongly correlated, it does not mean that one is the cause of the other. There may be some third variable, such as frustration, mental instability, or something else, that is causing *both* the exposure to pornography and the criminal behavior.

The *post hoc, ergo propter hoc* fallacy is also sometimes committed by reporters themselves. The press has interviewed persons suspected of or charged with the crimes and reported on their reading matter, hobbies, personal notebooks, and so on. In many cases, these reports seem to be an instant psychoanalysis, although clearly they were done by people without psychological training. The press reported, for example, that Lee Harvey Oswald had checked certain books out of the public library shortly before the assassination of President Kennedy. This kind of reporting seems to involve the *post hoc, ergo propter hoc* fallacy, even if the report did not say that there was a causal relationship. Surely the response of many readers must have been that possession of certain books and the assassination were related, or else why would the books even be reported?

Scientific Method

Wendell Johnson has given one of the better summaries of the scientific method:

> We may say, in briefest summary, that the method of science consists in (a) asking clear answerable questions in order to direct one's (b) observations, which are made in a calm and unprejudiced manner, and which are then (c) reported as accurately as possible and in such a way as to answer the questions that were asked to begin with, after which (d) any pertinent beliefs or assumptions that were held before the observations were made are revised in the light of the observations made and the answers obtained.[23]

The details of the scientific method can best be brought out by describing an example of a scientific investigation. The following discussion illustrates the key steps in the scientific approach by describing some research on the relationship between frustration and aggression. This research was conducted by psychologist John Dollard and his colleagues, and much of it was reported in the volume *Frustration and Aggression.*[24]

1. *Science begins with a problem or question.* This research began as an attempt to find a general explanation of human aggression, including "strikes and suicides, race prejudice and reformism, sibling jealousy and lynching, satirical humor and criminality, street fights and the reading of detective stories, wife-beating and war." [25]

---

[23] Wendell Johnson, *People in Quandaries*, Harper and Brothers, New York, 1946, p. 49.
[24] John Dollard, Neal E. Miller, Leonard W. Doob, O. H. Mowrer and Robert R. Sears, *Frustration and Aggression*, Yale University Press, New Haven, 1939.
[25] *Ibid.*, p. 26.

2. *A general or theoretical explanation is proposed.* The general explanation of aggression is the frustration-aggression hypothesis, stated more exactly this way: "The occurrence of aggressive behavior always presupposes the existence of frustration, and, contrariwise, . . . the existence of frustration always leads to some form of aggression." [26] This hypothesis was influenced by the theoretical ideas of Freud, who wrote of aggression being the "primordial reaction" to the blocking of pleasure-seeking or pain-avoiding behavior.[27]

3. *A specific test hypothesis is formulated.* Hovland and Sears derived a specific test hypothesis that suggested a relationship between economic depression as an indicator of frustration and the number of lynchings in the South as an index of aggression. More formally, their hypothesis stated "The strength of instigation to aggression varies directly with the amount of interference with the frustrated goal-response." [28]

4. *Careful observations are made to either confirm or refute the test hypothesis.* Hovland and Sears obtained data on the number of lynchings each year from 1882 to 1930 from the *Negro Yearbook,* published by Tuskegee Institute. As one index of the severity of interference with economic actions, they used the annual per-acre value of cotton for fourteen Southern states for the same period of years. The correlation between the economic index and the number of lynchings was $-.67$, indicating the number of lynchings increased during periods of economic depression.

5. *The general explanation is either rejected, seen as gaining further support, or revised on the basis of the observations.* In the research described, the Hovland and Sears study was interpreted as supporting the frustration-aggression hypothesis, although the link could be strengthened greatly by additional evidence that the societal "frustration" that erupted in lynchings resulted primarily from the economic pressures of falling cotton prices. During the same period, the South diversified its agriculture; perhaps that created tension and was also a factor.

---

[26] *Ibid.,* p. 1.

[27] *Ibid.,* p. 21.

[28] Carl I. Hovland and Robert R. Sears, "Minor Studies of Aggression: VI. Correlation of Lynchings with Economic Indices," *Journal of Psychology,* 9 (1940):301.

Journalists will rarely go through the entire series of steps that comprise the scientific method when they are researching and writing a news story. We are not suggesting that they attempt to use the scientific method to write news stories. Rather, what we are suggesting is that journalists can benefit from some of the ideas and techniques that the scientists also will find useful.

1. *Quantification and measurement.* Lord Kelvin said, "If you cannot measure, your knowledge is meagre and unsatisfactory." [29] Use of numbers, or quantification, is fundamental to scientific thinking for several reasons.

Quantification permits us to report more precisely; it permits subtle discriminations. The classic example is the measurement of temperature with a thermometer. Instead of the limited verbal descriptions (hot, cold, very hot, very cold, and so on), the thermometer gives us a scale with many different degrees of temperature. In measuring readability, scores from formulas like the Flesch Reading Ease formula permit more precision than verbal categories (such as difficult writing or easy writing).

Quantification also permits comparisons. Is Johnny taller this year than he was last year? Were there more major crimes in Philadelphia yesterday than there were on the same day a year ago? Do more people express approval of the way the President is handling his job this month than last month? Quantification provides the tool for answering questions of this type.

Quantification is also useful for reducing or summarizing data. Means, or averages, for instance, are useful to represent a large number of scores with a single number. The percentage serves a similar function of compressing or reducing data. Quantification lets us deal with realities that are not directly confrontable. Hans Zeisel has pointed this out in his valuable book *Say It with Figures:*

> Modern social life has become much too complicated to be perceived by direct observation. Whether it is dangerous to take an airplane, whether one kind of bread is more nourishing than an-

---

[29] Quoted in William O. Aydelotte, *Quantification in History*, Addison-Wesley, Reading, Mass., 1971, p. 49.

other, what the employment chances are for our children, whether a country is likely to win a war—such issues can only be understood by those who can read statistical tables or get someone to interpret them.[30]

Quantification permits the use of powerful statistical and mathematical techniques. The process of statistical inference, a powerful system for drawing conclusions, depends on quantitative information.

2. *Reliability and validity.* The *reliability* of a measurement may be defined as the extent to which the measurement remains constant. Frequently in the behavioral sciences, the primary concern for reliability is for *inter-observer reliability:* do different observers, using the same measuring tool, reach the same measurements?

The *validity* of a measurement may be defined as the extent to which it measures what it was designed to measure. One means of validating readability formulas, for instance, is to show that their scores correspond to reading comprehension scores when students are asked questions about material they have just read.

Reliability and validity can be applied not only to scientific measurement, but also as criteria for assessing the value of any information. The terms *reliability* and *validity* can be useful to the journalist as supplements for the much-heralded term *accuracy,* which is difficult to define in concrete terms.

Behavioral scientists customarily check for reliability of measurement when their research is based on observations that are difficult or that involve judgments. In a content analysis of the kinds of news found in newspapers, for instance, judges (or coders) may need to assign each story to one of twelve news categories. Such a content analysis only has scientific value if it can be shown that different coders categorize the stories in the same way. Therefore, in content analyses, it is often a standard procedure to compute a *reliability coefficient* to determine to what extent coders agree. This reliability coefficient could be simply the proportion of coding decisions on which two coders agree. A reliability coefficient of .90, for example, might be accepted as a satisfactory level of coding reliability.

---

[30] Hans Zeisel, *Say It with Figures*, 5th ed., Harper and Row, New York, 1968, p. xv.

The Worst American State

H. L. Mencken conducted the first study resulting in an article titled "The Worst American State" in 1931. Mencken obtained statistics for the forty-eight states on income, education, crime, and a list of other variables, and then ranked the states on each index. He then combined the rankings on the separate indexes to create one overall ranking of the forty-eight states. This gave him a ranking of the states from the "best to worse."

John Berendt repeated the Mencken study for *Lifestyle* magazine in 1972, comparing the states on forty criteria. He obtained his data from such sources as *The Statistical Abstract of the United States, The Information Please Almanac,* The Institute of Life Insurance, the R. L. Polk data bank (for information on the number of new Cadillacs and Lincolns registered in each state), A. C. Nielsen (for the percentage of homes with television sets), *Editor and Publisher Yearbook,* the Audit Bureau of Circulation, *Who's Who in America,* the Directory of the Performing Arts, the National Safety Council, *Uniform Crime Reports,* and *The Sometime Governments* (a study of the fifty state legislatures by the Citizens Conference on State Legislatures).

The following lists compare the rankings of the states for 1972 and 1931. The two rankings correlate with a Spearman rank correlation coefficient of .93, an extremely high correlation (a perfect correlation would produce a coefficient of 1.00). This suggests that the ranking of states did not change much over forty years.

But what does this rank-ordering of the states really mean? Is it simply a reflection of industrialization? How does this social indicator reflect the quality of life in the various states? For both the journalist and the behavioral

---

The weakness of a content analysis conducted without reliability checks is illustrated by Edith Efron's *The News Twisters,* a book purporting to show that television network newscasts were biased in favor of liberal candidates and issues.[31] The problem with this study was that only one observer—apparently Miss

---

[31] Edith Efron, *The News Twisters,* Nash Publishing, Los Angeles, 1971. For a critique of the Efron study, see Robert L. Stevenson, Richard A. Eisinger, Barry M. Feinberg, and Alan B. Kotok, "Untwisting *The New Twisters:* A Replication of Efron's Study," *Journalism Quarterly* 50 (1973):211–219.

FINAL STANDINGS

	1972 (Berendt)	1931 (Mencken)		1972 (Berendt)	1931 (Mencken)
1.	Connecticut	Massachusetts	26.	Maine	Missouri
2.	Minnesota	Connecticut	27.	Idaho	Maryland
3.	New York	New York	28.	Indiana	North Dakota
4.	Illinois	New Jersey	29.	South Dakota	Wyoming
5.	Massachusetts	California	30.	Alaska	Montana
6.	Hawaii	Minnesota	31.	Nevada	Idaho
7.	New Hampshire	Iowa	32.	North Dakota	South Dakota
8.	Rhode Island	Illinois	33.	Montana	West Virginia
9.	California	Oregon	34.	Florida	Arizona
10.	Utah	Rhode Island	35.	Virginia	Oklahoma
11.	Iowa	Michigan	36.	Missouri	Florida
12.	Washington	Maine	37.	New Mexico	Virginia
13.	Michigan	Washington	38.	Tennessee	Texas
14.	New Jersey	Wisconsin	39.	Oklahoma	New Mexico
15.	Maryland	New Hampshire	40.	Arizona	Kentucky
16.	Delaware	Ohio	41.	Texas	Louisiana
17.	Oregon	Nebraska	42.	West Virginia	North Carolina
18.	Wisconsin	Utah	43.	Louisiana	Tennessee
19.	Nebraska	Kansas	44.	Georgia	Arkansas
20.	Pennsylvania	Pennsylvania	45.	Kentucky	Georgia
21.	Ohio	Vermont	46.	North Carolina	South Carolina
22.	Colorado	Colorado	47.	Alabama	Alabama
23.	Kansas	Indiana	48.	Arkansas	Mississippi
24.	Vermont	Nevada	49.	South Carolina	
25.	Wyoming	Delaware	50.	Mississippi	

scientist these rankings of the best/worst states open a vast frontier for exploration.

SOURCE: John Berendt, "The Worst American State," *Lifestyle*, November 1972.

Efron—made the judgment of whether a given statement was favorable or unfavorable to a particular person or issue. Her book would have been much more useful if she had presented objective definitions of favorable and unfavorable coverage, and had then reported the extent to which two or more judges agreed in classifying statements according to the definitions.

Journalists are already aware of the importance of reliability, although they may not refer to it by that name. The journalistic concepts of *objectivity* and *attribution* are related to the scientist's concept of reliability. An objective news account is some-

The Best Professional
Football Team

Harvard statistician Frederick Mosteller has argued that the usual measure of a football team's superiority—the win-loss record—is not the most accurate measure because some teams do not play others at all and some teams have stiffer schedules than others.

Mosteller performed a statistical analysis of the 1971 and 1972 National Football League regular seasons to determine the genuinely superior team each year.

Mosteller's technique produced ratings of the twenty-six teams adjusted for their opponents' performances for the entire season.

His analysis indicated Pittsburgh was the strongest team in the NFL in 1972, even though Miami finished with a 14-0-0 record and became the first team in NFL history to be undefeated and untied in a fourteen-game season. Mosteller's report indicated Miami had the easiest schedule in the NFL in 1972.

The statistical analysis produced the following rankings of teams for the 1972 season. (Win-loss records and percentages for the season are listed for comparison purposes.)

National Conference	Mosteller Rank	Season Record	Season Percentage
Atlanta	17	7-7-0	.500
Chicago	15	4-9-1	.321
Dallas	5	10-4-0	.714
Detroit	8	8-5-1	.607
Green Bay	3	10-4-0	.714
Los Angeles	16	6-7-1	.464
Minnesota	7	7-7-0	.500
New York Giants	13	8-6-0	.571

New Orleans	23	2-11-1	.179
Philadelphia	25	2-11-1	.179
San Francisco	9	8-5-1	.607
St. Louis	22	4-9-1	.321
Washington	6	11-3-0	.786

American Conference	Mosteller Rank	Season Record	Season Percentage
Buffalo	21	4-9-1	.321
Cleveland	10	10-4-0	.714
Baltimore	20	5-9-0	.357
Cincinnati	11	8-6-0	.571
Denver	19	5-9-0	.357
Houston	24	1-13-0	.071
Kansas City	12	8-6-0	.571
Miami	2	14-0-0	1.000
New England	26	3-11-0	.214
New York Jets	14	7-7-0	.500
Oakland	4	10-3-0	.750
Pittsburgh	1	11-3-0	.786
San Diego	18	4-9-1	.321

SOURCE: Frederick Mosteller, "A Resistant Adjusted Analysis of the 1971 and 1972 Regular Professional Football Season," Memorandum EX-5, Department of Statistics, Harvard University, Cambridge, Massachusetts, January 1973.
"Final Standing of the Teams," *The New York Times*, December 18, 1972.

Minorities at the
University of Texas

Bringing information from different sources together in a summary table can be a useful technique for giving meaning to figures.

When University of Texas President Stephen Spurr released information on the number of minority students at the university and the amounts of financial aid they received, a guest writer for the student newspaper compared the figures with census figures for the state to give them meaning.

John Vrooman, a teaching assistant in economics, prepared an article for *The Daily Texan* showing the percentages of black and brown students attending the university compared with the percentages of black and brown people living in Texas.

His article included the following table:

Race	Total population 16–24	Those with 4 years of high school	Those with 4 years of college	Distribution of Univ. of Texas	Distribution of student loans
White	71.5%	74.2%	90.5%	94.0%	79.3%
Black	11.2%	12.5%	4.2%	1.1%	4.4%
Brown	17.5%	13.3%	5.3%	4.9%	16.3%
All races	100.0%	100.0%	100.0%	100.0%	100.0%

(Data source: U.S. Census: 1970, Detailed Characteristics, PC(1)-D45, *The Daily Texan,* Feb. 6, 1974.)

SOURCE: John Vrooman, "Pay Us Now or Pay Us Later," *The Daily Texan,* Feb. 14, 1974.

times defined as one that will be accepted by two different persons, even when they stand on opposing sides of a controversy. This is, in effect, a rather rigorous criterion of reliability. It is a requirement that only those aspects that are agreed upon by two observers should be included in a news story.

Attribution is making clear who or what is the source of a statement. The purpose of attribution is to make it possible for the reader or another reporter to verify that the source made the statement. In effect, attribution puts in the story the necessary information for a reliability check.

One of the criticisms that can be made of the New Journalists is that in some of their writings no reliability checks are possible. This is particularly true when "composite characters" are created. New Journalists often report the thoughts and sometimes even the dreams of persons they are writing about. Gay Talese reports the thoughts and feelings of characters throughout *The Kingdom and the Power,* a study of *The New York Times.*[32] These thoughts are sometimes quite intimate: Talese reports that when associate editor Clifton Daniel first met his wife, Margaret Truman, one of the things he was most impressed by was her "plunging neckline." Talese defends the accuracy of such reporting, stating that it is based on extensive interviewing. However, the accuracy of *The Kingdom and the Power* has been challenged by at least one of the principals whose "feelings" were described—former Sunday editor Lester Markel.

Tom Wolfe describes a hallucination by Leonard Bernstein in the beginning of *Radical Chic.*[33] The account of this "vision" is not attributed to Bernstein in any way, and the reader is left wondering if it is a fictional creation of Wolfe's or a description that he obtained from Bernstein through interviewing.

One example of a kind of information in news stories that is frequently unreliable is the estimation of crowd size. Researcher Gerald Sturges [34] reports that estimates of the crowd at a March for Victory rally led by fundamentalist minister Carl McIntire on October 3, 1970, varied from 7,150 (*Washington Post*) to between 200 and 250 thousand (*Christian Beacon,* edited by McIntire).

In the Public Broadcasting Laboratory documentary, "Journalism: Mirror, Mirror on the World," the investigating team attempted to show that reliable measurement could be made of the number of women arriving on trains to attend a march in Washington, D.C., by the Jeannette Rankin Brigade. They used three observers with hand counters. The three counters were in almost perfect agreement, and showed that 3,000 women attended the march. Washington police had estimated the number of women at 5,000.[35]

---

[32] Gay Talese, *The Kingdom and the Power,* Bantam Books, New York, 1970.

[33] Tom Wolfe, *Radical Chic and Mau-Mauing the Flak Catchers,* Bantam Books, New York, 1971, pp. 3–4.

[34] Gerald D. Sturges, "1000 + 1000 = 5000: Estimating Crowd Size," *Society,* April 1972, p. 42.

[35] "Journalism: Mirror, Mirror on the World," Public Broadcasting Laboratory film, 1968.

Estimating Crowd Size

The size of the crowd is often an important part of news stories, particularly those dealing with campaign speeches, political demonstrations, religious revivals, and rock festivals.

But how can the journalist obtain an accurate estimate of the size of a crowd?

Too often the journalist relies on the opinion of an expert, such as a police officer. These estimates are often grossly exaggerated. Herbert A. Jacobs, who has done research on estimating crowd size, states that police estimates are often double or triple and sometimes as much as twenty times the actual number.

A New York police commissioner, for instance, estimated that a crowd of eight million gathered to watch a parade for General Douglas Mac-Arthur in 1951. *The New York Times* later used official city maps, measured sidewalk widths, and calculated that a parade route from Battery Park to City Hall could hold no more than 141,436 spectators. Even allowing for people watching from windows and side streets, the *Times* estimated the total could not be more than 500,000.

Jacobs studied the sizes of crowds in Sproul Plaza at the University of California at Berkeley. He obtained the dimensions of the Plaza from architects' blueprints, and then counted the number of people in photographs taken from above the Plaza during various rallies. By dividing the area in square feet by the number of people, he came up with crowd density figures for different kinds of gatherings. Jacobs found densities ranging between 4 and 9.5 square feet per person. The usual density was between 6.5 and 8.5 square feet to a person.

On the basis of this research, Jacobs developed two formulas for estimating crowd size:

1. The standard formula. The reporter paces off the length and width of the crowd, multiplies these together to find the area, then divides the result by a crowd density figure (7 is suggested as an average). Jacobs states the resulting figure will probably be within 20 to 25 percent of an actual nose count.
2. The simpler formula, for crowds that are approximately square and between 500 and 5,000 people. The reporter *adds* the length and width, and multiplies by the density figure (7 if the crowd is loosely composed, 10 if the crowd seems more compact).

SOURCE: Herbert A. Jacobs, "To Count a Crowd," *Columbia Journalism Review*, Spring 1967, pp. 37–40; Gerald D. Sturges, "1000 + 1000 = 5000: Estimating Crowd Size," *Society*, April 1972, pp. 42–44, 63.

The criterion of validity has been elaborated, particularly by Campbell and Stanley [36] and by Webb *et al.*[37] to include *internal validity* and *external validity*. Internal validity refers to whether the difference found *within* an inquiry is genuine. An attitude-change experiment might lack internal validity, for instance, if subjects realized that it was an attitude-change experiment and deliberately "changed their attitudes" just to help the experimenter.

External validity refers to whether the differences found can be generalized outside the inquiry. A frequent source of external invalidity is the failure to study a sample that is adequately representative of the population about which the researcher wants to generalize. The best safeguard against this threat is to specify the population in advance and draw a *random* sample.

A sample is not random, and the term *random* should never be used, when the investigator has *any* choice in the selection of persons sampled. Everyone in the population being studied should have an *equal* chance of being picked. Also, a random sample is not one in which the selection is merely haphazard. This is the problem with the "man-in-the-street" poll—where you stand makes all the difference in the world.[38]

The concept of validity can be sharpened still further by pointing out a number of *threats* to valid measurement. One way to increase the likelihood that a given measurement is valid is to consider these threats and rule out the operation of as many as possible. One possible source of invalidity in interviews, for example, is reactivity—the awareness of the source that he is being interviewed. Particularly when the investigator is seeking information about unethical, illegal, or socially disapproved acts, interviews are not likely to produce valid information.

3. *Theory.* The goal of the practicing journalist is obviously not to build systematic scientific theory, and yet theory can be useful to the journalist for guiding the line of inquiry. Theory developed in the behavioral sciences can help the journalist decide what is

---

[36] Donald T. Campbell and Julian C. Stanley, *Experimental and Quasi-Experimental Designs for Research*, Rand McNally & Co., Chicago, 1966.

[37] Eugene J. Webb *et al.*, *Unobtrusive Measures: Nonreactive Research in the Social Sciences*, Rand McNally & Co., Chicago, 1966.

[38] For a detailed discussion of sampling techniques, see Chapter 6.

important and worth looking at in human behavior and what is
not.

John W. Riley, Jr. has suggested that journalists and sociol-
ogists should mutually agree on some theory or theories that
would stimulate more imaginative public and mass media uses of
the behavioral sciences.

> Such an effort need not be very definitive nor even very formal.
> What I have in mind is some elemental theory, let's say, of deviant
> behavior, a theory which could conventionally be used in reporting
> events having to do with crime, with race relations, with mental
> disorders, or drug addiction. Certainly, the current reporting on
> problems of this sort leaves much to be desired.[39]

Leo Bogart has described a situation in which a television
news team did not know what questions to ask in an interview,
and suggests that behavioral science theory would have helped
them formulate questions. The occasion was the power blackout in
New York in November 1965.

> A group of people had been trapped in an elevator overnight. The
> idea was to interview them the following day in order to make a
> documentary feature. The reporters and camera crews went out,
> but they found that they simply didn't know what questions to ask.

---

[39] John W. Riley, Jr., "A Review of Session One," in Yu, *Behavioral Sciences and
the Mass Media*, p. 53.

They asked questions like "How did you feel?" and "Didn't you get tired?" It did not occur to them to ask about how the individual members of the group related to each other, how they coped with the emergency, what tensions developed between what people, who took a position of leadership, and all the other questions which might occur to a social psychologist.[40]

4. *Hypothesis testing.* Charles Darwin observed, "How odd it is that anyone should not see that all observation must be for or against some view, if it is to be of any service." [41]

Hypotheses serve a number of purposes, one of the primary being that they *focus* an inquiry; they also help safeguard objectivity. The investigator who seeks knowledge by formulating hypotheses becomes used to saying: "This may or may not be true. Let's look at the evidence and see."

Curtis MacDougall, the author of a leading reporting-newswriting text and well-known journalism professor, has written:

> The journalistic fact finder does not begin with a hypothesis for which he seeks factual proof. Rather, he is an open-minded seeker after truth who explores every possible avenue of investigation; and only after he has exhausted every chance to obtain additional information does he attempt to draw conclusions regarding the accumulated data. This objective approach to knowledge is much sounder than that practiced by many researchers in other academic fields.[42]

This position seems to confuse *hypothesis-formation* with *conclusion-drawing*. Scientific investigators do not assume that their hypotheses are true; they only conclude that it is plausible after testing them with evidence. Journalists must have some hypotheses about what is important to a given story and what is not, or they literally would not know where to begin looking for information. These hypotheses might be in the form of unstated assumptions. One of the purposes of hypothesis-formation is to make these unstated (and perhaps unconscious) *assumptions* visible, so their full implications can be drawn out and they can be used to direct observation.

Philosophers Morris Cohen and Ernest Nagel have pointed out

---

[40] Bogart, "Social Sciences in the Mass Media," p. 160.

[41] Quoted in Morris R. Cohen and Ernest Nagel, *An Introduction to Logic and Scientific Method*, Harcourt, Brace and World, New York, 1934, p. 197.

[42] Curtis D. MacDougall, *Interpretative Reporting*, 6th ed., The Macmillan Co., New York, 1972, p. 20.

the importance of hypotheses and the difficulty with "letting the facts speak for themselves." Discussing Herodotus' attempt to explain the annual sudden rise in the Nile River:

> How important hypotheses are in directing inquiry will be seen clearly if we reflect once more on the frequent advice: "Let the facts speak for themselves." For what *are* the facts, and which facts should we study? Herodotus could have observed the rise and retreat of the Nile until the end of time without finding in that particular repeated fact the sort of connections he was looking for—the relations of the inundation to the rainfall in Central Africa, for example. His problem could receive a solution only with the discovery of an invariable connection between the overflow of the Nile and some other fact. But *what* other fact? The number of other facts is endless, and an undirected observation of the Nile may never reveal either the other facts or their mode of connection. Facts must be *selected* for study on the basis of a hypothesis.[43]

5. *Causal inference.* The word *cause* is used in at least three different senses, and journalists are at times interested in all three senses.

(a) Cause in the everyday sense. Nagel has defined the cause of an event in the everyday sense as "a particular occurrence (often, though not invariably, involving an overt manipulation of things by human beings) such that without it the event would not take place." [44] He gives the following examples of causal statements in this sense: The snowfall on December 12 tied up the transportation in New York City. The lights went on when Mrs. Smith turned the switch. The bank failed because of baseless rumors about its solvency.

Journalists seek to find a cause in the everyday sense when they answer "Why?" as one of the five W's in covering an ordinary news story. Why did the automobile overturn, killing its two occupants? Because a tire blew out. Other factors might be involved, such as the roads being icy, or the driver panicking. The journalist might find that several factors are causes in the everyday sense.

(b) Cause in the historical sense. Cause is used by historians to refer to the events or forces that led up to or produced a particular historical event. Historian David Hackett Fischer defines a causal explanation as "an attempt to explain the occurrence of an

---

[43] Cohen and Nagel, *An Introduction to Logic and Scientific Method*, p. 201.
[44] Ernest Nagel, "Types of Causal Explanation in Science," in Daniel Lerner, ed., *Cause and Effect*, The Free Press, New York, 1965, p. 19.

event by reference to some of those antecedents which rendered its occurrence probable." [45] The use of cause in the historical sense resembles its use in the everyday sense in that both generally refer to the cause of a particular event, a specific happening pinpointed in time and space.

Journalists are interested in the use of the word *cause* in more of a historical sense when they begin moving into investigative and interpretative journalism. What were the causes of the killings of four students at Kent State? The journalist who attempts to answer such a question may operate much like a historian, looking at many kinds of evidence and taking longer to write the piece than the reporter covering daily news stories.

(c) Cause in the scientific sense. Causal statements in science take the form of general statements rather than statements about a specific happening pinpointed in space and time. Examples of causal statements in science would be: frustration produces aggression; cross-fertilization causes superior plant growth to self-fertilization; perception is influenced by needs and values. Notice that these statements do not refer to a particular event located at one point in time, as do the previous kinds of cause.

Science requires three major types of evidence before it approves a statement of causality:

1. Evidence of concomitant variation, or that the causal variable and the dependent variable are associated.
2. Evidence that the dependent variable (the effect) did not occur in time before the causal variable.
3. Evidence ruling out other factors as possible determining conditions of the dependent variable.

Journalists seeking a rigorous causal explanation of something should ask themselves how they can obtain these three types of evidence.

The controlled experiment is the most powerful method developed to demonstrate causality in the scientific sense, because it simultaneously gathers evidence of all three types. (The controlled experiment is discussed in Chapter 10.)

---

[45] David Hackett Fischer, *Historian's Fallacies*, Harper and Row, New York, 1970, p. 183.

Threats to Causal Inference

The difficulty of making valid causal inferences is illustrated by a test of the effects of driving 50 mph conducted by the Associated Press and a criticism of that test expressed in a letter from an assistant professor of psychology.

The "test" involved having reporters drive from Fort Worth to Abilene at 50 mph and then from Abilene to Fort Worth at 70 mph. The test indicated the trip took 51 minutes longer at 50 mph and increased the gas mileage from 14.56 miles per gallon to 15.46 miles per gallon.

The letter from David B. Cohen, assistant professor of psychology at the University of Texas, made these points:

In order to demonstrate the effect of speed, one needs to keep constant all factors except speed. At least five other factors were varying along with speed (50 vs. 70 mph):

(a) Note that the car was driven uphill from Fort Worth (altitude approximately 617 feet) to "just west of Abilene" (altitude approximately 1,726 feet) at 50 mph, then downhill back to Fort Worth at 70 mph;

(b) Only one run each way was made under conditions that may have biased the results by many unknown factors: traffic conditions, driving style (especially through small towns where it is difficult to maintain a steady speed), different route each way, different weather conditions at different times of the day;

(c) Type of car used: different cars will realize different degrees of savings at different speeds;

(d) Possible bias from preconceived opinion or expectation of the drivers (what were their motives?);

(e) Errors in calculation.

It is clear that when there is systematic variation in factors other than the one whose effect you are studying, you cannot conclude much about the effect of that factor per se.

SOURCE: "One-Hour Loss Going 50 M.P.H. Saves 62 Cents," Associated Press, as printed in *Austin American-Statesman*, December 2, 1973; David B. Cohen, "Gas Test Inaccurate," letter to the editor, *Austin American-Statesman*, December 6, 1973.

Journalists are interested in using the word *cause* in the scientific sense when they are engaged in investigative or interpretative reporting that involves making general causal statements. Is a person with long hair treated differently by police than a person with short hair? The question is one of causality; it is asking what are the effects of hair length on how a person is treated by police. Why do citizens who witness a crime become involved in some situations but not in others? Does a person's race have an effect on whether or not he or she is shown a potential home by a real estate agent? These questions are timely enough to concern the journalist, but they are also at a level of generality that makes the scientific method the appropriate means of answering them.

A Note on Ethics

Since the atomic bombs were dropped on Hiroshima and Nagasaki in 1945 a number of physical scientists have shown especial concern for ethical questions regarding their research. One expression of this attention was the founding of the *Bulletin of the Atomic Scientists*. A similar concern for ethics has also developed in the behavioral sciences. Psychologist Herb Kelman and sociologist E. A. Shils have written sharp criticisms about the use of deception in behavioral science research.[46] There have also been extensive debates about psychological experiments, such as Stanley Milgram's studies of obedience in which subjects were made to think they were delivering shocks of lethal intensity to another person.[47]

Television station WCKT in Miami prepared an investigative story on citizen reaction at being present when crimes are committed, which illustrated the kind of ethical questions that can confront the journalist.[48] Newsmen from the station, with the cooperation of the police, staged a number of robberies, hold-ups,

---

[46] Herbert Kelman, "Human Use of Human Subjects: The Problem of Deception in Social Psychological Experiments," *Psychological Bulletin* 67 (1967):1–11; E. A. Shils, "Social Inquiry and the Autonomy of the Individual," in Daniel Lerner, ed., *The Human Meaning of the Social Sciences*, Meridian, New York, 1959, pp. 114–157.

[47] Stanley Milgram, "Behavioral Study of Obedience," *Journal of Abnormal and Social Psychology* 67 (1963):371–78; Diana Baumrind, "Some Thoughts on Ethics of Research; After Reading Milgram's 'Behavioral Study of Obedience,' " *American Psychologist* 19 (1964):421–423; Stanley Milgram, "Issues in the Study of Obedience: A Reply to Baumrind," *American Psychologist* 19 (1964):848–852.

[48] Gene Strul, "Partners in Crime . . . A TV Station Proves Public Apathy," *The Quill*, March 1968, pp. 16–19.

jail escapes, and so forth, to see if people would try to stop the crimes or would become otherwise involved.

Bystanders were obviously being deceived in these simulations, and it is possible that a bystander might have been injured in attempting to stop the "crime." A newsman who played the role of a thief breaking into a jewelry store actually cut his hand on the broken window glass. It is conceivable that a bystander could have been similarly injured. It seems quite likely that in this kind of situation, a television station could be held liable for such an injury.

Other questions of ethics, particularly involving invasion of privacy, are raised by the use of some kinds of unobtrusive measures. Does the journalist have the right to go through J. Edgar Hoover's trash (or Bob Dylan's, as A. J. Weberman did for a story in *Esquire*)? The ethical questions raised by these techniques have not been discussed to any great extent. The classic book on this research approach—Eugene Webb *et al.*, *Unobtrusive Measures: Nonreactive Research in the Social Sciences*—"purposefully" avoids consideration of the ethical questions it raises, stating that they would require another book.

Every journalist must weigh the public importance of a story against these ethical questions:

1. To what extent are you justified in deceiving people to gather information?
2. To what extent are you invading people's privacy in order to gather information that might be unobtainable in other ways?
3. To what extent are you willing to risk exposing people to loss of dignity or take a chance on inflicting harm on them in order to gather information?

Then each journalist must decide if a particular technique is appropriate for finding the information he or she is seeking.

Conclusion

The behavioral scientist and the journalist are alike in that both are trying to report important information about society and human behavior. The behavioral scientist has lessons to learn from the reporter about the timeliness of reporting and the need for addressing major problems that face society. The journalist has lessons to learn from the behavioral scientist about using theory and hypotheses to direct inquiries, making reliable and valid observations, using quantification to make more precise statements, basing conclusions on adequate samples, and making legitimate causal inferences.

Historically, the task of reporting and explaining community events has remained an ongoing challenge for every generation. But while the task has remained the same, the tools have not. Increasingly the perspectives of behavioral science have begun to alter our judgments of what constitutes solid community reporting.

We should set as one of our goals the acquisition of knowledge of relevant behavioral science techniques to improve accuracy, to answer questions that were difficult to answer before, and to deepen our ability to interpret the news about our communities. It seems likely that in the future the public will increasingly come to expect the journalist to possess these skills as part of the professional training.

Part 2

Methods of Reporting

Chapter 4

Reporting Surveys and Polls

G. Cleveland Wilhoit and
Maxwell McCombs

A familiar figure around the newsrooms of both newspapers and broadcasting stations has always been the politician, with publicity release in hand. Today, however, that handout often describes a public-opinion poll. And it shows . . . guess who . . . is in the lead.

What should a responsible journalist do with the poll? Should you simply run it, attributing the findings to the politician's pollsters? Or, should you carefully evaluate the poll—everything from the size of the sample to the wording of the question—*before* you run it? Increasingly, journalists are recognizing a responsibility to evaluate polls critically, the same as they would any other information, before carrying them as news.

This is not always easy. Skeptical insight into scientific polling is crucial, and if the politician brought you an unsound poll, you have to be willing to face an irate political leader to say, "We can't run that because . . . ."

A large number of the releases brought to newsrooms are based on surveys that are inadequately (or, on occasion, dishonestly) done. A rejection must be based on sound professional knowledge in order to weather the inevitable—and unfair—charge of political bias that will undoubtedly be hurled your way if you do not carry the results.

This is no small point. Much of contemporary political news coverage, especially by columnists and commentators, focuses on the "chances" a given candidate has to win or, say, that a bond issue has of passing, or simply how people feel about various public issues. One study showed that such coverage amounted to 35 percent for some candidates in the 1968 Presidential election.[1] Readers, viewers, and political leaders have come to expect this to be part of the political rhetoric, and it is an unquestionably important part of any public campaign that depends on public opinion.

News organizations have found no shortage of persons who are willing to supply their versions of polling data to feed hungry news machines pressed by deadlines. This chapter briefly outlines some important considerations for the journalist to keep in mind when poll results must be written. All polls that are soundly done have a few major things in common, or they simply do not deserve space in your news effort. Sometimes you may discover that it is fairest to your readers to send the candidate back home with the poll results still firmly in *his or her* hand.

Political Polls

Polls, of course, are used for many purposes. Basically, they are designed to assess public opinions on various issues, but they are also used simply to find out which television stations people watch or what kinds of refrigerators they own. As a research methodology, polling seems simple—just a matter of asking a few questions—but, in reality, it requires the same kind of skill and care that behavioral scientists regularly employ in their work. If it is done well, polling is not easy.

A majority of political candidates for major offices use private political polls in their campaign strategy.[2] The polls range from sophisticated, sensitive measures of public opinion to outright

---

[1] Maxwell E. McCombs and Donald L. Shaw, "The Agenda-Setting Function of Mass Media," *Public Opinion Quarterly* 36 (1972):176–187.
[2] Louis Harris, "Polls and Politics in the United States," *Public Opinion Quarterly* 27 (1963):3–8.

fraud, but they all seem to be treated as newsworthy. They typically wind up on the front page or in a prominent place in newscasts, regardless of whether the poll results are valid. About two-thirds of the political polls that appear in the media—quite often as a result of "leaks"—should have been tossed in the wastebasket. They should be discarded because their basic assumptions or methods are faulty, or there are so many unanswered questions about the methods that the information is likely to be worthless or misleading.

In other cases, even data from properly conducted polls sometimes have been manipulated to achieve political advantage, a sophisticated form of "dirty tricks." If a candidate turns up well in only two of the fifteen questions in the poll, it is not uncommon to find a leaked story or even an actual press release based only on the two good items. Everything else in the poll, of course, was simply not shown to the reporter, who should have asked.

Much of the unethical, questionable, and "self-selected-sample" use of polls by politicians and special interest groups might be prevented if reporters were better "watchdogs" of the polls in the same way they are for other types of news. Philip Meyer, a member of the Washington Bureau of Knight Newspapers and author of *Precision Journalism*, which concentrates on survey research methods, studied polls published during the 1968 Presidential primaries and concluded that many reporters and columnists had unwittingly used distorted polling information in their stories.[3]

Political scientist Nelson Polsby studied newspaper treatment of survey data released by a team of behavioral scientists at Stanford University and the University of California, Berkeley. He found extreme differences in media interpretation of the survey, which cast doubt on the accuracy of many of the stories that were published.[4] Gerhart D. Wiebe, a journalism researcher who analyzed *The New York Times'* treatment of polls during the Congressional elections of 1966, found that headlines were often

[3] Philip Meyer, "Truth in Polling," *Columbia Journalism Review* 7 (Summer 1968):20–23.
[4] Nelson W. Polsby, "Political Science and the Press: Notes on Coverage of a Public Opinion Survey on the Vietnam War," *Western Political Quarterly* 22 (1969):47–60.

misleading, that clarifying facts were omitted, and that interpretations of polls were frequently erroneous.[5] Even in the *Times*.

To avoid being taken in by a glib (or even dishonest) news source who is attempting to paint a rosy picture of public opinion or voting intentions, journalists must learn the basics of polling and be willing to ask tough questions. If the news source is honest and has valid data, the hard questions will provide information that, in the long run, will help educate readers to know a good poll from a bad one. If the source has something to hide, a few hard questions may incur the source's wrath, but readers or listeners will surely benefit.

In summary, reporters should scrutinize poll results with the same tenacity they would a report from a governmental official about whom they are skeptical. The basic objective is to determine the credibility and validity of poll results before they are printed or aired.

Some Key Questions About Polls

The basic idea of polling—asking specific questions of a sample group—is fundamental to journalism. Reporters have asked people to describe their opinions and behavior for years and, in fact, political polls have their historical roots in journalism.

In the Presidential campaign of 1824 the *Raleigh Star* and *North Carolina Gazette* and the *American Watchman and Delaware Advertiser* did the first "straw polls" of voter intentions by interviewing persons at a number of meetings and political rallies.[6] While the samples were extremely unscientific or "accidental" from our standpoint, the basic idea of the political poll was there.

What modern pollsters have added to that nineteenth-century journalist's approach to a survey is simply more systematic inquiry. They have introduced the ideas of *probability sampling*

---

[5] Gerhart D. Wiebe, "*The New York Times* and Public Opinion Research: A Criticism," *Journalism Quarterly* 44 (1967):654–658.

[6] James Tankard, Jr., "Public Opinion Polling by Newspapers in the Presidential Campaign of 1824," *Journalism Quarterly* 49 (1972):361–365.

Metropolitan Daily Newspaper Treatment of Political Polls During the 1970 Elections

The American Association for Public Opinion Research (AAPOR) in 1969 adopted a set of standards for disclosure of public opinion polls. Twenty-four major metropolitan dailies—representing seventeen states and ranging from the *Miami Herald* to the *Anchorage Daily Times*—were studied during the 1970 Congressional elections for inclusion of the AAPOR criteria in poll stories. Only one news story in the sample contained all eight of the AAPOR standards.

TABLE 1 *Percentages of Public Opinion Poll News Stories Meeting Specific AAPOR Standards for Disclosure of Polls*

Category	Percent
Sample size	55.8
Sponsor	44.2
Base of results	37.2
Timing of interview	32.6
How contacted	20.9
Definition of population	14.0
Exact wording of question(s)	13.9
Error allowance	9.3
N = 43	

SOURCE: Taik Sup Auh and G. Cleveland Wilhoit, "Metropolitan Daily Newspaper Treatment of Political Polls during the 1970 Elections." Paper presented at the Association for Education in Journalism Convention at Colorado State University, Fort Collins, August 1973.

and a greater concern for *reliability* and *validity* in *questioning* and *interpretation.*

So, a list of suggested questions reporters should ask about polls contains some familiar ones—who, what, why, where, and when and especially how—and others that relate to the more technical aspects of survey methods. Some of the answers should be included in the poll news stories. Others must be used by the reporter to evaluate the credibility of the research. These are some major questions you should ask:

1. Who sponsored the survey?
2. Who was interviewed? (What population is being described?)
3. How were the persons selected for interviews? (What was the *sample design?*)
4. How many persons were interviewed?
5. How accurate are the results? (What is the estimated size of the *sampling error?*)
6. Who were the interviewers?
7. How were the interviews conducted?
8. When were the interviews conducted?
9. What were the actual questions asked?
10. How are the data tabulated and analyzed?

You might use these ten questions as a checklist. They are closely related to a list of standards regarded by the American Association for Public Opinion Research as important for disclosure when publishing poll results. Not many newspapers have measured up as well as they should. Let's look at each checkpoint more closely.

WHO SPONSORED THE SURVEY?

In most cases, when reporters write stories based on poll results, the data have been gathered because of some need or interest of a potential news source. A typical example is the privately commissioned poll during an election campaign. Sponsorship of a poll may have a subtle effect on question wording and selection both in the interview schedules and in the publicity releases prepared from the survey data. Also, sponsorship may affect how the data are analyzed.

Clearly, sponsor identity is necessary if the reporter and the reader or listener are to be able to evaluate poll information properly. News sources may have righteous public relations objectives in conducting surveys of opinion, but the scientific validity may be abandoned in the hopes that the ends justify the means. Reporting who, literally, paid the piper is the first step in helping the reader evaluate what tune was called or played.

Reporters should not only ask who paid for the survey; they should also ask about the experience and reputation of the research firm or group that conducted the survey. Reporters should ask about the research firm's credentials. Be firm about this.

An extremely important item for poll stories is the way the sample to be interviewed was selected, which determines to what *population* the sample results may be generalized. The population is the aggregate of persons to which the sample survey data refer. For example, if a sample of the general "adult" population is interviewed in an election survey, the results for the *entire* sample may not be generalized to a different group, such as "registered voters." They are much more interested in politics than the general population. Who you ask makes all the difference in the world. If politicians poll members of their own party about their chances, the results may be quite valid, for members of their own party, of course! *Who* was interviewed?

Also, who was *not* interviewed? In all surveys, some persons who are in the original sample refuse to be interviewed or are never located by interviewers. This factor is called *non-response* bias and may affect the validity of survey results if those not responding are similar in age, socioeconomic class, or other characteristics pertinent to a particular survey. For example, lower socioeconomic types of persons are sometimes harder to contact than others and also may respond differently.

If socioeconomic status is correlated with the attitude or behavior being surveyed, a consistent non-response may affect the accuracy of results. The reporter should ask the news source about the size of the non-response and whether there is any reason to suspect that those who were not interviewed might differ dramatically from those who responded.

If the research firm or survey sponsor is reluctant to supply information about non-response, you should pressure the survey sponsor for an answer or be challenged in the news story for not telling enough. If the source refuses to disclose the information, the reporter can try to use census data for the community to assess the representativeness of demographic characteristics that are reported in the survey.

A polling organization or news source must be willing to give the reporter complete details about the type of sampling used in a poll. Even if the reporter or editor does not wish to use *all* the technical details in the poll story, the news source should be pressed hard for sampling information so that the reporter and others may assess validity of the data and make thoughtful decisions *whether* to write a story based on them.

Is the sample a *probability scientific random sample?* That is, did every eligible person in the community have an exactly equal likelihood of being picked to be interviewed? Or, was the method a "convenience" sample, in which the interviewers went to factories, street corners, and offices, talking to persons they happened to meet? Or, did they ask for only volunteers (self-selected samples)?

If the sample is a probability sample, what sort of sampling design and source were used to provide the list from which the sample was drawn? Telephone directories, city directories, and county maps with the housing units labeled are common sources from which a sample is drawn. Each has its particular set of biases and problems (such as unlisted numbers, costs), so the reporter must try to evaluate whether important groups of people have been overlooked just by virtue of the sampling approaches used. (Sampling designs are covered in more detail in Chapter 6.)

HOW MANY PERSONS WERE INTERVIEWED?

In general, the larger the sample, the more accurate are the results. However, a carefully constructed probability sample that is small in size is likely to be much more accurate than a larger non-random (convenience) type sample because it insures that the sample represents the population more accurately.

Here is a general rule for any reporter or editor to keep in mind in considering whether the size of a sample is adequate: If opinion or behavior appears to be evenly divided in the community—that is, if the reporter's best information suggests opinion is equally strong on all sides of the issue or the candidates are very close—a larger sample is required to give an accurate picture of the community. The closer the opinion, the larger the sample. In addition, the closer two candidates or sides of an issue appear to be in an actual survey result, the larger the sample required to be sure the small differences suggested in the survey are real and not a result of *sampling error.*

HOW ACCURATE ARE THE RESULTS?
(WHAT IS THE ESTIMATED SIZE
OF THE SAMPLING ERROR?)

Reputable survey research firms willingly supply estimates of sampling error—the percentage or numerical range of accuracy *within* which any survey estimate of the whole population may be expected to fall. While sampling error is tied to sample size—that is, if everything else remains the same, sampling error goes down as sample size goes up—a specific estimate of the error may provide an easy way to tell the reader when an election or an issue is too close to call. For example, if poll results show candidate A with an expected 48 percent of the vote of registered voters and candidate B with an expected 52 percent of the vote, the crucial next piece of information is the sampling error. If the error reported is 6 percent, this means the "true" vote from the voting population—*not* the sample— could vary as much as six points from the expected vote estimated from the poll. Candidate A might even win, with 54 percent of the vote, while B goes under with only 46 percent of the vote.

With a larger sample, the margin of error could be reduced, but even national polls which sample (generally) about 1,600 do not reduce the margin of error much below 3 percent. As Chapter 6 points out, samples of enormous sizes would be required to reduce the margin of error much below this 3 percent; it would not be worth it.

WHO WERE THE INTERVIEWERS?
HOW WERE THE INTERVIEWS CONDUCTED?

Good reporters know from their own interviewing experience that survey research is no better than the quality of the interviews. Information about the types of

How Sex in U.S. Has Changed

The U.S. is in the midst of a "vast, profound, and unprecedented" sexual liberation movement, according to a survey published in *Playboy* magazine yesterday.

The survey said that premarital sex has become both acceptable and widespread, with the change most noteworthy in women.

The "social changes related to sexual liberation have been vast, profound, and unprecedented," the survey said. "Americans are more tolerant of the sexual ideas and acts of other persons than formerly and far, far freer to envision various previously forbidden acts as possible for themselves."

The Playboy Foundation commissioned the survey, which was conducted by the Research Guild, Inc., a private research organization.

The survey indicated that, although sexual attitudes of Americans have gone through radical changes since the Kinsey study twenty-five years ago, the changes have not destroyed "institutions necessary to the stability of society itself."

The survey included interviews with 2,026 persons over the age of seventeen—982 men and 1,044 women—living in cities and suburbs. Seventy-one percent of those surveyed were married, 25 percent single, and 4 percent divorced.

In his sexual behavior study a generation ago, Dr. Alfred Kinsey reported that one-third of single women in his study had had intercourse by the age of twenty-five.

The *Playboy* survey found that about 75 percent of single women admitted to having premarital relations before twenty-five, and said they were having relations more frequently.

In other findings, 32 percent of the married men under age twenty-five in the survey said they had engaged in extramarital relations, only a slight increase over the Kinsey figures.

However, 24 percent of wives under age twenty-five admitted extramarital affairs, a jump of about 15 percent since Kinsey's study.

In contrast, the survey said, "The great majority of people still feel that love and sex are too closely interwoven to be separable at will or for fun. Anywhere from 80 to 98 percent of the men and women in our study say that they or their mates would object to any kind of extramarital sex experience by their partners. . . ."

SOURCE: *United Press International*, September 13, 1973.

Sex Survey "Ripoff"

The *Chicago Daily News* said yesterday *Playboy* magazine used questionable methods in its current survey of sexual behavior in the 1970s.

The newspaper, in its Sept. 29–30 edition, said respected experts, including those associated with the Kinsey Report, "have doubts about the credibility of the survey and the methods used in doing it."

The Daily News headlined its report "The Sex Survey Rip-off" and subtitled it "or . . . How the Playboy Foundation spent $100,000 to Find Out Everything They've Always Wanted to Say About Sex."

The newspaper said research experts did not quarrel with the *Playboy* conclusions published in the October edition and to be followed in five more editions.

The *News* said the findings indicate "that premarital and oral sex are on the increase, women are having more orgasms than in the past, and the homosexuality rate has remained stable."

But, the newspaper said, experts question whether the survey reached people really representative of the nation's population.

The research was conducted by the Research Guild Inc. of Chicago "not a clinical assembly of scholars," unlike Dr. Albert S. Kinsey who used five other scientists, the *News* reported.

SOURCE: *San Francisco Sunday Examiner & Chronicle,* September 30, 1973.

---

persons conducting interviews, the extent of their training, and whether the interviews were done in person should be considered essential in evaluating the validity of a survey.

Were the interviewers experienced and professionally trained? Were they persons who would have a reasonable chance to establish rapport with the type of person they interviewed? Were there any problems with incomplete or unclear responses? If minority-group members were included in the sample, were interviewers of the same minority assigned to them?

If the interviewing was conducted by telephone, or by a mail questionnaire, the journalist should report these facts. The mode of the survey has crucial effects on the answers. If someone shows you the results of a survey into people's deeply personal lives based on a telephone survey, be particularly suspicious.

But all three types of interview techniques—person-to-person, telephone, and mail—may be used effectively for certain subjects or issues. Obviously you need to know how the interview was conducted. Look at the questions asked, too.

WHEN WERE THE INTERVIEWS CONDUCTED?

The timing of interviews in relation to other things going on in a community may have a great effect on the results. For example, if a major disclosure about a political candidate's honesty occurs in the news during the time interviewing about voter intentions is taking place, the disclosure may seriously affect the remaining interviews. Also, if interviewing is done early in a political campaign, but the results are not publicized until much later, obvious distortions in the meaning of the data are possible. In one extreme case, a political candidate released a poll shortly before election day showing him substantially ahead of his opponent. What was not reported was that the poll was six months old. When the poll was taken, the candidate's opponent was not even a declared contender for the office. No wonder he was ahead! So, if events have changed the issue since the interviewing was conducted, the reader should be informed about the possibility of misinterpretation of the poll. *Or,* perhaps, you shouldn't even run the poll.

WHAT WERE THE ACTUAL QUESTIONS ASKED?

It makes a lot of difference if someone asks you: "Don't you like strawberry shortcake?" as contrasted with, "Do you, or do you not, like strawberry shortcake?" As any reporter knows, wording can be all important. Technical aspects of polls, such as sampling technique, are easier than framing questions, contrary to popular view. A reporter should always ask any polling news source for a complete copy of the questionnaire used so that exact wording of crucial questions may be checked for loaded words and unclear and poorly worded questions. Also, the reporter may determine if potentially embarrassing results may have been left out of the publicity release by checking the entire questionnaire.

If the questionnaire or interview schedule is unavailable to the reporter, the source should be asked to provide the exact wording of crucial questions. If the source is unwilling to give exact wording, the reporter should include that fact in the news and note why it may or may not be important. Or, of course, the reporter may recommend that the survey be rejected for publication.

FINALLY . . . HOW ARE THE DATA
TABULATED AND ANALYZED?

Have any special tabulation or analysis techniques been used? Although technically pure, poll findings that result from the presence or absence of various data manipulations may mislead audiences and journalists alike. Poll predictions on an upcoming election, for example, based on the entire sample versus only those members of the sample most likely to vote may yield drastically different news stories!

Finally, if you have checked out a poll and found that it is sound, readers do not have to be told everything. But you must provide them with enough details that they, too, can evaluate the results of the poll. That is only responsible journalism. The answers to most of our checklist questions can be skillfully slipped into your stories at crucial places. Or, they can be placed in a sidebar, as some newspapers do it, but they must be put somewhere.

Don't let the city desk or copyeditors put you down with this response: Our readers or viewers can't understand the technical stuff, so cut it! In too many cases that happens, but this information is *an inherent part* of a story based on poll results. Without it, you have told an incomplete story.

The print and electronic journalists must argue that including this information can be done simply and that the reader—not to mention the person who brought in the poll data—must be educated to read survey stories more critically. That is part of the media responsibility in an age in which people are deluged with all kinds of persons trying to "shape" their opinions. The responsible press must act more as a filter, less as a conduit.

Only journalists with a strong sense of responsibility and thor-

Standards for Disclosure of Polls as Reported in the *Miami Herald* during the 1970 Elections

Here's How *Herald* Polled Florida Voters

sponsor
type sampling

The Miami Herald's survey is based on a *modified probability sample* of *registered voters who say they plan to vote in the Nov. 3 general election.*

definition of population

The survey *was designed by Philip Meyer of Knight Newspaper's Washington Bureau, who has studied public opinion research at Harvard* under a Nieman Fellowship and who served last year as a project director of the Russell Sage Foundation.

experience and reputation of person directing the survey

identification of interviewers

when survey was conducted

Nine reporters interviewed *600 people between October 14 and October 19* in *precincts scattered from Pensacola to the Florida Keys and from Cape Coral to Jacksonville.*

sample size

The voters were handed paper ballots and asked to *"suppose elections were being held today. Please mark the ballot as you would in a real election for the candidate or party you would like to see win in each contest."* Those who were in doubt were asked to mark the ballot for the candidate or party *"toward which you lean, as of today."*

exact wording of crucial question

ough insight into surveys will really be in a position to say no, when necessary, to those who promptly will charge "news bias." But the journalist, as a professional, must simply be able to evaluate surveys on a scientific basis and then make a decision whether or not to run survey stories—which is a press, not a political, judgment.

error
allowance }

probability
level }

    In a survey of this type, the expected *error allowance is five percent.* For example, if the survey shows a candidate to have the support of 60 percent of the voters, *the odds are nineteen to one* that his true support is between 55 and 65 percent. *The error margin is greater for percentages based on less than the full sample.* } *warning about base changes*

identification
of interviewers {

    Reporters who took part in the survey are Juanita Greene, Susan Burnside, Heath Meriweather, June Kronholz, Don Bedwell, Capital Bureau Chief William Mansfield, William Malong of the capital bureau[sic], *Monte Hayes of the Broward County Bureau and Bob Burdick, Boca Raton Bureau Chief.*

SOURCE: *Miami Herald,* October 25, 1970.

Chapter 5

Conducting a Survey

Maxwell McCombs and
G. Cleveland Wilhoit

Journalists have been doing survey research for decades. That hoary journalistic tradition, the "man-in-the-street" interview, is extensively used whenever a major news story breaks. Passersby have been queried about their feelings when political leaders were assassinated, about their preferred candidates in numerous upcoming elections, and about every other subject that has come to a reporter's or editor's mind.

This is survey research, albeit of a very unprofessional quality, as the reader who has read the last chapter on evaluation of polls knows. But with an appreciation of research methods any reporter or editor can design a rigorous set of interviews that are a valuable lode of information about public responses to topics in the news. And newsroom applications of systematic, scientific survey research can go far beyond the traditional approach exemplified by "man-in-the-street" interviews.

Because polling and "man-in-the-street" interviews have a long history in journalism, survey research is the area where journalists are likely to feel most comfortable initially in applying the lessons of behavioral science to news reporting. Chapter 4 has already demonstrated the importance and value of methodological rigor in polls and surveys. In training a journalist how to evaluate polls, the rudiments of survey research have already been presented. The checklist of questions in the preceding chapter, used in evaluating a poll, lists the essential facets of survey research. The agenda is set; what remains here is to delve deeper into the items on this agenda so that journalists can move from evaluating someone else's survey work to creating and carrying out their own surveys.

Mode of Interviewing

The first question a journalist must ask in planning a survey is: "How will the interviews be conducted?" Interviews with a sample of respondents can be con- ducting the interviews has key implications for question and questionnaire design, determination of the mode is the first major decision. What are the criteria that influence a reporter's decision on the mode of interviewing? There is no fixed, magic number of criteria to be weighed. Six will be suggested here for considera- tion.

Obviously, in actual time the interviewing follows the design of the questionnaire. However, since the mode selected for conduct- ing the interviews has key implications for question and question- naire design, determination of the mode is the first major decision. What are the criteria that influence a reporter's decision on the mode of interviewing? There is no fixed, magic number of cri- teria to be weighed. Six will be suggested here for consideration.

COST

There are significant differences in the costs of face-to-face, telephone, and mail interviews. Cost looms large in any newsroom, which is another reason to decide on the mode of interviewing at the very first stage of planning. Suppose the reporter's goal is to complete interviews with a ran- dom sample of 200 voters in the city. For the moment, we will ig- nore such factors as non-response and refusals and just consider the cost of obtaining 200 voter interviews. Considering the cost alone, the *face-to-face interview* is the most expensive. An inter- viewer must travel to the residence of each voter who is to be interviewed, and if the respondent is not at home, *callbacks* are necessary.

Once the interviewer has found the voter, then time is required to complete the interview. Even if this is only ten to fifteen minutes, we must also pay for the travel and searching time, plus the expenses of the travelling. And callbacks add to the costs. If the sample is spread over a large area—such as an entire county or entire state—these travel costs can be substantial. In our example where the sample is 200 voters from a single community, travel costs are much smaller. Nevertheless, a ten or fifteen minute interview will cost an absolute minimum of $2.50 each. If one hires a professional interviewing organization or market research firm to do the interviewing, the costs are likely to be $10 or more per interview. Even using the minimum cost figure, we must budget $500 to $600 for direct out-of-pocket interviewing costs. Most news directors and city editors do not easily allocate that kind of money.

If cost alone is the criterion, a *mail questionnaire* is the cheapest form to use. The clerical cost of stuffing 200 envelopes is small. One can probably find someone around the newsroom who will do it free. So the only real costs are the envelopes, reproduction of a cover letter explaining the survey, and the first-class postage out and back. Remember you have to pay the postage both ways. Few voters are so loyal to your newspaper or broadcasting station, or interested enough in your survey, to pay for the return postage. Typically, twenty-five cents or so will cover the costs. For 200 interviews, this means only about $50. (This figure does not include the printing costs for the questionnaire itself, because that cost is common to all modes of interviewing. There has to be a supply of questionnaires to be filled out.)

In between the cost of the face-to-face interview and the mail questionnaire is the *telephone interview*. Newsrooms are already well equipped with telephones, including WATS (the acronym for wide area telephone service) lines in many cases, when one is considering a regional or statewide survey. This eliminates any direct costs for telephoning, leaving only the costs of the interviewers' time. Even at the same rate of pay as for face-to-face interviews, the costs are substantially less. An interviewer who must travel from house to house and return several times to many of these addresses will do well to average two interviews per hour, even though the interview itself takes little more than ten or fifteen minutes. In contrast, a telephone interviewer can easily average three or more interviews per hour. In most survey situations, the ratio of productivity is considerably higher than the three to two just described. A more typical ratio is probably closer to five to one. That is, in a given period of time for which an interviewer is being paid, the telephone interviewer will produce five interviews for every one completed by the face-to-face interviewer.

Cost is not the only criterion for selecting a particular mode of interviewing. There are a number of interrelated factors that must be considered simultaneously. For example, before giving the mail questionnaire a high positive rating and the face-to-face interview a rather negative rating, we must consider the response rate. How many people in our selected sample of voters will be successfully interviewed? The discussion of sampling in Chapter 6 shows how to select a representative sample of whatever group the journalist is interested in. But if interviews are not successfully completed with most of that sample, the resulting information may be totally invalid. Perhaps there were only a few elderly people at home on the afternoon the reporter called. That would hardly be a representative sample of the whole community.

Response rates for face-to-face interviews and for telephone interviews are about the same. In both cases, the trick is to find people at home and complete an interview. *Non-response*, resulting from not-at-homes and refusals, is rather small for both modes. But for mail questionnaires non-response is a serious problem. Mail questionnaires are perceived by many respondents as another piece of "junk mail" to be thrown in the waste basket. Even for those that survive initially, how many will ever be filled out? There is little in the mail questionnaire to demand immediate attention to the interview; it can be deferred. In short, responding to a mail questionnaire requires substantial motivation and interest in the topics of the survey. The typical result is that 10 percent or fewer are ever returned. Even if the response rate reaches 50 or 60 percent, the replies may still be a biased sample of the community under study. Since the return of a mail questionnaire does require substantial motivation, the replies often overrepresent those with intense interest or with extreme views on the topic.

Finally, there is the problem of identifying who really filled out the questionnaire. With the face-to-face or telephone interview we have reasonable knowledge of who gave the answers. But when a mail questionnaire goes into the mailbox we lose control of it. The response—if there is one at all—*may* be from the registered voter to whom the questionnaire was addressed. Or it may have been filled out by a teenage daughter, or spouse, or other relative. In short, the mail questionnaire is often an unreliable device for gathering representative information about a community or group because of the poor response rate.

The complexity of the questions to be asked also determines the best mode for interviewing. In general, as we move from mail questionnaires to telephone interviews to face-to-face interviews, we can increase the complexity of questions posed. In the mail questionnaire, the instructions and the questions must be relatively simple. If they are not, respondents will either answer incorrectly or will give no answer at all because they do not understand what is being requested. Over the telephone, we can explain things a bit more and adjust the explanation to fit each respondent. But there are still many kinds of questions that are too complex to use in a telephone interview. Even something as common as a rating scale is difficult to communicate successfully over the telephone. With a printed rating scale to look at and hold, a respondent can easily make a check mark. This cannot be done over the telephone.

In the face-to-face interview, we have all the advantages available to pose difficult and complex questions. Instructions can be adjusted to take account of respondent difficulties. Training aids—ranging from a printed card given to the respondent to detailed charts or photographs—can be used. A face-to-face interview can become like a classroom if the survey topic demands it. The freedom of the face-to-face interview to delve into all kinds of topics, at all levels of complexity, using a wide variety of observation and measurement techniques, accounts for its extensive use despite the high financial costs.

NUMBER OF QUESTIONS

The overall length of the questionnaire that can be used varies considerably among the three modes of interviewing. Few people will have sufficient motivation to fill out a twenty-page, quarter-inch thick questionnaire that arrives unsolicited in the mail. Mail questionnaires are best limited to two or three pages. In other words, twelve to fifteen questions is an optimum length for a mail questionnaire. The rule of thumb on length is about the same for a telephone interview. Five to ten minutes is the upper limit for a telephone interview. Few persons will stay on the telephone very long answering a stranger's questions. And remember, it is very easy for the respondent to terminate a telephone interview.

In contrast to the mail questionnaire and the telephone interview, the face-to-face interview can go to considerable lengths. It is not uncommon for a face-to-face interview to last half an hour. And interviews lasting from one to two hours are possible. The tolerance of the respondent is considerably greater in the face-to-face situation. And, considering the high fixed cost of these interviews in terms of travel costs and so on, the additional costs of another dozen or so questions is quite small. In short, the high costs of the face-to-face interview are balanced by the larger volume of information that might be secured.

SOCIAL DESIRABILITY BIAS

Most persons like to project a favorable image—even to a stranger who is interviewing them briefly in a survey. Therefore, the positive answers are inflated about such things as voting, viewing educational television, reading serious books, and reading editorials in the newspaper. Much more behavior of this type is reported by survey respondents than actually occurs. For example, in a statewide survey of Louisiana voters during 1968, more than two-thirds reported that they had voted. Official election returns, however, showed that only about half the state's eligible voters actually went to the polls. In another survey, 32 percent reported viewing educational television during the past week. But when they were asked to name a program they had seen, only 19 percent of the sample could actually name any program on educational television.

In the telephone and face-to-face interview we can build in follow-up questions like "Which program did you watch on educational television?" and so limit the inflationary effects of *social desirability bias* on our data. But in the case of the mail questionnaire, remember that we lost control of the questionnaire when we dropped it in the mailbox. Regardless of any number of follow-up and probing questions, respondents can think out their answers carefully—even look up supporting information—in order to project the best possible image. In short, it is exceedingly difficult, if not impossible, to control the effects of social desirability bias in the mail questionnaire.

REPRESENTATIVENESS OF THE RESPONDENTS

It has already been noted that the *external validity* of the mail questionnaire may be seriously compromised by the problem of non-response. So many of the respondents selected in the original sample design typically are lost at the data-collection stage of the mail interview that the final available set of data is quite unrepresentative of the population or group that we set out to describe.

Neither the telephone survey nor the face-to-face survey has this difficulty to such an extreme degree. But the telephone survey is limited by the availability of telephones. In most geographic areas and for many groups of people this is not really a problem. But for some groups—such as urban poor or migratory workers—it is extremely serious. They cannot be reached by telephone. The telephone survey also has another problem that at least potentially limits the representativeness of the data obtained—the problem of unlisted telephone numbers. In the average city less than 10 percent of the telephones have unlisted numbers, but in a city like Washington, D.C., the proportion of unlisted numbers is closer to 50 percent. One possible way around this problem—albeit a somewhat tedious one—is to have a computer generate random four-digit numbers, representing the last four digits of a telephone number. (We know what the first three digits—the exchange—are for each area.) Every telephone number, regardless of whether it is published or unlisted, has an equal chance of turning up in such a sampling. Of course, it also means that the interviewers will dial many nonexistent telephone numbers.

In terms of representativeness, then, the face-to-face interview will typically yield the best set of data. The only serious constraint is social desirability bias, and this can be dealt with extensively during the interviewing period.

The six categories discussed are not the only criteria to be considered when designing a survey. But they are some of the more important ones. Considering the three modes of interviewing vis-à-vis these six criteria leads to the conclusion that the mail questionnaire is the least desirable for carrying out a survey. While the mail survey does rank well on cost, it receives low marks on response rate, kinds and numbers of questions, social desirability bias, and representativeness of the respondents in journalistic types of information gathering.

This leaves the face-to-face interview and the telephone interview as the major tools a reporter can best use in conducting survey research. The face-to-face interview has the advantage in terms of the kinds and numbers of questions that can be included and sometimes in terms of the representativeness of the respondents. For response rate and social desirability bias there is little difference between the two modes.

In many reporting situations the key criterion is likely to be the cost. Here the telephone interview has a distinct advantage. Most of the costs are already part of the overhead cost of the newsroom and do not have to be reflected in the project budget. Telephone interviews can also be conducted more rapidly than face-to-face interviews. In newsrooms where costs and speed are prime considerations, the telephone interview is the likely choice.

Translating Reporting Goals

Having decided on the mode of interviewing, the reporter now begins to consider the actual questions to be asked in the interview. Just as in reporting, a key ele-

Strip-mining Opposed by
50 Percent in Coal Areas

The Coal Mining Attitude poll was conducted for the *Courier-Journal* and the *Louisville Times* by Unidex Corp., a three-year-old opinion and market analysis company based in Bloomington, Ind. Unidex is best known for its college student opinion poll, the results of which are published by fifty-six newspapers.

Personal interviews were conducted with 601 persons in their homes, 301 from six coal-producing counties in eastern Kentucky and 300 from four coal-producing counties in western Kentucky. The counties, chosen because they were the top ten in coal production in the 1966 Department of Commerce tonnage report, are Floyd, Harlan, Knott, Letcher, Perry, and Pike in the east and Muhlenberg, Hopkins, Ohio, and Union in the west.

The interviews were conducted between July 28 and August 25.

To obtain the opinions, the pollsters used random methods of selection, and the sample was designed to be representative of the total population (eighteen years and over) in the ten-county area.

When figures from the eastern counties were combined with those of the western counties, the eastern figures were weighed to reflect the larger population proportion as compared with the western counties' population. This is a standard polling technique.

The margin of possible error varies with each different answer in a poll. According to Unidex, the most extreme margin of possible error for this size and type of poll is 4.5 percentage points, but most of the answers are closer to a margin of 2 or 3 percentage points.

Among the survey's findings were:

One out of every two residents interviewed in the eastern Kentucky counties favor a statewide ban on strip-mining as compared with a little over one out of four in western counties who favor a ban.

In the western Kentucky counties, considerably more persons interviewed oppose strip-mining than favor it, but not to the point of banning it.

Strong anti-strip-mining sentiment is found among underground coal miners.

Older residents in the coal fields are more likely to oppose strip-mining than the younger residents.

About three of every ten persons interviewed feel that new laws are needed to control strip-mining. The greatest number of these people feel that the companies should be made to restore the land they have mined.

More than 90 percent of those interviewed felt a coal company, even though it holds a broad form deed to the minerals, should get the permission of the land owner before mining the land.

Attitudes toward strip-mining in Kentucky's 10 top coal-producing counties

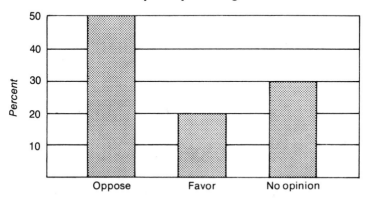

Attitudes toward banning strip-mining, by place of residence (percentage of those that favor ban)

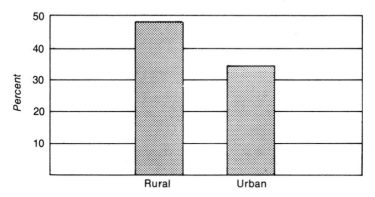

SOURCE: *Louisville Courier-Journal & Times*, October 8, 1972. Copyright © 1974, The Courier-Journal & Times.

ment in survey research is specifying the *focal question* to be asked. Each item in a questionnaire stands or falls on whether it can shed light on the major question or theme at issue. The focal question may be a *hypothesis* or it may be a *community characteristic* that the reporter wishes to estimate. Since a hypothesis—a statement of the possible relationship between two variables— can subsume estimates of community characteristics, the advantage lies with hypothesis testing. Hypotheses help the reporter define the limits of an investigation. Who am I to talk to? Which documents shall I seek? What shall I ask? And, how shall I link my information to the focal question? In short, determination of the focal question is important both for the design and analysis of the questionnaire—our concerns here—and for the sample design—the concern of Chapter 6.

Developing the Questionnaire

The typical reporter thinks questionnaires are easy to design. Fortunately, the reporter's training in clear and concise writing does present a head start in developing questionnaires, but there is much more to it than just good, clear writing. Framing questions is both an art and a science.[1]

The focal question phrased by the reporter early in the survey project is the key to questionnaire design. Specific questionnaire content is derived from the focal question. Each specific questionnaire item must be evaluated against the criterion: What can this item potentially contribute to answering the focal question?

The process begins with a clear understanding of the meaning and scope of the focal question. The newspaper morgue, the local public or college libraries are starting points for background information about a particular problem. The reporter's first-hand experience and insights may be helpful and often may be the only information at hand. Just as reporters research regular news stories, they must do a great deal of leg work in putting together all the information known about the survey problem before drafting a questionnaire.

---

[1] Stanley Payne, *The Art of Asking Questions*, Princeton University Press, Princeton, 1951.

In almost every survey project, the reporter's thinking about the focal question is likely to be *causal*. That is, the reporter has in mind a set of factors that are possibly related to or that predict another set of things. Suppose, for example, the reporter was interested in skepticism or cynicism about the criminal justice system. He thinks the views of young persons are different from those of older persons and has a hunch that the difference is related to perceived or actual inequities in the sentencing of young and old.

The reporter's causal thinking is often clearly separable into *independent* factors (such as age and perceived inequities) and *dependent* factors (skepticism, cynicism, and other opinions). Independent (or predictor) factors are often demographic characteristics such as age, sex, and socioeconomic levels. Dependent (or response) factors that a questionnaire attempts to gauge are often more complex behaviors, such as opinions.

When opinion assessment is a major goal, four critical elements of an opinion must be probed, usually with separate questions. First, a question may be designed to assess *opinion direction*— whether the person is favorably, unfavorably, or neutrally inclined toward an issue. A second query seeks the *degree of favorability*—extreme, moderate, or slight. Intensity—how strong the person feels about an expressed position—is also usually dealt with in one or more questions. This third dimension gives an idea of how crystallized the person's opinion is and the likelihood of opinion change. A fourth dimension, *saliency,* is harder to assess than the other elements, but it is often an important predictor of effective public opinion. Saliency—how important or pertinent an issue is for a person—is usually asked about in terms of how much the respondent perceives the issue as involving or affecting him or her personally.[2]

Drafting questions is easier if one thinks in terms of independent and dependent factors because it helps to focus on the research question and avoids unnecessary time spent on unrelated questions. Question-drafting sessions are often sidetracked by the excited query: "Wouldn't it be great to find out if . . . ?" A

---

[2] Further discussion of the relationship between these factors and the opinion process is available in Robert E. Lane and David C. Sears, *Public Opinion,* Prentice-Hall, Inc., Englewood Cliffs, N.J., 1964.

counter-query may save time: "What does that tell us about our independent or dependent factors?"

Deciding on the Question Mix

Questions for both independent and dependent factors may range from completely structured to completely open. Each question has two parts, a stimulus range (the query) and a response range (the answer). The reporter's objective is to have as much control as possible over both those parts without putting words into the respondent's mouth.

Question forms

SO-RO Stimulus open Response open	**SO-RC** Stimulus open Response closed
SC-RO Stimulus closed Response open	**SC-RC** Stimulus closed Response closed

SO-RO Questions Investigations that need to remain as unobtrusive as possible may use completely unstructured questions. This question form placed early in the interview allows the interviewees to define the story area in their own terms. The structure-free question is usually a probe about a broad topic that allows the respondent to say whatever comes to mind:

> What do you consider to be the most serious problems facing the people of this city?

Respondents are free to define "serious problems" in their own terms. Local problems or national problems with local implications could be mentioned. Social problems or political problems may be raised. Both the question and the potential answers are extremely open.

Other questions may focus on particular problems or aspects of them in which the journalist is interested, but the unstructured probe allows the interviewer to assess the meaning of problems as first defined by the respondent, not the interviewer.

The structure-free question may also be used as a reliability or validity check at the end of a highly structured questionnaire. "Is there anything else you would like to mention?" is a common way of allowing respondents the opportunity to contradict themselves, expand, or cite important areas the questionnaire may have missed.

SC-RO Questions Respondents may be asked about a specific problem or issue in a structured query, but permitted to phrase an answer in their own terms:

> Some persons say racial strife is the most pressing problem facing the people of this city. Others disagree. What do you think?

This form retains maximum authenticity of the form and content of the response, assuming the question is asked properly and the interviewer is able to record the answer accurately.

SO-RC Questions Some transitional situations in a questionnaire may use the open query and closed response:

> In thinking about the major problems facing the people of this city, do you happen to be aware of any actions taken by elected officials during the past year in response to those problems?
> _____ Yes _____ No

This question may lead the interviewer to a further question about which problems and which attempted solutions are perceived as relevant by the particular respondent. The other question forms are likely to be used more often, however, because a closed response is often inappropriate to an open question. Also, the either/or response used in the above question should be used with caution. Most issues are too complex to force respondents into a yes-no answer.

SC-RC Questions The most frequently used question form is the completely structured item. Both the query and the range of response are limited by the interviewer. A question just cited may be changed to fit the SC-RC form by limiting the terms of the response:

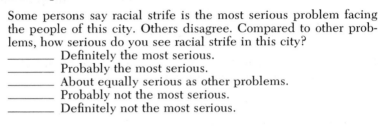

Some persons say racial strife is the most serious problem facing
the people of this city. Others disagree. What do you think?
_____ Racial strife is definitely the most serious.
_____ Racial strife is probably the most serious.
_____ Racial strife is probably not the most serious.
_____ Racial strife is definitely not the most serious.

But structured questions such as this are subject to greater
peril than other forms. As the reader has probably realized, the
forced choices in this answer exclude the possibility that racial
strife is only *as important* as some other problem. The question
can be improved:

Some persons say racial strife is the most serious problem facing
the people of this city. Others disagree. Compared to other prob-
lems, how serious do you see racial strife in this city?
_____ Definitely the most serious.
_____ Probably the most serious.
_____ About equally serious as other problems.
_____ Probably not the most serious.
_____ Definitely not the most serious.

The principal advantages of the completely structured question are economy of interviewing time and efficiency in recording
and tabulating the response. In subject areas where the reporter
has established that the respondent's knowledge or opinions are
pertinent, the closed question can provide valid results. If the
respondent is not qualified to answer because the issue is not
salient or because important knowledge is lacking, the closed
question may distort the respondent's actual position. For example, for persons with low awareness of racial and other major
problems, the question above is likely to exaggerate the apparent
awareness of the racial problem. The question could provide valid
results if it is used along with the open (SO-RO) question phrased
above. The proper blend of structured and open questions depends upon the focal research question and survey objectives.
Usually, practical limitations such as experience of the interviewers, time requirements, and ease of coding dictate greater
structure than the reporter may ideally desire.

                           Scales and Indices Some in-
dependent and dependent factors are so complex that a single,
isolated question vastly oversimplifies the respondent's answer.
Most social and political problems have numerous facets. Watergate, race relations, and environmental problems are good ex-

amples. A single item in a questionnaire does not tap the vast domain of these topics. Using a single item imposes a simplistic perspective on complex subject matter.

One solution to the problem of oversimplifying the response is to develop a number of *related items* (often called a *scale* or *index*) that measure the factor. These items can be combined to form a single variable so that the reporter is labeling a sample of the respondent's behavior rather than the response to a single item. Reporters can develop a scale suited to their purposes, but their first thought should be: Has anyone else studied this problem? In many cases, the answer is yes. A scale or index that has been pretested is often available in the behavioral science literature.

Remember, to be valid the combined items must be related. If you develop your own scale or index, this relationship must be established. Items that *appear* to tap the same topic or concept often do not actually relate to each other. Scales from the literature have already been pretested to establish this homogeneity.

The Handbook of Research Design and Social Measurement,[3] for example, lists thirty-six scales and indices covering such diverse variables as social status, group structure, community solidarity, and religious identification. There are numerous other sources.[4]

Typical of multiple-item measures prepared by behavioral scientists is Bosworth's Community Services subscale, which consists of twenty items. Survey respondents are asked to indicate for each item whether they "strongly agree," "agree," "disagree," "strongly disagree," or are "undecided." Responses can be scored from 0 ("undecided") to 4 ("strongly agree"), and the sum of each respondent's scores can be calculated. This sum (total of scores across all items) represents the community services measure for the respondent. Obviously, a score based on twenty items covering numerous facets of community services is more valid than data obtained from a single indicator.

---

[3] Delbert Miller, *Handbook of Research Design and Social Measurement,* David McKay, New York, 1964.
[4] For example, John P. Robinson *et al., Measures of Political Attitudes,* Survey Research Center, University of Michigan, Ann Arbor, 1968; and *Measures of Occupational Attitudes,* 1969.

Community Attitude Scale

1. The school should stick to the 3 R's and forget about most of the other courses being offered today.
2. Most communities are good enough as they are without starting any new community improvement programs.
3. Every community should encourage more music and lecture programs.
4. This used to be a better community to live in.
5. Long-term progress is more important than immediate benefits.
6. We have too many organizations for doing good in the community.
7. The home and the church should have all the responsibility for preparing young people for marriage and parenthood.
8. The responsibility for older people should be confined to themselves and their families instead of the community.
9. Communities have too many youth programs.
10. Schools are good enough as they are in most communities.
11. Too much time is usually spent on the planning phases of community projects.
12. Adult education should be an essential part of the local school program.
13. Only the doctors should have the responsibility for the health program in the community.
14. Mental illness is not a responsibility of the whole community.
15. A modern community should have the services of social agencies.
16. The spiritual needs of the citizens are adequately met by the churches.
17. In order to grow, a community must provide additional recreation facilities.
18. In general, church members are better citizens.
19. The social needs of the citizens are the responsibility of themselves and their families and not of the community.
20. Churches should be expanded and located in accordance with population growth.

SOURCE: *Handbook of Research Design and Social Measurement,* Delbert C. Miller, copyright © 1964, 1970 by David McKay Company, Inc. Used with permission of the publisher.

Pretesting

Reporters are always concerned about the reliability of sources and the validity of information obtained from them. In the same way, a reporter should evaluate a questionnaire for reliability and validity before the research is undertaken. Does the questionnaire measure consistently? Would similar results be obtained from the same questionnaire in repeated uses with the same respondent? Is it measuring the factor for which the study was designed?

Pretesting a questionnaire is essential. Not only should reporters be concerned about the reliability and validity of various sections of the questionnaire, but they should be concerned also about simpler problems such as order of presentation of questions, length of time required to answer, clarity of questions, and errors in meaning and syntax.

A common way of pretesting a questionnaire is to have a small group (like those to be interviewed in the survey, but not the same persons) respond to the questionnaire. In-depth interviewing of these persons about the meanings they attach to various terms or questions, difficulties they may have with the instructions, and their general reactions to being interviewed about the topic will provide invaluable information for revising and improving the questionnaire. Pretesting a questionnaire is an eye-opening experience. The reporter is likely to be amazed at the ambiguity, semantic fuzziness, and syntactical snags that escape the critical eyes of the questionnaire-drafting team, only to be picked up immediately in the pretest!

Once the pretest has been done and changes have been made in the questionnaire, the reporter is ready to design the final version to be used by the interviewers. The sequence of questions in the interview depends upon the effect various questions may have on each other. Questions at the beginning are usually selected to help build rapport with the respondent. Questions that are possibly embarrassing to some persons should obviously not be first in the interview. Items that are comfortably answered should come first.

If the study requires the respondent to have specific knowledge or characteristics, appropriate *filter questions* are asked early so the interviewer will not waste much time. The interview may be terminated early if the filter questions suggest that the person is not eligible to respond. The major objective in deciding questionnaire format is the ease with which the interviewer and interviewee may exchange the necessary information to obtain a reliable and valid response.[5]

Selection of Interviewers

Whether a reporter is designing an original survey and actually hiring interviewers to do the field work or simply verifying the quality of someone else's survey to use as a news source, Chapter 8 on interviewing should be carefully studied. There are numerous sources of error than can affect the accuracy and completeness of the data gathered in a survey.

A survey interview is a pseudo-conversation between two strangers, a person selected at random from some public or group and a paid professional interviewer. While the interview questions and instructions are typically couched in a conversational style, in part, to facilitate rapport, it is nevertheless a pseudo-conversation because the interviewer is adhering to a carefully designed· script. Only the respondent is really in the conversational mode.

This pseudo-conversation brings together two individuals with myriad characteristics that may or may not match in a contrived setting designed to generate data on a topic designated by an absent third party. The interaction resulting from this situation has important consequences for the accuracy and completeness of the data collected. Characteristics of respondents that can lead to incomplete and inaccurate answers include: poor memory; negative attitudes toward the topic, interviewer, or sponsor of the research; inarticulateness; lack of knowledge; lack of motivation to respond fully; desire for the interviewer's approval; and reluctance to divulge socially undesirable information. Characteristics of the interviewer that can affect the data include: poor understanding of

---

[5] For extensive discussions of questionnaire development, see: Claire Selltiz *et al.*, *Research Methods in Social Relations*, Holt, Rinehart and Winston, New York, 1967, pp. 235–278; and Fred N. Kerlinger, *Foundations of Behavioral Research*, Holt, Rinehart and Winston, New York, 1964, pp. 392–410.

the interview procedures and instructions; inability to record answers accurately; opinions or expectations about the respondent's behavior; and an interest in having the survey come out "right."

Survey procedures that can affect the accuracy and completeness of the survey data include: the mode of the interview; the kinds of information requested; the form and wording of the questions; the length of the interview; and the setting of the interview. Most of these potentially distorting characteristics are properties of the respondent, interviewer, or questionnaire/interview procedures.

When we go beyond these properties and begin to consider the relationships among these elements, we can enumerate new sets of potential sources of distortion in our survey data. It will suffice here as an introduction to consider the match, or lack of match, between the interviewer and respondent on a number of demographic characteristics.

While a review of the extensive literature in this area turns up divergent findings regarding the effects of interviewer-respondent similarity in age, sex, race, social class, education, and religion,[6] the overall trend is an increase in validity with increased similarity. This occurs primarily when the topic of the interview is directly related to the demographic attribute. For example, in a survey of 1,200 residents of low-income neighborhoods, blue-collar interviewers obtained more politically liberal responses than did white-collar interviewers.[7] In a National Opinion Research Center survey, anti-Semitic prejudices were expressed more readily to interviewers with Gentile names than to interviewers with Jewish names.[8]

However, too great a similarity, too perfect a match between the respondent and the interviewer, also leads to bias in the responses. If one thinks of these comparisons of respondent and interviewer on various demographic characteristics as indicators of *social distance*, then the best current evidence suggests that a

---

[6] Carol H. Weiss *et al.*, "Respondent/Interviewer Interaction in the Research Interview: Abstracts," Bureau of Applied Social Research, Columbia University (1971) PB—204 597.

[7] Daniel Katz, "Do Interviewers Bias Poll Results?" *Public Opinion Quarterly* 6 (1942):248–268.

[8] Duane Robinson and Sylvia Rohde, "Two Experiments with an Anti-Semitism Poll," *Journal of Abnormal Psychology* 41 (1946):136–144.

moderate amount of social distance produces the most valid data. When the social distance is zero, there seems to be as much distortion as when the social distance is great.

Weiss, for example, examined the validity of welfare mothers' responses to five questions with objective answers: voting in the last Presidential election, voter registration, receipt of welfare, having a child who ever failed a grade in school, and having a child fail a subject on the last report card. All of these responses could be validated in external data sources. Contrary to the folk-wisdom of surveying based on the earlier studies of discrepancies between respondent and interviewer characteristics, Weiss found a higher error rate when the respondent and interviewer were highly similar in age, education, and social status.[9]

More recent work has incorporated these seemingly contradictory findings into a curvilinear model of social distance and its effects on the validity of survey data. That is, both zero and very high social distance lead to invalidity. The middle range produces the fewest errors. The reporter who is working with survey data should carefully study this literature and its implications for both surveys and the more idiosyncratic journalistic interview.

From Data to Information

Considering the vast amount of effort that goes into the planning and field work of any scientific survey, it is surprising how little time is spent analyzing the data and converting the raw data into information. Planning and field work represent extensive investments of time and money. The analysis is the payoff from this investment. Most surveys do not yield a level of profit anywhere near what could be extracted from them. For creative reporters with some knowledge of survey research, their own surveys and those of others represent highly profitable sources of analysis.

In many instances, little more is ever reported than the basic tabulations of the answers given to each question in the survey. While these descriptions, these estimates of some population char-

---

[9] Carol H. Weiss, "Validity of Welfare Mothers' Interview Responses," *Public Opinion Quarterly* 32 (1968–69):622–633.

acteristics, are usually interesting and of some use, they barely scratch the surface of a rich lode of information. Opinion polls, a long-time staple of journalism, seldom do more than report the percentages favoring or opposing a particular issue. For years we were told how many people supported the government's Vietnam policy and how many opposed it. Sometimes the descriptive detail included five or six alternative stances on Vietnam, ranging from immediate withdrawal to use of nuclear weapons. Over time, the trends in these descriptions shifted, and finally a majority moved from support of the war to opposition. The descriptions— especially their time trends—are interesting, but are highly limited information.

Similarly, we are told periodically what percentage of Americans approve and disapprove the President's performance. Again, the temporal trends are interesting but represent limited bits of news. And we have long known that these public-opinion poll referenda on a President are influenced by his public relations effort. A nationally televised Presidential address sometimes can be worth 20 or 30 percentage points gain in the next Gallup Poll.[10]

Tabulation of the answers to poll questions are simple surface descriptions of public opinion. Reporting these results often follows the traditional event orientation of the press. The question tallies are simply another event to be noted in the news. When there is any analysis of the results, it is typically that of an expert—either self-selected or nominated by the reporter—giving a subjective interpretation of what the poll means. Or else, the analysis is a simple *demographic analysis* of the findings. That is, the tallies are broken down to show the percentages of males and females, Democrats and Republicans, Northerners and Southerners, and so on, who answered the questions.

Demographic analysis is better than nothing because it often yields some hints or clues about the explanation for the descriptive pattern turned up by the poll. But demographic analysis, especially very mechanically applied demographic analysis, is rather simplistic. It might falsify some of the experts' guesses or intuitions about why the poll shows certain patterns, but it does not directly offer any evidence about the explanation. Demographic

---

[10] Leo Bogart, *Silent Politics: Polls and the Awareness of Public Opinion*, Wiley-Interscience, New York, 1972, pp. 51–52.

variables are good *locators* or *predictors*, but they are not true independent variables. They do not explain the causes for the pattern of results measured by the survey.

Here, again, hypotheses play an invaluable role in guiding the reporter's explorations. If the reporter has framed explicit hypotheses about the explanations for the opinions or behavior being studied in the survey, then the analysis can move quickly beyond a mechanical demographic/locator variable level of analysis. Furthermore, the hypotheses will systematize the search of the data, the conversion of raw data into newsworthy information. In the typical survey, there are so many trees that can be examined that it is quite easy to wander and never see the forest.

Consider the simple matter of two-way *cross-tabulations*. A tabulation of opinions about the President separately for male and female respondents is a two-way cross-tabulation, the opinion question cross-tabulated by the question on the respondent's sex. In a survey containing fifteen questions, there are 105 potential two-way cross-tabs. With twenty-five questions the number jumps to 300. For *n items* the number of cross-tabs is $(n)(n-1)/2$. Computers can quickly and tirelessly produce these vast quantities of data; but for the reporter to mentally digest them is quite another matter. For the reporter with a deadline a week away, hypotheses are invaluable guides in the data "forest."

Assuming that hypotheses have been stated and the cross-tabulations appropriate only to those hypotheses have been created by the computer, let's examine this cross-tabulation and the information it contains. Basically, a cross-tabulation is a set of pigeon holes. Suppose the cross-tabulation is voters' feelings about the *importance of Watergate* by their *use of news media*. The categories for these variables define the pigeon holes into which each voter is sorted or classified. Suppose each voter was asked to rate Watergate as "very important", "somewhat important", or "not important at all." These three possible responses to that question define the three columns. The three responses to a question about how frequently political news is read in the newspaper define the three rows. The answers given by a particular voter to each of the two questions then uniquely determine which *one* of the nine pigeon holes he falls in. (In the event a respondent fails to answer one of the questions, he or she is discarded from the analysis.)

Opinion About the Importance of Watergate by Voters' Use of News Media

Importance of Watergate

Media Use	COUNT ROW PCT COL PCT TOT PCT	*Not at all important*	*Somewhat important*	*Very important*	*Row total*
	Low	6 15.4 85.7 7.5	15 38.5 55.6 18.8	18 46.2 39.1 22.5	39 48.8
	Moderate	0 0.0 0.0 0.0	11 52.4 40.7 13.7	10 47.6 21.7 12.5	21 26.2
	High	1 5.0 14.3 1.2	1 5.0 3.7 1.2	18 90.0 39.1 22.5	20 25.0
	Column Total	7 8.7	27 33.7	46 57.5	80 100.0

Chi square = 16.34 with 4 degrees of freedom ($p < .01$)

Looking at the Watergate illustration, we see a number of pieces of data in each cell. The first figure is the actual number of respondents falling into each of the nine categories. For example, there are fifteen low media users who rate Watergate as "somewhat important." This is the basic bit of information in the cross-tab but far from the most interesting. The next two percentages in the table progress from data to information. Their origin is quite simple. In the first instance the number (n) in each cell is divided by the total n for that row to form a percentage. The second figure is the cell n divided by the column total, again to create a percentage.

In the typical data set, only one of these percentages is useful and correct; the other should be discarded. The logic of cross-tabulations is simple. For each separate value of the independent or locator variable—in this case, use of news media—the pattern of responses to the dependent variable is described in percentages. Here we see that less than a majority of low media users (46.2 percent) consider Watergate "very important," whereas 90 percent of the high media users view Watergate as "very important."

One pattern of percentages can be compared to the pattern for the other value(s) of the dependent variable. In this example there are interesting differences in assessments of the importance of Watergate among people who differ in their use of news media. It can be argued from the evidence in this table that heavy media play of Watergate influenced the views of those most frequently exposed to this material.

In most instances, it is quite clear which is the independent and which is the dependent variable. There could be a question here about the order of variables. Which came first, interest or media exposure? Many times the true time order is unknown, but either a plausible assumption can be made or the hypothesis assigns the variables. Since the mechanical production of the data on the computer might result in the independent variable sometimes being in the rows (as here) and sometimes in the columns, the computer produces both sets of percentages. The user of the data selects the appropriate set and discards the other.

This computer printout of the cross-tabulation of media use by opinion on Watergate also contains two other major sets of information. The right-hand column of the table and the bottom row of the table show the totals used to calculate the percentages just discussed. These are the simple tabulations for each variable, sometimes referred to as the *marginals* for each variable. So a cross-tab also contains the simple descriptive information about how many gave each answer to each question.

But more importantly, the cross-tab includes a statistical analysis of the relationship between the two variables included in the table. The *chi-square* (χ^2) value generates a *probability estimate* of the likelihood that the *empirical pattern* of the relationship between use of news media and opinion on Watergate is due to chance. Here we see that the probability of such a pattern or relationship occurring by chance alone is only one time out of 100.

Most analysts looking at that chi square would conclude that the relationship is not due to chance; in other words, that it is *statistically significant*.

What the chi-square statistic literally does is to compare the number of respondents empirically found in each cell of the table with the number that would be expected there just by chance. As that difference increases, the probability (p) decreases that the results are due to chance.

Chi square is not the only statistic used to analyze survey data, but it is about the most common one. It represents a good foothold in statistical analysis of survey data for the reporter who is new to this area. From this modest beginning the inquisitive reporter can go on to other statistical techniques and forms of data more complex than the two-way cross-tabulation. Once the simple answers are obtained, reporters will find themselves generating more complex hypotheses about explanations of community opinion and behavior. Evidence bearing on these hypotheses will lead the reporter deeper into behavioral science methodology. Two-way cross-tabulations and chi-square analysis barely scratch the surface. But since most survey data is simply reported in verbatim descriptions of the marginals or mechanistic demographic analyses, even this represents a significant step forward.

PRESENTING TABLES

Tables are self-contained. The reader should be able to look at a table and understand the data *without* referring to the text of the news story or listening to the newscaster's description. The title of the table, then, must completely explain the categories and types of information contained in it. The independent and dependent factors should also be labeled.

Using tables in news stories based on survey data have two important advantages. They enhance the precision and clarity of the findings. They enhance the readability or listenability of the news story. It is difficult to present the data succinctly and clearly from a cross-tabulation in verbal form. Data tables can do this job, leaving the reporter free to describe their meaning and implications to the audience.

TABLE 1 *Opinion About the Importance of Watergate by Use of News Media*

	Not at all important	Somewhat important	Very important
Low	15.4	38.5	46.2
Moderate	0.0	52.4	47.6
High	5.0	5.0	90.0

EDITORS' NOTE: This data table was prepared from the computer printout shown in the preceding box.

Summing Up

Journalists who have added this information on survey research to their reporting repertoire will have moved up to the frontier of in-depth news reporting in their communities. But this chapter leads only up to the frontier. The other books and sources cited here will help the journalist cross that frontier and create new techniques of journalism.

Chapter 6

Sampling Opinions and Behaviors

Maxwell McCombs

As reporters and as ordinary individuals we constantly sample the world around us. In the morning most of us look out the window to see what kind of day it is. On the basis of that tiny sample—a few seconds of time and a small portion of the environment—we select our wardrobe and make plans for the day. Reporters take only slightly more "sophisticated" samples of the world when they dash into the streets to learn the local reactions to the latest economic controls or the mayor's most recent pronouncement.

Most of our ideas about the world, in fact, are based on samples. The evening news on television or the total news content in one issue of the *New York Times* is only a tiny sample of what is happening in the world. Of necessity, our pictures of the world have to be based on samples. No one has the time, opportunity, ability, or even inclination to take on all of reality. We sample those aspects we are interested in and generalize from that sample to the whole. This is true for our conventional folklore about the world and how it works and for the more formal reports of journalism.

Therefore, sampling is not something new that behavioral science brings to journalism. Behavioral science methodology only introduces a more orderly version of a procedure we all use. Like many other aspects of scientific methodology, the significant difference is in the degree of orderliness imposed. Since journalists already sample among people, public records, and events to report the news, a systematic knowledge of sampling can enhance the precision of their reporting.

Implicit in this discussion is the decision to *sample* rather than to conduct a *census*. A sample selects a few from a larger group. A census represents every member of the group. In the vast majority of cases the cost in time and money dictates a sample rather than a census. When the population of people, documents, or whatever is large, it is impractical to attempt to collect data from each unit. No news agency has the time or resources to collect each voter's opinion on an issue or to determine the effects of price controls on every service station operator in the community. So we settle for a sample. Only when the population is small are censuses usually attempted. Censuses are the exception and samples are the rule when we are collecting facts about our communities.

However, we pay a price for this efficiency in collecting news. The price is accuracy. Obviously, information collected from everyone is more accurate than information collected from a few and *projected* to everyone in the population. Cost and accuracy are directly related. To obtain the highest degree of accuracy, we must be willing to pay the price both in time and in money. In most cases, a compromise is reached. Some precision will be sacrificed in order to reduce costs. However, we shall see that it is not too bleak a situation since one can obtain a substantial degree of precision while enjoying the economies of sampling.

Probability Versus Non-Probability Samples

Whether a reporter is simply evaluating a survey or poll as a potential news source or is actually considering an original survey, the question of *sample design* is crucial. How was the sample of persons selected? Or, if a survey is being planned: How shall we select the actual sample of people to be interviewed? For both questions the major criterion is the *representativeness* of the sample. Does the sample from which our data came accurately represent a larger population? After all, it is in this larger population that we really are interested. The news story is to describe the *population*. The specific individuals who actually answered questions are of interest only because they reflect the larger group, a point that is sometimes overlooked. How representative the sample is of the larger group is determined by the decisions made about the sample design.

Sample designs fall into two distinct groups: *probability samples* and *non-probability samples*. Most of the advantages lie with probability samples. Probability sampling is the only approach that yields estimates of the extent to which the sample findings differ from the results that would have been obtained from a census. Exact statistical statements can be made about the precision of the results. No such estimates can be made about the precision of non-probability samples. We shall discuss these estimates later, but first let us examine the actual designs themselves.

Although probability samples are superior data sources, non-probability samples should be considered first because journalists have encountered them and used them far more frequently. The "man-in-the-street" interview is an excellent example of a non-probability sample. Whether it is the typical half dozen or less interviews or a straw poll in which thousands of ballots are collected, there is nothing in this design to even remotely suggest that it is representative of any larger population. These respondents represent themselves and no one else. This is a "catch-as-catch-can" design in which respondents are obtained in a haphazard way. Any resemblances between the respondents and the larger community is purely coincidental. "Man-in-the-street" interviews are poor reporting because of the high risk of inaccurate impressions. How could six individuals represent the public opinion of an entire community on some issue of the day? Six people hardly represent all the subgroups present in any community's population.

Typically, such interviews and the larger-scale straw polls are conducted in locations where large numbers of people are available, which eliminates many logistical problems. But how representative are the noon-hour shoppers downtown? Numerous people who work far from the downtown area are clearly excluded from the sample, thus biasing the results and any generalizations made from the findings. Or, if the interviewing is done at a suburban shopping mall, just how representative are these people? Suburbs are typically quite different from the central city and often from each other. In short, neither the data-collection locations nor the people available are likely to be representative of any larger group we are interested in. As Senator Robert F. Kennedy remarked about a 1,500-interview straw poll conducted by the Chicago *Sun-Times:* ". . . the newspaper had taken its poll standing outside banks and polling all the bank presidents, and my God, the Republican was ahead." [1]

Straw polls abound at election time, and are simply expanded versions of "man-in-the-street" interviews. The sample design, here too, is haphazard. There is little assurance that such a sample is representative. One's best bet, in fact, is that it is *unrepresentative.*

Roll [2] has pointed out that the extraordinary success of the *New York Daily News* straw poll can be accounted for largely by the wide margin of victory in most of the elections predicted. Even a crude poll could have predicted that Nixon would win in 1972. By contrast very precise polls had difficulties calling the close 1960 race between Kennedy and Nixon. But the polls in that race, based on highly representative samples, did correctly report the closeness of the race.

The 1969 *Daily News* straw poll, which correctly called the winner in the New York mayoral election, although with little precision in its estimate of the vote, also resulted in a ludicrous law suit. In the election, Mayor John Lindsay ran for re-election against both Republican and Democratic candidates. Conventional political wisdom held that an independent candidate had no chance against two organization-backed candidates in New York City.

But the initial *Daily News* straw poll appearing less than two weeks before the election showed Lindsay with a commanding lead. Democratic candidate Mario Procaccino was outraged. Obviously, he charged, the straw poll was unrepresentative of New York City voters. Furthermore, he said that his own polls taken at a chain of movie theaters showed him ahead. So into court went Procaccino and the *Daily News* to argue the relative merits of their

---

[1] Gerhart D. Wiebe, "The New York Times and Public Opinion Research: A Criticism," *Journalism Quarterly* 44 (1967):655.

[2] Charles W. Roll, Jr., "Straws in the Wind: The Record of the *Daily News* Poll," *Public Opinion Quarterly* 32 (1968):251–260.

data. To anyone with the most basic knowledge of sampling and polling, this was an absurdity—a heated argument in which the contending sides both based their position on worthless data.

Election day vindicated the *Daily News* in terms of who won. But it was hardly a precision job of political reporting. The election-eve *Daily News* straw poll reported a whopping twenty-one-point spread between Lindsay and Procaccino, predicting that the mayor would receive 48 percent of the vote and Procaccino 27 percent. In the actual balloting this twenty-one-point spread shrank to a seven-point margin. Lindsay received only 42 percent of the vote and Procaccino received 35 percent. If the margin had been much closer, the *Daily News* might have been as red-faced as many other straw pollers of the past.

To offset the vagaries of unplanned sample designs some pollsters have used *quota samples* to insure representation among a variety of subgroups in the population. This form of sample design came into wide use after the debacle of the 1936 *Literary Digest* straw poll. That poll forecast a crashing defeat for Franklin Roosevelt in his 1936 bid for re-election. Unfortunately, the *Literary Digest* sample was drawn largely from its own subscription lists, from telephone directories, and from automobile registrations. During the depths of the Depression it is little wonder that such a sample was overwhelmingly Republican. To insure greater representativeness of their samples, pollsters turned to quota samples. That is, quotas were set for interviews with various subgroups. The quotas might be structured in terms of income and level of education or in terms of past voting preferences.

The basic idea of quota sampling is to balance the distribution of interviews across various important population subgroups. The basic idea is sound, but the implementation is difficult. What population characteristics should be used to define the quotas? How many variables should be used? If too many are used, finding people to fit such complexly defined subgroups will be difficult for the interviewers.

Filling a quota, say, of below age thirty, white, Catholic males, with some college education earning over $10,000 a year— matching on six variables—is not a simple undertaking. And in filling these quotas—even if more parsimoniously defined—there is another methodological problem. Final selection of respondents is left to the interviewers. As a practical matter, interviewers usually select the most accessible members of a subgroup. A campus interviewer who is assigned a quota of six freshman girls will most likely head straight for the freshman dormitory to fill the quota. This excludes all freshman girls who do not live in that dormitory from the sample, and so begins to distort its representativeness. Because of these methodological problems, quota sampling has been abandoned by most survey researchers.

Random Samples

The most straightforward type of probability sample is the *simple random sample*. Lotteries and drawing names from barrels are familiar examples of simple random samples. In such a selection procedure the names (or numbers, or whatever the population consists of) are thoroughly mixed and one or more are selected. Under such a procedure *each unit has an equal chance of being selected*. Intuitively, most people regard this characteristic as essential in insuring the fairness of the selection.

In a lottery or drawing for prizes only a few winners are selected. For an opinion poll or some other survey, we typically select more "winners" or respondents, say one or two hundred. But the principle is the same. Each unit in the population under consideration (for example, all registered voters in Syracuse, all the mayor's political speeches, every family with children in the Fairfield School District) has an equal chance of being selected for examination by the reporter. Ultimately, only a small portion of the population is actually selected, but under the conditions of the selection procedure, every unit had an equal chance of being selected.

Think back for a moment on straw polls and quota samples and note why everyone in the population does not have an equal chance of being selected under those procedures. With a random selection procedure the odds of drawing a highly representative sample are exceedingly high. The distribution of different kinds of people, of people with various opinions or intentions, seldom deviates more than a few percentage points from the total population. Most importantly, when random sampling is used, we are able to state quite precisely what the odds are of any significant deviation from the actual population values. (More on this in a moment.) But first let us examine some typical sample designs that reporters will encounter or that they might consider using in their own surveys or in content analyses, which is the subject of Chapter 7.

While the simple random sample is the prototype or the ideal, it is seldom used because of the logistical difficulties. For any large population it would be exceedingly cumbersome to list out all the names on slips of paper and mix them up in a large barrel. Furthermore, there is no roster listing all the members who exist for many of the populations we are interested in. So other designs yielding similar results are more commonly employed.

If a roster or directory does exist, a *systematic random sample* is a more convenient design. Suppose the goal of a survey is to interview 250 people out of a population of 10,000. In other words, the goal is to interview every fortieth person. Since the names are listed systematically in a file or directory, we can draw a number at random between one and forty. Random number tables found in most survey research and statistics books are convenient for this purpose. This randomly selected number is our starting point. Then every fortieth name thereafter is selected, yielding a total of 250 names by the time the end of the roster is reached. If the starting point drawn at random was "fourteen," then the fourteenth, fifty-fourth, ninety-fourth names, etc. in the list would be selected. Since the starting point was selected at random, this insures that every individual in the population had an equal chance of being included in the sample.

However, there are numerous survey situations where no roster exists. In these situations some type of *multi-stage sample design* is used, based on a series of random selections at several different stages in the procedure. Suppose, for example, that the goal is to draw a statewide random sample of adults. The first step might be to compile a list of the counties in the state. This is stage one. But we would not want to draw a simple random sample of counties because their populations differ tremendously. Most states have a number of densely populated urban counties and many sparsely populated rural counties. So the counties should be weighted according to their populations, and a systematic random sample drawn.

If the goal is 500 interviews in a state with a population of

4,000,000, then the *sampling interval* is 8,000. We wish to interview every 8,000th person. As before, a starting point between one and 8,000 is selected at random, and every 8,000th person is selected. In this case, two things will be noted about our list of counties. First, in which counties does the sampling interval fall? Second, how many times does it fall in a particular county? Some counties with less than 8,000 population will not fall into the sample at this stage, but some will. Why? Also note that every county with more than 8,000 population will fall into the sample at least once. Many will have weights of "2" or more. Why?

It is important to keep in mind at this stage that the ultimate goal is a representative sample of *persons*. To the extent that the stage-one sample is "biased" toward larger counties, remember that they are where the majority of the people live. A representative sample of most states will have considerably more urban than rural respondents.

At stage two, the counties selected at stage one are typically subdivided further into smaller geographic units such as townships or boroughs. Then the same systematic random sampling procedure used in stage one is repeated on these geographic units. If the weight of the county is "1", then a single subunit is selected. If the weight is "2", two are selected. The outcome of this stage is another set of geographic units with various weights.

At stage three, the *sampling unit* might well be the individual household. With a small number of county subunits from across the state to work with, it is feasible to obtain maps showing actual household locations. At this stage, actual households can be sampled. We are now ready to assign interviewers to specific addresses across the state. These addresses represent a random sample of the state's population selected in a multi-stage random sample.

For many surveys, a close approximation to the procedure just described is the complete sample design. Other surveys take the design one step further to insure actual random selection of the respondent within the household selected for interviewing.[3] Some

---

[3] Verling C. Troldahl and Roy E. Carter, Jr., "Random Selection of Respondents Within Households on Phone Surveys," *Journal of Marketing Research* 1 (1964):71–76; W. J. Paisley and E. B. Parker, "A Computer-Generated Sampling Table for Selecting Respondents Within Households," *Public Opinion Quarterly* 29 (1965):431–436.

instruct their interviewers to talk with whomever comes to the door or use a simple quota sample, such as alternating between males and females. The argument in favor of these latter techniques centers on the ease of administration in the field. When a specific individual must be interviewed, *callbacks* will be required frequently. Where any adult will suffice—or simple quotas are used—interviewing will be completed more quickly and inexpensively. But this gain may be at the cost of some representativeness in the resulting sample of respondents.

The reporter who uses survey data as a news source will encounter a number of other terms in probing the details of sample design. Two features likely to be encountered are *cluster sampling* and *stratified sampling*. These are additional procedures that can be used with any of the sample designs already discussed. For example, a survey might be based on a stratified systematic random sample or on a multi-stage cluster sample or even a stratified multi-stage cluster sample. If each of the terms appearing in a sample design name or description is understood, there is no problem in comprehending the overall design.

A stratified sample means that the population has been divided into subgroups, or strata, and separate samples drawn from each stratum. For example, a campus survey might be based on a stratified sample in which separate samples were drawn of the freshman, sophomore, junior, and senior classes in order to insure proportional representation of each. If each stratum is large, then stratification is usually unnecessary because you will obtain enough of each subgroup anyway.

Commonly, stratification is used when one stratum is small and the survey wishes to obtain sufficient numbers of respondents from it to insure adequate analysis. For example, in a statewide survey of North Carolina or New York the number of Indians likely to be selected in a straight random sample is on the order of about one percent. In a survey with 300 respondents, that represents only about three Indians. If one is especially interested in comparing Indians to other groups in the state, then some form of stratification is needed. Those few counties with sizeable Indian populations could be grouped in a separate stratum and a separate subsample drawn. If a subsample of 100 is drawn from three counties where the Indian population is about 15 percent of the total population, then with random sampling procedures we would expect about fifteen of those respondents to be Indians. That is still quite small and suggests that a stratum composed of yet smaller geographic units would be necessary. Also, disproportionate numbers of these smaller units might be selected.

Cluster sampling means taking clusters of interviews from communities rather than randomly dispersed respondents. Rather than 100 respondents residing on 100 randomly selected blocks, a survey might interview ten people on each of ten randomly selected blocks across the city. The number of respondents (n) is still 100. Obviously, cluster sampling is more efficient in terms of time and interviewer expense. But again, these savings are at the expense of some reduction in representativeness. The great strength of a purely random sample is its heterogeneity, while clusters taken from the same block, or neighborhood, are far more homogeneous. In terms of *sampling error,* which we shall discuss later, cluster samples have a higher error rate than straight random samples.

The purpose of using samples is to describe economically the behavior or opinions of many on the basis of a few representative observations. The purpose of this brief overview of sample designs is to insure that a reporter's poll or survey is in fact based on *representative* observations.[4]

Sampling Documents for Content Analysis

The reporter who wants to use documents as the data source for a news story confronts the same problems as the reporter who wants to write a public-opinion story. How does one adequately sample the population? This assumes that the first decision point—census versus sample—has led to the decision to use a sample.

Documents can be sampled in exactly the same manner as people can. Any of the sample designs just described can be used. If documents are serial numbered, as most public files are, then either a simple random or systematic random sample can be drawn. In other cases where the files are complex or the documents them-

---

[4] For additional background on representative sampling, see Leslie Kish, *Survey Sampling,* John Wiley & Sons, New York, 1965.

selves are lengthy, some type of multi-stage sample design probably will be used.

Suppose one set out to sample police arrest reports that were
filed chronologically for each precinct. One might begin by sampling precincts (stage one), and subsequently sample reports
within precincts (stage two). Of course, these records also could
be stratified by the type of crime involved.

Or, take another example—a story based on material from the
annual reports of various public agencies. One might begin with a
census of the reports from certain agencies for the past ten years
and then sample within the reports themselves. Or, one might
stratify the activities reported and sample only certain strata or
sample only certain events from certain strata. There are numerous possibilities. The design selected will depend on what the
reporter is looking for and how much material must be examined
to yield the story. A wide-ranging story might sample departments, years, and activities (a three-stage sampling design). Another reporter with a different purpose in mind might narrow the
population and take a census at one or more stages.

The purpose of sampling is to insure a representative set of
documents and facts on which to base a story without the reporter
having to read every word of every document in a voluminous file
of documents. Time is an important commodity to both behavioral
scientists and journalists.

Validating a Sample

The representativeness of a sam-
ple can be assessed in two ways. The *characteristics of the sample* can be compared to the *characteristics of the population,* and
the expected *sampling error* for the sample can be calculated.
Recall, however, that the sampling error can only be calculated for
probability samples.

We have a few facts already in hand for nearly all populations.
For cities, counties, and states we have U.S. Census data on the
number and proportion of men and women, of blacks and whites,
of young and old, and so on. Similar information exists about voter
lists. Every survey should include a few of these items in the
questionnaire or record them on the face sheet when the inter-

view is assigned. When the interviewing is completed, these items should be tabulated for the sample. This tabulation should then be compared to the population percentages.

Note the example from a *Winston-Salem Twin City Sentinel* election survey. The discrepancies between the population figures and the survey figures are small, typically less than three percentage points. The only large discrepancy is in the sex distribution. While women compose only 53.1 percent of the Forsyth County voters, they compose 59.6 percent of the sample. (This oversampling, or overrepresentation, of women is a fairly common phenomenon in survey research. Why?) Through such a comparison, the reporter and the readers can make an intelligent assessment of the representativeness of the sample on which the survey results are based.

Reporters and audiences must also consider the size of the sampling error. Survey findings are estimates, not precise statements, of fact. Their great virtue is that rather precise estimates can be made on the basis of a small number of observations. For example, the Winston-Salem newspaper made a highly accurate estimate of the 1972 Presidential vote in Forsyth County on the basis of only 280 interviews from the county's more than 75,000 registered voters. On election day in 1972 they split their vote 67.7 percent for Nixon and 30.5 percent for McGovern. This was very close to the 64.3 percent estimated for Nixon in the poll and 24.3 percent estimated for McGovern.

Actually, the precision of the poll estimate is even greater than it appears in this comparison. On November 1, when the poll was conducted, 10.6 percent of the Forsyth County voters were still undecided. On election day these undecideds became either nonvoters or supporters of a Presidential candidate. Apparently, a majority went for McGovern, a plausible outcome in a region with a long Democratic tradition.

Sampling Error

Exactly how precise is any sample likely to be? The major determinant of sampling precision is the number of persons interviewed. Intuitively, one would expect that a sample of 1,000 persons would yield a more accurate estimate than a sample of only ten persons. And, as exact statistical calculations will bear out, that intuitive belief is quite correct.

To avoid a total "cookbook" approach to the idea of sampling, it is necessary to digress for a moment and consider some brief aspects of statistics that do not require any mathematical background beyond simple arithmetic. Suppose your task was to estimate the proportion of red and green marbles filling a railroad boxcar. One could set out to actually count the marbles, arduously tabulating each red and green. But, as our previous discussion suggests, a quicker and more efficient procedure would be to take a sample as an estimate of the proportion of red and green marbles.

The accuracy of this sampling could be investigated by taking a large number of samples and examining the variation in their estimates. If, in fact, a large number of random samples were taken of the marbles in the boxcar—say 100 samples of fifty marbles each—and the proportion of red marbles were noted in each sample, it is an *empirical fact* that a bar graph plotting the sample estimates would form a perfectly *normal distribution* (symmetrical bell-shaped curve) centering on the true population value. The most frequent estimate in our 100 samples would be the actual population value. The next most frequent estimates would be immediately adjacent to the actual population value. Most of the estimates would fall very close to the true population value.

The actual amount of *dispersion* in the estimates is primarily a function of the number of units observed (marbles in our example, people in a survey). In statistical terms, the value of the *standard deviation* of the set of sample estimates is largely determined by the number of units on which each estimate is based. In our marble estimate, the number is fifty. Where we are dealing with percentages—as is usually the case with survey materials used by journalists—the formula for the standard deviation (σ) is

$$\sigma = \sqrt{pq/n}$$

As we already know, n is the number of units (persons or marbles or whatever) in the sample. The p and q are the proportions that fall into the two categories: red and green in the case of the marbles, pro X and anti X in a public-opinion survey. The actual proportions for each question in a survey can be entered, or the calculation can be done once for the entire survey. Usually, the calculation is done only once. Since the value of the standard deviation is greatest when p and q are each set at .5, we can replace pq with a constant, .25 (.5 × .5), and the value of the standard deviation is now wholly dependent on the n.

One additional piece of information and you are ready to calculate the sampling error for any survey based on random sampling. The sampling estimates will vary. While the true population value is the most frequent estimate, many other estimates occur, and their total occurrence far exceeds the true population value. Therefore, we use a *confidence interval* to state the likely error of our *single* survey sample. The most commonly used confidence interval is the 95 percent level of confidence. What we are doing is calculating the range of percentages that would encompass 95 percent of the sample estimates if we repeatedly took samples of a given size from some population. As we have already said, the extent of this range depends on the size of the sample. For a small sample, the range is quite large. For very large samples, the range is quite small.

To find out what the range of the sampling error is at the 95 percent level of confidence, this calculation is carried out:

$$\text{Sampling error} = 1.96\,\sigma$$

or

$$\text{Sampling error} = 1.96\,\sqrt{.25/n}$$

The table shows the results of this calculation for various size samples.

**Sampling Error at the 95 Percent
Level of Confidence for
Samples of Various Sizes**

Sample Size	Sample Error *
50	.139
100	.098
150	.080
200	.069
250	.062
300	.056
350	.052
400	.049
450	.046
500	.044
550	.042
600	.040
650	.038
700	.037
750	.036
800	.035
850	.034
900	.033
950	.032
1,000	.031

* Assumes simple random sampling.

For a sample of fifty the sampling error is .139 or 13.9 percent. This means that the true population value may lie as much as 13.9 percent above *or* below the estimate obtained from your sample of fifty. If the sample estimate of the proportion of red marbles is 45 percent, the true answer, at the 95 percent level of confidence, lies somewhere between 31.1 percent and 58.9 percent (45 percent ± 13.9 percent). That is a considerable sampling error. But, as the size of the sample is increased, the error is reduced. For a sample of 500, the sampling error is only .044 or 4.4 percent, a much more precise estimate. Note that the reduction in sampling error is not directly proportionate to the increase in the n. When the sample size was increased ten times (from fifty to 500), the error was reduced by only two-thirds. Another example: doubling the sampling size of the sample will not halve the sampling error. Check it out!

Finally, a note on population size. The size of the sampling error does *not* vary with the population size. A sample of 300 voters in New York has the same error as a sample of 300 voters nationwide. The size of the sample error is reduced significantly only where the sample is some significant proportion of the total population. You can prove this for yourself by applying the correction for population size to the previous formula for sampling error. The correction is:

$$(1 - n/N) \text{ (sampling error).}$$

The n is the sample size and the N is the population size. If n were half of N, then the sampling error would be cut in half. But in the typical survey where 500 voters out of 150,000 are interviewed, the correction is only .003. For a sample error of 4.4 percent, that is a reduction to 4.39 percent, hardly worth all the arithmetic.

A statement of sampling error is the key fact in any survey report or news story based on a survey because the information being reported is only an estimate of the true situation in the population. Audiences should be told just how accurate these estimates are. The whole purpose of surveys and polls is to obtain representative samples. Sampling design insures a high degree of representativeness. Sampling error states its level of precision.[5]

---

[5] For additional background on the statistical aspects of sampling error, see William L. Hays, *Statistics for the Social Sciences*, 2d ed., Holt, Rinehart and Winston, New York, 1973.

Chapter 7

Mining Community
Records and Documents

Donald Lewis Shaw and
G. Cleveland Wilhoit

Ron Ziegler—*"I could . . . two options:
One would be to say that* (unintelligible)*;
the other would be to say that* (unintelligible)*."*
The White House Watergate Transcripts

Journalists, public officials, scholars, and, in fact, most American
citizens in 1974 were astonished
when Richard Nixon released transcripts of various tape recordings
made in his office related to the
so-called Watergate scandal.
Filling hundreds of pages, words
spilled forth to reveal the innermost workings of the Presidential
mind and the minds of his top aides.

Mr. Nixon reportedly reviewed the documents personally prior
to their release to the U.S. House of Representatives Judiciary
Committee. That, of course, put Mr. Nixon in the position of controlling some of the evidence that might be used against him in
impeachment proceedings. Never before had reporters been confronted with such a document, and they quickly went to work analyzing it.

What, they asked, did the transcripts say? Was the President
personally involved? Did he participate in a "cover up" for those
who had actually ordered (or carelessly allowed) Watergate? Even
with the published transcripts, answers remained ambiguous. In
some coverage, the news media employed *content analysis* to
"mine" the lengthy document for buried meaning. Were such
words as "unintelligible" or "inaudible" inserted more often into

the dialogue of Mr. Nixon and more often at crucial places than for other people? At least one television network counted the "unintelligibles" and tentatively came to such a conclusion. How often and in what places was dialogue omitted because it was judged not relevant to the Watergate break-in?

These transcripts are an unusual type of public document, revealing the decision-making process of the White House at a crucial time. Insightful reporters can, and did, make skillful use of such public documents by using content analysis to examine them for meaning. Most public documents, of course, are not so dramatically produced, but they still can be useful to journalists focusing in depth on their own communities.

Just as glaciers move slowly across the earth leaving enduring traces of their progress, human beings leave behind momentous records of their activities. For journalists, there are numerous documents that can be used as sources for social indicators of various aspects of community life—records of birth, marriage, and death fill dusty courthouse shelves. And every governmental agency or office regularly compiles records of its activities. Businesses, factories, and universities do the same, not to mention the massive outpouring from the media themselves. There are numerous outcroppings of community activities, situations, and problems.

Words—our world is full of them. Most words in records, moreover, were gathered for official reasons without regard to how a journalist might use them. So these words can often provide a *nonreactive* way to test community problems and values.[1] But one must have a sense of how to apply content analysis skillfully. Content analysis applies the same kind of systematic, careful observation to records and documents that is used when gathering information scientifically from other sources.

Content Analysis—What Is It?

Content analysis helps us cope with the flood of words in records and documents. Journalists live in a sea of words. We use words to inform others and to tell them

---

[1] Eugene J. Webb *et al.*, *Unobtrusive Measures: Nonreactive Research in the Social Sciences*, Rand McNally, Chicago, 1966, chapters 1 and 2.

what we think. Conversely, the words of others inform us, tell us what they think and feel. We are concerned about the effect of words. What, women ask, will be the effect on little girls when they read this sentence in a fourth-grade reader: "Oh, Raymond, boys are much braver than girls," or this one from a third-grade reader: "You're certainly not up to a man's work, so you'll start as a scrubwoman." [2]

In addition to words, facial expressions, gestures, and, at another level, paintings, music, sculpture, and architecture all communicate. How much of this can be dug out to help explain our local communities? Content analysis is an observation technique designed to take a sample of language (or paintings or music) and analyze that language for the messages it carries. The goal is to be able to *infer* from objective, hard evidence what the sender of the message really means or to obtain some idea of the effect the sender intends. It is not always obvious or easily determined simply by reading. The Watergate transcripts underscore this point.

Of course, drawing inferences is not a new procedure for journalists. They do it all the time. "What did the senator really mean?" "Why is the governor doing this?" Such questions are commonplace, and often the journalist can make shrewd guesses on the basis of what the senator or governor may have said or done; or *failed* to say or do. This was the challenge to journalists in the Watergate transcripts. The word symbols of our language portray events or persons that we do not personally see yet that are nevertheless real to us. One can sit in a peaceful, isolated mountain cabin and, from reading newspapers or watching television, get a sense of violent change in the world. For such an isolated individual it is not really the world itself but the word symbols representing the world that are changing. This is not a minor point. We live in a symbolic world. Furthermore, we personally see very little of it no matter how widely traveled we may be.

Content analysis is a tool to analyze this symbolic content of communication.[3] Through the years, the technique has been applied to such diverse content as suicide notes, paintings, and writing styles of major writers. In those situations, as in content

---

[2] "Sexist Texts," *Time*, November 5, 1973, p. 66.
[3] The variety of possible studies is evident in George Gerbner *et al.*, *The Analysis of Communication Content: Developments in Scientific Theories and Computer*

Patty's Voice, Tania's Rhetoric

For a Sunday feature on the lengthy drama of Patricia Hearst's kidnapping, a *San Francisco Examiner* reporter analyzed the content of tapes received from her. This simple, intuitive content analysis attempts to trace the changes in Patricia Hearst's views during four months. While a systematic, scientific content analysis might have yielded even more information, nevertheless, here is a feature story based on content analysis that appeared in the newspaper of her father, Randolph Hearst.

It's a sweet little voice, a ladylike one.

The inflections are proper and clear. The tones are warm and gentle, even a little bit diffident, and very earnest.

In this almost dreamy way, the little-girl voice of Patricia Hearst might be that of a young person in school, reciting a well-studied lesson.

This only compounds the brutal incongruity of what she is saying. This schoolgirl's sing-song recitation is about "watching our comrades die, murdered by pig incendiary grenades" and is sprinkled with vulgarities and obscenities in the mildest and most cultivated of tones. . . .

It is hard for most people to understand or even to try to analyze the metamorphosis of Patty Hearst, . . .

The only things to go on are the statements by Patty herself, in the strange language of the tapes. . . .

Remember how she sounded in the beginning?

Unquestionably a captive, held against her will but anxious to reassure her parents.

On the tape delivered Feb. 12, she said:

"Mom, Dad, I'm OK. I had a few scrapes and stuff, but they washed them up and they're getting OK.

"I'm not being starved or beaten or unnecessarily frightened . . . .

". . . And I want to get out of here but the only way I'm going to is if we do it their way. And I just hope that you'll do what they say, Dad, and just do it quickly. . . ."

Four days later Patty was again reassuring:

"Dad, Mom, I'm making this tape to let you know that I'm still OK and to explain a few things, I hope. . . ."

In this message there was the first faint inkling that Patty was being subjected to some persuasive influences by the SLA. She

Techniques, John Wiley, New York, 1969. Also see Ithiel de Sola Pool, ed., *Trends in Content Analysis,* University of Illinois Press, Urbana, 1959. Another excellent, but more complicated, source is Philip J. Stone *et al., The General Inquirer: A Computer Approach to Content Analysis,* M.I.T. Press, Cambridge, 1966.

said the SLA was "very annoyed about attempts by the press and by authorities to turn this into a racial issue. It's not. This is a political issue and this is a political action that they've taken."

She referred to the "People in Need" food distribution program demanded by SLA chieftain Donald DeFreeze as a gesture of good faith on which to base negotiations for her release.

"When it's necessary, the people can be fed," she said, "and to show that, it's too bad it has to happen this way to make people see that there are people who need food."

But she was still primarily an abducted girl who wanted to go home. . . .

But by April 4, after a gap of about six weeks, there was a turnabout, harsh and bitter. Patty called the $2 million food distribution program "a sham." . . .

On this tape Patty announced that she had been given a choice: to be released in a safe area or to join the SLA.

"I have chosen to stay and fight," she said.

She announced she had assumed the name Tania, after a woman follower of Che Guevara. The message ended with the revolutionists' rallying cry: "Patria o muerte. Venceremos."

It was still thought to be possible that Patty was saying what she said only in self-preservation, but the tape of April 24 pulled no punches at all.

"On April 15 my comrades and I expropriated $10,660.02 from the Sunset branch of Hibernia Bank," said "Tania." "Casualties could have been avoided had the persons involved kept out of the way and cooperated with the people's forces until after our departure."

She said she willingly took part in the robbery. Her words portrayed her as, by now, a devoted adherent to the SLA philosophy.

"Consciousness is terrifying to the ruling class and they will do anything to discredit people who have realized that the only alternative to freedom is death and that the only way we can free ourselves of this fascist dictatorship is by fighting not with words but with guns."

Last Friday's statement was even stronger.

It was angry, harsh, bitter, hurtful. Patty said she died in the gunfight and fire in which six SLA members were killed on May 17, in Los Angeles, "but out of the ashes I was reborn."

"Patria o muerte. Venceremos," she said in the soft little voice. . . .

SOURCE: Jane Eshelman Conant, *San Francisco Examiner*, June 9, 1974.

---

analysis studies that use the media to probe community opinion, the studies sought to *infer* answers to such questions as Why do people commit suicide? What kinds of people are most likely to do so? What do certain styles of painting or writing tell you about the age in which they were produced? What was a national leader's "state of mind" at selected times of national crisis? Crucial to content analysis is the design of a scientific study procedure, which will allow you to make inferences about the content you are studying.

A widely adopted definition of content analysis is that by Ole Holsti: [4]

> Content analysis is any technique for making *inferences* by *objectively* and *systematically* identifying *specified* characteristics of messages. [emphasis added]

This definition, like others, emphasizes inferences and systematic and objective observation. It is the rigor of *controlled* observation that differentiates content analysis from often shrewd, but armchair, guessing. Content analysis is, then, the scientific study of messages.

INFERENCES

You can draw inferences from the information collected only after you first focus carefully on a precise question or *hypothesis* to be answered. Probably more than any other information-gathering technique, content analysis requires journalists to make clear just what they are searching for *before* starting. Content analysis is often tedious and becomes even more so if, at the end, the results do not make the effort worthwhile. It is better to be clear at the start about what you intend to look for in the messages you have chosen to examine.

OBJECTIVE OBSERVATION

One commonly agreed upon creed of American journalism is that the journalist should not allow

---

[4] Ole R. Holsti, *Content Analysis for the Social Sciences and Humanities*, Addison-Wesley, Reading, Mass., 1969, pp. 2–3. An earlier and influential definition is one by Berelson: "Content analysis is a research technique for the objective, systematic, and quantitative description of the manifest content of communication." Bernard R. Berelson, *Content Analysis in Communication Research*, The Free Press, Glencoe, Ill., 1952, p. 18. The beginner will find these both useful plus Wayne A. Danielson, "Content Analysis in Communication Research," in *Introduction to Mass Communication Research*, Ralph O. Nafziger and David Manning White, eds., Louisiana State University Press, Baton Rouge, 1963, pp. 180–206.

purely personal biases to color or distort a report of events. This applies even more to the journalist as a content analyst. You have to specify carefully what you are seeking. If you are classifying words into different categories, you must explain those categories so well that another journalist would be able to classify them in almost the same way after hearing or reading your explanation. To the extent another journalist could, the study is judged *reliable*— two or more people agree with the basic observations made.

This means that content analysis often is not a good tool to study highly intuitive, personal themes in documents because it is difficult to get two or more coders to agree on meaning. But the journalist usually is more interested in the manifest, more commonsense interpretation of documents. If you cannot explain your project well enough so another journalist could obtain about the same results, how could you ever explain your findings to your audience?

SYSTEMATIC OBSERVATION

After you formulate a research question or hypothesis and locate an appropriate body of documents to answer it, you must study the material according to a formal, relatively fixed, unbiased plan. As you sort words, phrases, or paragraphs into categories, you may find, sometimes surprisingly, considerable evidence *against* your hypothesis. Count it. Systematic observation *forces* you to hold back your intuitive judgment until all the evidence is in. It makes you follow the evidence like a pilot who has to rely upon instruments when the weather will not permit unaided visibility. And like the pilot, you are surer to arrive safely at your goal if you use instruments than if you rely upon "seat-of-the-pants" flying. For journalists, that goal is reliable and valid reporting of community news.

Analyzing Your Community

Your community is more than a configuration of buildings, streets, schools, and factories. From the news point of view, it is mostly people. And when it comes to people, how does your community rate on health, education, mobility, age, income, employment? As uniquely as the pattern of streets, a community is characterized by these less visible variables. Skillful mining of records can tell you much about these variables, which really indicate a community's quality as a place to live.

For years journalists have rolled up their sleeves on occasion to dig into police, court, or tax records to check out facts or to do "trend" stories. It is in analyzing these records that content analysis sometimes can provide insightful alternative paths to community understanding if only print and electronic journalists would learn how to *analyze* words systematically as well as they spin them out.

What words or points does the mayor constantly use when making a public speech? What themes, ideas, or goals emerge from speeches or other records/documents when you sit back and take a systematic critical look at them? Three political scientists collected the Presidential nomination acceptance speeches of Republican and Democratic candidates from 1928 through 1964.[5] Using a computer, they were able to count the frequencies of key words (those referring to foreign policy, economics, and selected other areas) in order to study how the parties differed from each other and how they changed over time. Among their findings was the decline, in both parties, of concern about domestic economic issues. Likewise, they discovered that recent speeches emphasized direct persuasive appeals much less, and more often referred to "needs" and "desires" of their political audience. In other words, both parties more often used *indirect* persuasion. Not only were the themes of the speeches changing, but so was the tone of their rhetorical delivery.

Has the mayor of your community subtly changed his or her attitude during the course of office? How have different mayors touched on different community problems, and who was most successful in meeting those problems? You do not necessarily need a computer to study emphasis on changing themes; paper and pencil will be sufficient.

Language reflects change, and change can be measured in two major ways. First, you can study change *across cultures* (or across subcultures, groups, or different institutions within the same en-

---

[5] Marshall S. Smith, Philip J. Stone, and Evelyn N. Glenn, "A Content Analysis of Twenty Presidential Nomination Acceptance Speeches," in Stone, *The General Inquirer*, pp. 359–400.

compassing culture). Anthropology is an example of a field devoted to studies of cultural diversity. Secondly, you can study change *across time,* as the historian does. Or, thirdly, you can study change simultaneously across both culture and time. It may seem to expect a lot, but journalists are expected to be able to compare institutions and explain events across recent history in their news stories.

The study of major party political acceptance speeches did both. These speeches and documents, which are often reprinted in their entirety in newspaper stories, reflect subjects and themes that are important at the moment. But for a longer range analysis of the shifting perspectives of your community, the news value is still there. The ideas and values of your community trail behind it in a barely submerged stream, much of it captured in news stories as well as in public and private records.

The Media as Community Reflectors

The media, themselves, provide a rich hunting ground for the insightful content analyst. There are nearly a thousand commercial and educational television stations, about 7,000 commercial radio stations, and nearly 1,800 daily newspapers in the United States. In addition, there are thousands of magazines and weekly newspapers. While we often think of the media as engaging in one-way communication, it is clear that readers and viewers provide important feedback information to the media. Our own organizations, the news media, can tell us important things about our communities.

Are the people who are really powerful in your community the ones who get the most coverage in local news? One study showed that a U.S. senator who came from a large state and had been in office for a long time was more apt to get personal news coverage.

In another content-analysis study, journalism professor Walter Gieber decided to study the lovelorn columnists, a fixture of the American newspaper since the close of the nineteenth century.[6]

---

[6] Walter Gieber, "The 'Lovelorn' Columnist and Her Social Role," *Journalism Quarterly* 37 (1960):499–514.

How You Get in the News
. . . Regularly?

Two communication scientists decided to see what type U.S. senator is most likely to make the news on a regular basis. After carefully sampling from all the stories coming over the AP wire for a given period and counting the number of references to various U.S. senators in these stories, they discovered that the population size of a senator's state and his seniority correlate best with AP wire "news visibility." Uncorrelated with news visibility are such factors as

By size of state population

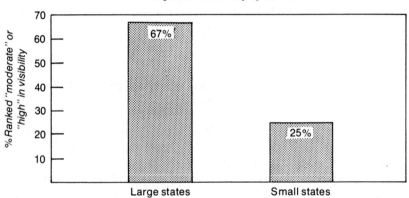

By Senate seniority ranking

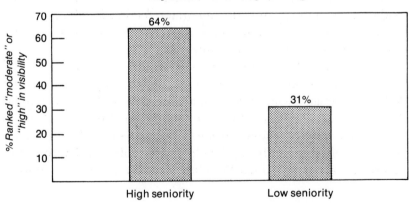

"importance" of Senate committee assignments or recognized prominence as a representative of various points of view. The authors conjecture that news visibility for U.S. senators is related to the generally better Presidential chances of large-state senators plus the wire service effort to serve the larger audiences in those states.

SOURCE: Adapted from G. Cleveland Wilhoit and Kenneth S. Sherrill, "Wire Service Visibility of U.S. Senators," *Journalism Quarterly* 45 (1968): 42–48.

He obtained the letters sent to a prominent (unnamed) columnist and analyzed them for the type of problems people write about. He also sought to discover what kinds of people write letters.

Gieber found a wide range of problems expressed in the 420 letters he sampled. In addition to the expected problems of courtship, sex, and marriage, a number of writers asked about psychological counseling, social relations, and various community resources. Gieber pointed out that answering questions about community resources represented one positive community function of the columnist. These particular writers wanted help in locating the proper community resource or agency for their problems. In some cases, they complained of obtaining inadequate help at these agencies. Why couldn't they find help? Could they in your community? And what they did *not* complain about may be as important as what they did complain about.

Findings of Gieber's research are limited in their ability to be generalized. Those who wrote in were most often female, single, young, and of lower socioeconomic background—not a picture of the typical American newspaper audience. But for that audience, the study did reveal leads for possible community problems. Traditional interviewing can be combined with content analysis to follow up why people of lower socioeconomic background feel they have to write a distant columnist to obtain information about local community help. Are your community problem-solving agencies functioning properly? Many newspapers, radio stations, and television stations have columns or programs that could provide rich data sources for this kind of journalistic analysis.

Let us examine another example of content analysis of media content. Although constrained by similar sampling limitations, letters to the editor provide another way to study your community. More than eight million people a year write letters to editors of newspapers and magazines. And many now write to their local television station managers.

Three communication researchers studied mass magazines to discover how well letters to the editor mirrored national concerns.[7] They sampled letters to the editor in five national magazines and used *cluster analysis* to find how often key words grouped together around reader concerns. They found that reader worries—about Vietnam, crime, inflation, race relations, pollution—very closely paralleled findings of a National Opinion Research Center survey done in the same time period. The authors suggest not only that the content-analysis approach is cheaper, but also that it has great potential in studying letters over time, another way of charting community moods. In applying this analysis to your community media, the *persistence* of the same local problems, call them moods if you like, would suggest an inability somewhere in the community for solving those problems, at least in the view of those who typically write or call in.

Those who write letters to the editor tend to be male, well educated, older, and long-time residents in the community, which is nearly the opposite of those who write to the lovelorn columnist. Letter writers feel a stake in their communities. Generally speaking, they can also be divided into those who want to "change things" and those who merely want to express themselves.

While journalism researchers David Grey and Trevor Brown are disturbed by the unrepresentative sample of people who write in during emotionally intense political campaign situations (plus the fact that many editors "choose" the letters they want to print),[8] others have cited the possibility that editorials stimulate reader response and that letter writing provides a cathartic release for "steamed up" readers.[9] Community issues boil up. This unrepresentative but articulate minority of letter writers may provide an

---

[7] Donald F. Roberts, Linda A. Sikorski, and William J. Paisley, "Letters in Mass Magazines as 'Outcroppings' of Public Concern," *Journalism Quarterly* 46 (1969):743–752.

[8] David L. Grey and Trevor R. Brown, "Letters to the Editor: Hazy Reflections of Public Opinion," *Journalism Quarterly* 47 (1970):450–456, 471.

[9] Hal Davis and Galen Rarick, "Functions of Editorials and Letters to the Editor," *Journalism Quarterly* 41 (1964):108–109.

insight into the changing mind and concerns of your community. It is a beginning that you will probably have to supplement with interviews with selected community leaders.

The imaginative reporter might even make use of obituaries. One editor of a Montgomery newspaper recently sought to find where central Alabama blacks went when they moved away. The U.S. Census documented the exodus of blacks from the farms of central Alabama. Where had they moved? There were no increases in the black population of Montgomery, Birmingham, or other Southern cities to account for the migrants. So the editor carefully studied the obituaries of blacks in his newspaper, systematically recording where the out-of-town survivors came from—mostly, though not entirely, from several industrial cities of the North and Midwest, he discovered. Not all local "theories" about where central Alabama blacks moved—"everybody's going to Detroit"—were correct. Content analysis provided information that would have been difficult and expensive to obtain from other sources, and shows a good example of studying a readily available outcropping to chart mobility.[10]

Decision Points in Content Analysis: A Case Study

Perhaps an actual ongoing journalism investigation that used content analysis can help illustrate the technique and some important methodological decisions that have to be made as the journalist goes along. There are six major decision points you will need to consider carefully.

1. Specify the *objectives* of your study, normally in the form of questions or hypotheses.
2. Locate the relevant *universe* or population of documents that will answer the study objectives.
3. Determine which documents you actually will study (normally a *sample* from the population of all the relevant documents).

---

[10] This was part of a study of mobility done by editor Ray Jenkins and reported in the *Alabama Journal*. Jenkins discussed the methodology at a workshop in Chapel Hill, North Carolina, in December 1971.

4. Collect the data.
5. Analyze the data you gather to answer your study objectives.
6. Report your findings clearly for a general community audience.

We can briefly illustrate each of these steps with a project done by Arlene Jacobson and Jan Johnson of the *Raleigh Times*.[11] These journalists had an idea that content analysis, if applied in the right place, could tell them something about Raleigh. And it did. Here is a step-by-step report.

SPECIFYING STUDY OBJECTIVES

These journalists became curious about the type and frequency of different requests to the "Hotline" column of the *Raleigh Times*. Such columns, under titles like "Action Line," "Call Quest" and "Live Wire," have recently earned high readership in newspapers. Many radio and television stations have similar programs. Requests range from complaints about products purchased to requests for birth-control information. The range, in fact, can be staggering. But, asked Jacobson and Johnson, what *kinds* of problems are most *frequently* raised? And what kinds of people in Raleigh seek information through this unofficial community problem-solving medium? Is it possible that the frequency of selected problems mentioned (say, about paving streets or fixing stoplights) is so great that it suggests a breakdown of important community problem-solving mechanisms? So Jacobson and Johnson formulated their study objectives.

They decided first to locate the type and frequency of community problems mentioned, and second to find as best they could the type of people (men or women, rich or poor, black or white) who appealed to their newspaper for information or help. They hypothesized that those who wrote in would be of lower socioeconomic status and, in Raleigh at least, more often would be black than white. In short, they wanted to know if those least likely to know which government or private agencies could help them (or those

---

[11] Ms. Jan Johnson is a reporter and Ms. Arlene Jacobson was then a copyeditor for the *Raleigh Times*. Both are graduates of the University of North Carolina School of Journalism. Ms. Jacobson now works on the copy desk of the *Charlotte Observer*.

with least "power" with those agencies) would be most likely to appeal to the newspaper as a public ombudsman.

What data are needed to answer the study questions, and are these data available from a reliable source? Jacobson and Johnson had an advantage in working for the newspaper. They arranged with the editor in charge of the column to obtain copies of all requests that came in. Nearly all requests came by telephone, so they excluded the few letters received. For a study of Raleigh problems these were judged as sufficient data. But these data would not have been enough if our journalists intended to generalize findings to similar columns that appeared in other community newspapers.

The *Raleigh Times* receives more than 100 inquiries each week, and the file soon builds up. Jacobson and Johnson decided to use *sampling* to cut down their work load. In this study, the *total number* of requests coming in by phone represents the *universe* of requests that came to the newspaper, *not just those published.* Our journalists sampled from this universe because they wanted to know what people phoned in about, *not* what the editor in charge of the column thought was important enough to publish from day to day. Any good editor will exercise judgment to avoid treating the same topic constantly and to provide a reasonable variety of treatment to different types of requests. But *repetition* of selected problems/requests was one of the variables Jacobson and Johnson sought to find. The more frequent the mention, they reasoned, the more likely a possible community problem lies underneath.

For two months, October and November, they randomly selected 500 requests from the approximately 1,000 that were telephoned to the *Times* during that period. They recognized that requests during these months might be seasonally influenced in terms of the type requests which came in, requests related to heating systems with onset of winter, for example. They did not consider this possible bias great enough to mar their study, but they kept it in mind when they looked at their results.

Using a "Coding Sheet" to Keep Track

Arlene Jacobson and Jan Johnson of the *Raleigh Times* used a coding sheet to analyze and tabulate the number of different kinds of requests coming to their newspaper's "Hotline." Each informational request telephoned to the newspaper that fell into their sample was judged to fall into one of the following categories and merited one check.

The coding sheet left room for some information such as sex or age of caller, to be added later when they tried to match the name of the person who called in with the same person at the county Board of Elections in order to find out better what kind of person asks "Hotline" for help.

Coding sheets are an important part of content analysis and justify thoughtful planning and thorough testing out early in any journalistic study.

CODING SHEET

_____ Date of call   _____ Number of call

_____ Sex of caller   _____ Age of caller

_____ Is the caller one
                with problem?

TYPE OF PROBLEM

PERSONAL

Consumer problems:
  House
    Payment _____
    Repairs _____
    Quality _____
    Service _____

  House trailer:
    Payment _____
    Repairs _____
    Quality _____
    Service _____

COMMUNITY

Traffic _____
Pollution _____
Law enforcement _____
Compliments, feedback _____
Criticisms, feedback _____
General community
  information _____
General city services _____

Motor vehicles:
    Payment _____
    Repairs _____
    Quality _____
Merchandise:
    Local: Payment _____
          Quality _____
          Service _____
    Mail order: Payment _____
            Quality _____
            Service _____
Other appliances:
    Payment _____
    Quality _____
    Repairs _____
Other:

_____

General information:

_____

Family problems:
    Credit _____
    Salary, income tax _____
    Veterans, army _____
Birth control:
    Vasectomy _____
    Tubal ligation _____
    Contraceptives _____
    Other _____
Legal information _____
Insurance _____
Addictive substances:
    Liquor _____
    Drugs _____
    Other _____
Marital problems:
    Divorce _____
    Child support _____
    Alimony _____
    Other _____
Health _____
Other _____

Query, Hotline _____
Compliments, Hotline _____
Criticisms, Hotline _____

OTHER _____
Can't determine _____

"Operational Definitions"
Simply Defining Exactly
What You Mean

For every category on the coding sheet where you need to put a check mark, you need a solid definition of that category to go by. Jacobson and Johnson wrote out and tested for clarity a definition for every major and minor category listed on the coding sheet.

This is one of the most crucial parts of content analysis and the area where experienced content analysts would caution you about going astray. If you cannot define what you want clearly enough so that *someone else* can do it, do not use content analysis. The effort will not be worth it and, more importantly, your results will not be reliable.

Defining what you want is what behavioral scientists call making *operational definitions*. In reality, it means carefully defining what you want and making sure you are understood, which is scarcely a new task for a good journalist. Examples of definitions used in the Raleigh study are:

(From coding sheet)	*(From operational definitions)*
PERSONAL	"This major category relates to those informational requests or problems that affect an individual's immediate environment or possessions."
Consumer problems:	"This subcategory is for those requests or problems relating to goods or services owned or rented by an individual or partic-

COLLECTING THE INFORMATION
FOR THE STUDY

How does one analyze so many requests into intelligible categories? Especially, as was often true, how does one classify the language of inarticulate people who had trouble making clear over the telephone (answers were recorded verbatim) just what information they wanted? Our journalists scanned the data to get a sense of the broad types of informational requests made. Then, they carefully defined each *category* of in-

	ipated in by a neighborhood or community. This includes services presumably offered to anyone in the public domain."
House	"A house is any apartment, home, or permanent dwelling place other than a trailer or tent."
Payment _____	"Any informational request or complaint related to either buying or renting a house or paying for home repair."
GENERAL INFORMATION	"Any questions pertaining to where or how to find an article; definitions of terms; requests for statistical information; almanac-type questions; very comprehensive questions not relating to any specific event or problem. ("Who won the World Series in 1951?" "What is the capital of Canada?" "Where can I buy pressed butterflies?")" [Editors' note: Using examples like this is an excellent way to help get across what you mean.]
Family problems	"Those requests that pertain to problems personally affecting the individual calling in, his family, kin, or close friends."
Credit _____	"Any request or complaint relating to any kind of credit problem or situation of the person calling in, his family, kin, or close friends."

formational request and devised a *coding sheet* to keep them on the track in collecting it.

Well-designed content analyses always involve at least a simple coding sheet with everything you are looking for carefully defined. The boxes show their basic coding sheet and examples of their definitions for various categories shown on the coding sheet.

After compiling the coding sheet and definitions of each category, Jacobson and Johnson carefully tested them to make sure they would be clearly understood. This is called the *reliability* check. Each reporter read a randomly selected sample of the requests independently to find how closely two observers agreed. This enabled them to spot ambiguous definitions or to discover the need for additional or fewer categories.

When you do a content analysis, you *must* conduct some kind of reliability check. It is a way of showing that you have kept your observation under tight control. Jacobson and Johnson used a simple formula and discovered they agreed 88 percent of the time in their judgments of how to classify each informational request, indicating that almost anyone could follow their classifications relatively easily.

On a simple project like this, they would not have wanted to fall below 80 percent agreement because that would indicate that the definitions were too ambiguous and were hard to follow. It is the reliability check that makes content analysis different from just reading through some documents. If someone is going to check you, you have to spell everything out carefully.

After the reliability check, Jacobson and Johnson began to classify all the remaining 500 informational requests according to the system they had devised and checked out. Like everyone else, they found that content analysis is often very slow going at first, but they speeded up considerably with a little experience. For journalists who become discouraged at this step there is a simple rule: Stick at it.

ANALYZING STUDY INFORMATION

Jacobson and Johnson broke the analysis into two parts. First, they had asked, what kinds of problems would surface in the column about Raleigh? In this kind of study, one normally makes the *assumption* that the greater the frequency of mention—of words, themes, types of stories, or informational requests, or whatever is your *criterion variable*—the more important it is. Otherwise, why would it be mentioned so often? (But remember that in some propaganda studies, for example, the most significant aspect of a public address may be what the leader did *not* say. Television journalists and newspaper columnists are particularly attuned to what leaders chose *not* to talk

Keeping on the Right Track
with a Reliability Check

One feature of content analysis that distinguishes it from simply reading a body of material is the *reliability check*. If you assert that your observations are scientific and reliable, you assert that others who *use your rules carefully* and *look at the same data* will come up with almost the *same results*. (That is why journalists who use this method must formulate rules so carefully and spend some initial time checking them for clarity.)

Our *Times* journalists independently examined twenty-five of the 500 "Hotline" requests and coded them. Then they used a simple formula to find their *percentage of agreement*. That formula (a commonly used one) is:

R (% of agreement) =

$$\frac{2 \text{ (the number of requests coded the } same \text{ way by coders A and B)}}{\text{(the total number coded by A)} + \text{(the total number coded by B)}}$$

Jacobson and Johnson each coded 25 items so the bottom part of the formula equals $25 + 25$, or 50. Of the 25 Jacobson (coder A) classified, 3 were classified differently from the way Johnson (coder B) had classified them. Altogether, however, they still agreed upon 22 of the 25 requests— that is, they coded them the same way. Hence, the top part of the formula becomes 2×22, or 44. Now we have everything we need. Their percentage of agreement is:

$$R = \frac{2\,(22)}{25 + 25} = \frac{44}{50} = .88 \text{ or } 88\%$$

SOURCE: This formula on reliability is adapted from R. W. Budd, R. K. Thorp, and Lewis Donohew, *Content Analysis of Communications*, Macmillan, New York, 1967, Chapter 8.

about as well as what they did, and sometimes it can be very revealing.) [12]

Table 1 shows their findings, with all the original categories collapsed into the major categories shown on the coding sheet.

[12] See Charles E. Osgood, "The Representational Model and Relevant Research Methods," in Pool, *Trends in Content Analysis*, pp. 33–88.

TABLE 1 *Distribution of Major Problems/Inquiries*

Type of Problems/Inquiries	Total Content Analysis Sample (%)	Subsample of Registered Voters (%)
Consumer problems	25	29
General information	27	25
Family information	17	17
Community issues	16	13
Compliments, criticisms, inquiries to "Hotline"	8	9
Other	8	7
Total percent	101 *	100
Total N	500	136

* Does not sum to 100 percent because of rounding.

The left-hand column in the table shows that "Hotline" was used most frequently (27 percent) by those seeking general information. But consumer problems accounted for nearly as many inquiries, and about one of every five persons requested information related to family problems. ("My husband left me and has not been making his alimony payments. What can I do?")

Our journalists were careful to keep in mind that these results may have been influenced by the kind of questions most often answered in the column because people with that kind of problem would be most tempted to phone in. Other than for the requests for which an answer was published, "Hotline" made no attempt to solve problems or provide information. But keeping this in mind, who did phone in?

Recall that Jacobson and Johnson, in part, conducted this study because they wanted to know what kinds of persons in Raleigh felt the need to complain publicly or to seek information about their problems. It was possible without compromising the confidentiality of the requester to cross-check many names against the voter registration information at the county Board of Elections.

For many, of course, they could find nothing. Those who wrote in sometimes lived out of town or the spelling of their names over the phone could not be matched against the voter registration records. The researchers could, of course, have tried to send out postcards for some background information, but they deliberately decided to use only existing, *unobtrusive* measures in their study.

This part of their study was, as they describe it, a "bit of a hassle," but for 136 of their sample of 500 they located additional information in the voter registration records. For these 136 callers there was information on age, race, sex, extent of voting, and address (used to determine the economic class of neighborhood in which the requester lived). With this information they could tell something about what kind of person wrote in or telephoned "Hotline," but they had to be careful. Those who register to vote may be very different from those who do not and about whom they could not find any additional information. Their only defense against claiming too much on the basis of these 136 callers was that this group complained or sought information on similar topics as did the entire group of 500.

The right-hand column of Table 1 shows how this special group distributed its requests to "Hotline." There is not much difference. Journalists who use content analysis, like those who use other methods of observing the community, must always be aware of potential weakness in sampling or interpretations and *frankly* make them clear to the reader without overdoing it. That is the essence of responsible behavioral science and journalism.

Tables 2 and 3 have information about the type of person phoning in according to several of the background variables. For the 136 special "Hotline" callers, Table 2 does not show clear trends according to age, except that those who are older more often tend to seek family-type information. This is particularly true (26 percent) of those in their forties. People of all ages seem to be having consumer problems.

Table 3 shows that men were somewhat more interested in community issues, while women more often sought family information. This also seemed true for the small number of blacks about whom Jacobson and Johnson could obtain information.

They were also able to match the addresses of those phoning in against economic data provided about Raleigh neighborhoods by the U.S. Census. They could determine if a "Hotline" respondent

TABLE 2 *Distribution of Major Problems/Inquiries in the Voter Subsample by Age*

Type of Problems/Inquiries	29 and Below	30–39	40–49	50 and Over
Consumer problems	35%	27%	23%	33%
General information	24	30	17	30
Family information	13	11	26	18
Community issues	16	11	20	4
Compliments, criticisms, inquiries to "Hotline"	3	16	6	11
Other	8	5	9	4
Total percent	‚99 *	100	101 *	100
Total N	37	37	35	27

* Does not sum to 100 percent because of rounding.

TABLE 3 *Distribution of Major Problems/Inquiries in the Voter Subsample by Sex, Race, and Income*

Type of Problems/Inquiries	SEX		RACE		INCOME	
	Men	Women	White	Black	Below Median	Above Median
Consumer problems	31%	28%	30%	22%	29%	37%
General information	24	26	28	6	13	35
Family information	11	21	11	56	39	5
Community issues	17	11	14	6	16	9
Compliments, criticisms, inquiries to "Hotline"	13	6	9	6	3	7
Other	4	8	7	6	0	7
Total percent	100%	100%	99% *	102% *	100%	100%
Total N	54	82	118	18	31	43

* Does not sum to 100 percent because of rounding.

lived in a neighborhood characterized by a median income above or below that for Raleigh as a whole. The results, as Table 3 shows, indicate that those of higher income are more interested in consumer problems, while those of lesser income more often seek family information.

What does this analysis add up to? Jacobson and Johnson undertook the content analysis to find out something about the range of community problems in Raleigh. They suspected the column was heavily serving those who could not find the proper community resources or could not get action out of them. While they were surprised by the number of requests relating to consumer problems and general information and the smaller number of requests that dealt with community issues, they were not surprised to find that those phoning in about more personal family-oriented problems tended more often to be poor, black, women, and those of "middle age." These are important problems to individuals in Raleigh. Is someone, our journalists asked, letting them down? Content analysis provides an intriguing indicator. Perhaps interviews with key community leaders can complete the answer.

Jacobson and Johnson decided to supplement their content analysis findings with information obtained from selected community leaders. They planned to combine the information into a story that focused on both community problems and the efforts of the community to help with those problems. This would provide a balanced analysis. Armed with the findings of their research, however, they found they could more skillfully plan the questions they would ask. Maybe, for a change, they also could tell community leaders a thing or two . . . to really get the interview going.

REPORTING FINDINGS TO A GENERAL AUDIENCE

In the Raleigh study, as in any good journalistic exploration, the results of the investigation must be written for a general audience. Our journalists considered using both data tables and an accompanying text, which would have to be done carefully. Tables can overwhelm the average reader. You need to be selective. But bar charts, graphs, and tables can help the reader visualize the point you are making and can help provide your newspaper with more visual impact as well.

Look at the results of the computerized study of Philadelphia's

An *Inquirer* computer study of the city's criminal courts, specially designed to measure those influences affecting the administration of justice, was based on the cases of 1,034 persons indicted during 1971 for one of the four major crimes of violence.

The 1,034 defendants represent a 39 percent sampling of all persons indicted that year for murder, rape, aggravated robbery, and aggravated assault and battery.

Data used in the computer study was gathered by an *Inquirer* investigative reporting team from more than 10,000 court documents and some 20,000 pages of notes of testimony concerning trials and other legal proceedings.

The chart . . . shows a breakdown of the race and sex of both offenders and victims of violent crimes in the *Inquirer* computer analysis, as well as the victim-defendant relationship and prior record of the accused.

For example, the defendant was white in only 9 percent of the cases. Similarly, the defendant was a woman in only 7 percent of the cases, but was a victim in 32 percent.

Although there were 1,034 defendants in the study, the actual number of cases used in the computer analysis totaled 1,374. Most of the difference was accounted for by those defendants who were charged with two or more violent crimes against different victims.

The survey included 62 percent of all persons indicted for rape; 52 percent of all persons indicted for murder; 44 percent of all persons indicted for aggravated robbery, and 16 percent of all persons indicted for aggravated assault and battery in 1971.

SOURCE: Adapted from an investigative story by Donald L. Barlett and James B. Steele in the *Philadelphia Inquirer*, 1973.

criminal justice system for 1971. That study sought answers to these questions:

1. Are blacks and whites treated equitably by the judicial system?
2. To what extent are sentences for the same crime similar among all judges in Philadelphia?

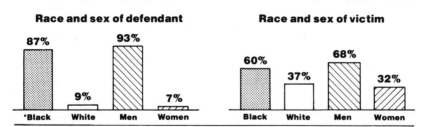

Race and sex of defendant

87% 'Black
9% White
93% Men
7% Women

Race and sex of victim

60% Black
37% White
68% Men
32% Women

Intra-racial crime

71% of cases, defendant and victim were members of same race
28% of cases, defendant was black and the victim was white
1% of cases, the defendant was white and the victim was black

Victim-defendant relationship

71% of cases, victim and defendant did not know each other
23% of cases, victim and defendant were acquaintances or knew each other by sight
6% of cases, victim and defendant were related

Prior arrest record of defendant

78% had at least one prior arrest
22% had no prior arrest

* Remaining 4 percent of defendants were of other races.

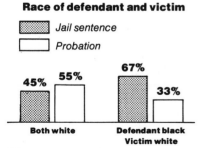

Race of defendant and victim

▨ Jail sentence
☐ Probation

45% 55% Both white
67% 33% Defendant black Victim white

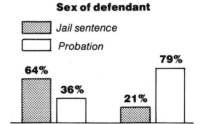

Sex of defendant

▨ Jail sentence
☐ Probation

64% 36% Male
21% 79% Female

When both the defendant and the victim in a violent crime are white, the offender is sent to jail in 45 percent of the cases. When the defendant is black and the victim is white, the defendant is sent to jail in 67 percent of the cases.

Men who plead guilty or are convicted of a violent crime are sentenced to jail in 64 percent of the cases, while women who plead guilty or are convicted of a violent crime are sentenced to jail in 21 percent of the cases.

3. Do certain types of crimes result in harsher sentences even though they are of the same legal seriousness as other crimes?

By using bar graphs the *Philadelphia Inquirer* tried to provide answers that were visually informative as well as providing solid reporting.

Race of defendant

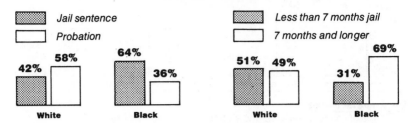

Jail sentence
Probation

	White	Black
	42% 58%	64% 36%

Less than 7 months jail
7 months and longer

	White	Black
	51% 49%	31% 69%

Blacks who plead guilty or are convicted of a violent crime are sentenced to jail in 64 percent of the cases, while whites who plead guilty or are convicted are sentenced to jail in 42 percent of the cases.

Blacks are sent to jail for seven months or longer in 69 percent of the cases, while whites are sent to jail for seven months or longer in 49 percent of the cases.

Jail sentences imposed by race of judge

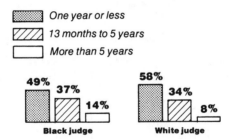

One year or less
13 months to 5 years
More than 5 years

	Black judge	White judge
	49% 37% 14%	58% 34% 8%

White judges sentence defendants convicted of a violent crime to jail terms of one year or less in 58 percent of the cases, while black judges sentence defendants convicted of a violent crime to jail terms of one year or less in 49 percent of the cases. White judges impose sentences of more than five years in 8 percent of the cases, black judges in 14 percent of the cases.

What information would you choose to run from Tables 1 through 3, and how would you present it? With graphs, bar charts, simple tables? Or, would you just mention relevant information in the story text? You can do this kind of study of your own community issues.

In the Raleigh "Hotline" study, two skilled journalists used content analysis *plus* interviewing to find out something about their community's problems. They used only available records. They spent about thirty hours in content analysis and initial interviewing, probably six times the amount of time needed if they had decided to use interviews alone. But the content analysis provided them with a central focus for interviewing. They did not have to depend entirely on what community leaders told them were the problems. They had their own independent information as a start.

Using Traditional Community Records

What can you do? You can use content analysis wherever your imagination leads you. You do not have to wait for your community to produce a local "Watergate" tapes transcript. Behavioral scientists and journalists have used the method of content analysis in many ways. They have compared the number of column inches given to different political parties by newspapers during campaigns or the treatment of different candidates on television news as a measure of "fairness." [13] They have studied all kinds of written and pictorial records as measures of how a communicator thought or felt during a particular time.[14] Many public documents related to the life of your community are available as social indicators for you to use through content analysis.

The School of Public Communications at Syracuse University has assembled information about some good starting places for reporters who want to dig into the public information already gathered in most communities. Let us evaluate some of these sources

---

[13] For the study of CBS news coverage based on content analysis see Edith Efron, *The News Twister*, Nash Publishing Company, Los Angeles, 1971. But also see Robert L. Stevenson *et al.*, "Untwisting 'The News Twisters': A Replication of Efron's Study," *Journalism Quarterly* 50 (1973):211–219. Many studies employing content analysis can be seen in *Journalism Quarterly* and *Public Opinion Quarterly*. The use of content analysis to measure "bias" in newspapers especially was prevalent in the 1950s and early 1960s.

[14] Several studies that particularly demonstrate the sophisticated range of content analysis are reprinted in Stone *et al.*, *The General Inquirer*, pp. 281 ff.

from the point of view of the interpretative journalist who commands the skills of content analysis.[15]

NEWSROOM LIBRARIES

From the records of your own newspaper or television station you may find old stories, film, or photographs that provide useful tips to guide your search for new or follow-up information about (or different angles to) community issues. Many files will provide useful background for community trend stories. One problem exists. Like American journalism in general, these files are often personality and event oriented rather than trend oriented.

THE PLAIN OLD TELEPHONE BOOK

Here you can find names, addresses, and telephone numbers of individuals and institutions. You can also find what kind of services or products are offered by many community businesses. Concentrating on various kinds of social indicators, one behavioral scientist has compared the "profiles" of different communities that emerge by studying the range of goods and services offered in the yellow pages.[16]

CITY DIRECTORIES

Many cities have directories that list by name every occupant of every street address in the city. (As a cross-check, many reporters regularly compare a person's address in the phone book with that in a city directory to make sure they are talking about the right person.) If your community

---

[15] The material discussed in this chapter is adapted from "Information About People: Where to Find It in Syracuse, N.Y.," S. I. Newhouse School of Public Communications, Syracuse University, Syracuse, N.Y., April 1973.

[16] David Heise, a sociologist at the University of North Carolina-Chapel Hill, has conducted such community comparison (thus far unpublished) studies. An insightful recent book, which outlines some social indicators of cities and regions, is David M. Smith, *The Geography of Social Well-Being in the United States: An Introduction to Territorial Social Indicators*, McGraw-Hill Book Company, New York, 1973.

has these directories for several years back—they probably are filed in your community library—you can do a simple piece of analysis by seeing how the number of business addresses have increased or decreased in selected areas of the city. But be careful! Like the telephone book, this source is always a little out of date.

PUBLIC LIBRARIES

In addition to a variety of reference sources, many libraries also keep their own "morgue," or archives, relating to community issues. This may include everything from genealogical information about local families to detailed information about local issues that have been emphasized through the years. (And sometimes libraries will assemble massive information on an issue or topic in which an individual librarian is interested. One of the authors of this chapter once met a reference librarian with one consuming interest beyond her work—local flowers.) One advantage of the public or college library morgue over that of the newspaper is that the library information is normally based on a wider variety of information.

COUNTY CLERKS' OFFICES

This important official, the clerk, may have different names in different places, but his or her office normally keeps community records on marriages, divorces, property deeds, business licenses, civil court case dispositions and judgments, mortgages, and even dog and fishing licenses.

In one way or another all newspapers try to cover this important office on a regular basis. For the interpretative journalist in search of indicators on his unique community, its files are very rich. Has your community had more or fewer than the national average of divorces? Are the people in your community getting married at younger ages than was true, say, five or ten years ago? Simple content analysis applied to the documents of this office can provide you with many interesting community stories.

Health departments contain many vital records relating to community health. Officials of such departments can give you vital statistics (or good estimates) relating to the extent of community inoculation against certain diseases or the "threat" posed to the community by a suddenly rising and spreading disease. Often these records are kept for many years back. And comparative figures for other areas are usually available.

CHAMBERS OF COMMERCE

Most organizations make it a point to collect many different kinds of community statistics—everything from average temperatures to opportunities for industry. Reporters need to be cautious because most groups naturally emphasize the "good" side of everything. Better Business Bureaus will sometimes make available such information as how a business was financed or the extent of products and services offered. In addition, credit bureaus may provide some limited economic information for properly authorized reasons. They are not likely to let you spy on individuals, but you could probably do trend stories relating to how solidly based is the financial rating of local businessmen as a group. One limitation: many of these records are not kept long; they are valuable only when current.

TAX OFFICES/BOARDS OF ASSESSMENT

Although it may be called by different names, this office keeps records of the amount of tax assessed against a specific piece of community property and whether or not that tax has been paid. Often these records also show the uses of property—residential, commercial, industrial. A skillful application of content analysis to these records will allow you to document long-term trends in rising or falling property values and the uses of property in your community.[17]

---

[17] Caution! Tax assessments are rarely the true value of property. And both tax rates and assessment ratios change over time. But assessment figures can be used to document trends and comparisons so long as these sources of distortion are explicitly taken into account.

POLICE AND SHERIFF'S DEPARTMENTS

In these departments, as in fire departments, numerous records relating to public safety are kept. If a warrant for arrest has been sworn out and served against an individual, this becomes part of the public record, and you can use it. Likewise police and sheriff's departments have to account regularly to community boards of aldermen about what they have been doing. This is also true of fire departments. So they regularly compile statistical summaries of various kinds of crimes committed (and solved) and types of fires extinguished. Often these records are kept for several years.

These records can help you answer such questions as these: Is serious crime rising in your community? How effective are your police in solving crimes? Using the accident reports of police, you could discover the traffic intersections at which people are most likely to get killed. But remember that content analysis will not produce evidence stronger than the documents you are studying. There is a natural tendency for police to *under*estimate the number of crimes committed and *over*estimate the number solved and for fire departments to *under*estimate fire damages. And, as is well known, many crime victims do not complain to the police. Content analysis can help you spot many interesting trends in these police and fire documents, but be on guard to spot built-in biases in the documents.

COURT RECORDS

Community courts are called by many names—city, municipal, state, county—and all except those at the lowest levels are required to keep some basic record of their actions. These records provide the basic information upon which an appeal can be judged. These records also provide a gold mine for community analysis if you are interested in any aspect of this question: What *kinds* of people (the young or blacks?) are charged with what *types* of crime (is it "rape" when you are black and "aggravated assault" when white?) with what kinds of *conviction rates* by what *specific courts* (or judges)? In the courts, community problems and issues regularly can arise. Content analysis can help you sort them out.

What Documents Tell (and Don't Tell) You

While the FBI and other law enforcement agencies are charged with the task of keeping tallies on the number of serious crimes committed, summary documents of these agencies have to be used with a reporter's skeptical insight. Many crimes go unreported because people may decide it's not worth it (minor larcenies), or they may be ashamed (rape) or afraid (assault) to report it.

A recent federal study of eight major cities used *survey research* to discover if people would anonymously admit to being crime victims. The results were compared with the actual statistics for selected crimes for the same period. The graph shows the differences.

In the case of auto theft, everyone reported it, probably for insurance reasons. But reporting of serious personal crimes is far from complete. Documents are great for showing trends, *but* they must be used with care. Results of content analysis with documents should be compared, where possible, with the findings of other reportorial techniques.

SOURCE: Adapted from "8 Cities Show a Crime Disparity," *The New York Times*, January 27, 1974. © 1973–74 by The New York Times Company. Reprinted by permission.

It Is Up to You

In the end, it all boils down to you, the journalist. Communities vary greatly in terms of the issues that need reporting, and journalists similarly vary in their interests. For the journalist with a bent for digging up the trend story, content analysis will supply some useful technique, and the community will supply the relevant body of documents, whether it be a series of mayoral addresses through the years or a file of old city directories.

The trick is to see the story, apply the proper reportorial technique to gather and analyze the facts, and present them interestingly to the increasingly sophisticated American reading and viewing news audiences.

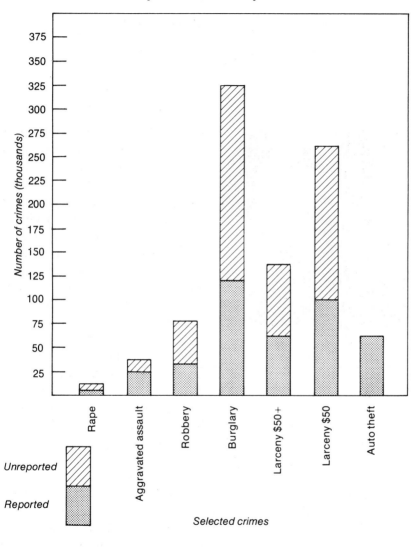

Reported versus unreported crimes

Number of crimes (thousands)

Rape · Aggravated assault · Robbery · Burglary · Larceny $50+ · Larceny $50 · Auto theft

Unreported

Reported

Selected crimes

Chapter 8

Interviewing

Peter Johansen

Sherlock Holmes solved mysteries uncommonly well. The opening pages of *The Hound of the Baskervilles* show us the key to that success. An unknown visitor forgot his walking stick at Holmes' house, and from it the detective deduced the stranger's occupation and several personal characteristics. Engraved on the stick was "To James Mortimer, M.R.C.S., from his friends of the C.C.H." and "1884." From that single stick, Holmes suggested that the visitor was a country doctor who walked a lot, that he once worked at Charing Cross Hospital, that he was a young man, that he was amiable, unambitious, absent-minded, and possessed a dog. Holmes' amazed friend, Dr. Watson, consulted his medical directory, found Mortimer's biography, and confirmed many of Holmes' conclusions. Finally, Mortimer himself returned, and a brief conversation confirmed or modified the remaining points.

Sherlock Holmes would have made an "ace" reporter. Relying on no one method, he gathered information by whatever approach was appropriate to the task at hand, and confirmed what he learned by a second method where possible. Thus, observation, reading, and interviewing combined to tell Holmes a good deal about his unknown visitor.

Journalists today should heed Holmes. They rely too much in each assignment on just one information-gathering tool. Too often that tool is the interview. Unlike Holmes, the typical reporter is

Getting Away from the Interview

Interviewing isn't always the most reliable way to gather information. Consider the 1973 professional baseball season, when Cleveland Indians pitcher Gaylord Perry was accused by many professional rivals of throwing outlawed spitballs. One of the complainants, Bobby Murcer of the New York Yankees, was even fined during the verbal fray after claiming that baseball commissioner Bowie Kuhn was "gutless" for not prosecuting Perry.

In interview after interview, Perry denied the charge. But were the denials true? The answer will never be conclusively established, but a *New York Times* story threw Perry's position into doubt:

> According to a secret report leaked to the *New York Times,* Gaylord Jackson Perry, the Cleveland operative, threw thirty spitballs against the New York Yankees on Friday night. . . .
>
> Most of the fans, and Perry, were unaware that a Yankee pitcher secretly prepared a pitching chart for this paper of Perry's deliveries to the Bronx Bombers during the game, which the Yanks won, 7–1.
>
> When the game ended the chart was quietly handed to a *Times* reporter in the Yankee locker room. The newsman then took the chart to the American Broadcasting Company television studios, where the tapes were replayed of Perry's motion before every pitch.
>
> It was discovered that there was one constant before every alleged "spitball"—Perry tugged the inside of his left sleeve with his right hand. That's the one that throws the ball. He did not touch the inside of the sleeve before throwing balls that the Yankee pitcher said were not spitters.

SOURCE: Gerald Esekenazi, "The Great Spitball Controversy," *The New York Times*, July 1, 1973. © 1973–74 by the New York Times Company. Reprinted by permission.

---

frequently satisfied when each party to a dispute has been asked for its opposing viewpoint. The reporter then weaves these few strands into a completed story, and any embellishments that appear are likely to be background material culled from the previous day's paper.

But interviewing is sometimes a notoriously unreliable method of finding out what *really* happened or what people *really* think. It finds favor with working journalists, however, because it is the quickest way to get information. It is faster to ask the city manager about this year's municipal budget than to pour through pages and pages of accountants' tables and make sense of them. After all, the reporter deals with contemporary events, and today's budget has to be in tonight's paper. Besides, the reporter—harried and harassed—probably has a half-dozen *other* stories due that day. That is why one reporting text states that 12 percent of the news stories in a metropolitan daily are openly based on interviews and that an additional 38 percent are partly based on oral sources.[1]

We do not think journalists should abandon the interview even if they could. Despite its faults, interviewing is indispensable. What we do advocate is the thoughtful use of the interview *in concert with other methods of information gathering.*

Consider what the local congressman has to say about urban renewal costs; if government statistics back him up, there is supporting evidence that the politician is correct. Behavioral scientists call this approach *multi-operationism* and *convergent validation.* We call it good sense.

Reporters cannot use the interview correctly, however, if they are blind to its dangers. A study of reporters in Ottawa, Canada, indicates that many do not know these weaknesses. Of the twenty-one journalists surveyed—including reporters for two local dailies and those from the parliamentary press gallery—only one had sampled extensively the interviewing literature and four others had a "nodding acquaintance with an article or two." Eight were clearly not aware of the biasing effect of providing a source with alternative answers to a question; thirteen did not know the pitfalls of leading questions; six saw nothing dangerous in double-barreled questions.[2]

It seems appropriate, then, to map some of the pitfalls of interviewing, caused by both the reporter and the source, and to provide suggestions for avoiding them.

When to Interview

Too often, journalists jump into an interview when it is not clear that that method will elicit

---

[1] Mitchell V. Charnley, *Reporting*, 2d ed., Holt, Rinehart and Winston, New York, 1966, p. 189.
[2] Alan Arbuckle, "The Incomplete Interviewer," *Content: For Canadian Journalists*, March 1972, pp. 12–13.

sound information. Sometimes the source has forgotten facts—names, dates, figures—that are crucial. Written records are more reliable, although occasionally the reporter is interested in a person's recollection, accurate or not. Sometimes a source will pretend to know information in order to conceal his or her ignorance. Sometimes a source has ulterior motives in granting an interview; the facts given are pre-selected to promote personal goals, and reporters do not always "flesh out" those facts before rushing such stories into print.

As reporters face those who refuse interviews, they develop techniques to break down their resistance. They may bluff, convincing the source that the sought-after information would be better corrected or fleshed out than publicized in the form that already exists. They may appeal to the source's vanity, suggesting they have the *other* side's story and it would be to the source's advantage to tell *his* side, too. They may threaten the source, suggesting that a "no comment" would look incriminating, regardless of its intent. They may invoke the power of the medium for which they work, agreeing with journalism professor Curtis Mac-Dougall that men in public life for any length of time "realize the power of the press and respect it." [3] Useful as they may be, however, such ploys may taint the information the reporters obtain. Surely honest reporters do not want to do that.

Still the fact remains: there are times when reporters must interview particularly reluctant individuals. What can they do? One successful technique is to seek out some information from lesser sources first. Piecing bits together, reporters can then confront the person with a partial story and argue that the story would be more "correct" if the source would flesh it out.

This procedure was used by Pulitzer Prize winners Carl Bernstein and Bob Woodward in their investigations of the 1972 Watergate break-in. Early stories were attacked by the White House, and these denials were traced to the President's chief-of-staff at the time, H. R. Haldeman. The *Washington Post* reporters then knew the story reached that far up in the hierarchy, but they "did not make a direct assault on the 'Berlin Wall' at the White House. They went around the wall, and then began to work their way up

---

[3] Curtis D. MacDougall, *Interpretative Reporting*, 4th ed., Macmillan, New York, 1963, p. 35.

from the bottom." [4] And work they did. Woodward and Bernstein visited at least fifty homes of staff members of the Committee to Re-elect the President to get information before interviewing higher-ups.

Woodward and Bernstein found that information from a number of sources was more reliable than from a single person. That is usually the case. The reporter's job, however, is to check the validity of that generalization in every instance.

Frequently, the reporter's topic is so sweeping, so complicated, that one or two persons could not possibly know everything. Other times, there is one unchallenged authority. Even here, though, the reporter must not confuse the expert's views with "truth." *New York Times* columnist Tom Wicker wrote:

> We tend to give weight to the official source, as if we believe that the man wouldn't be there if he didn't know what he was talking about; the institution wouldn't be functioning if it didn't have a certain relevance to whatever area it is functioning in.[5]

But, Wicker notes, experts—especially those affiliated with institutions—are sometimes irrelevant or out of touch with world events, and are not the locus of many non-establishment forces in the world, like women's liberation and the counterculture.

The reporter, then, must take a cue from Lewis Dexter, who urges his fellow political scientists to evaluate each interviewee. Suppose, he writes, some congressmen claim great outside pressure in a particular area of public affairs, while others say they receive little pressure. Dexter observes that if the latter group appears to have more influence in legislation, then their assessments of pressure may lead to more understanding of the political system than would the averaging of all congressmen's reports. One must have a test independent of what the majority say, Dexter concludes.[6] The newsmen, too, must make this decision when determining who to interview and when evaluating the relaibility of the information obtained.

---

[4] James McCartney, "The Washington 'Post' and Watergate: How Two Davids Slew Goliath," *Columbia Journalism Review*, July/August 1973, p. 15.

[5] Tom Wicker, "The Greening of the Press," *Columbia Journalism Review*, May/June 1971, p. 9.

[6] Lewis Anthony Dexter, *Elite and Specialized Interviewing*, Northwestern University Press, Evanston, 1970, p. 7.

Who Should Conduct Interviews?

When riots shook Washington after the assassination of Martin Luther King in 1968, both the *Washington Post* and *Washington Star* sent black reporters into the streets. As a result, these papers ran stories that all-white news bureaus could not get. A year earlier in Detroit, black newsman Ray Rogers accompanied a black sniper to a rooftop, and got a real exclusive. And fighting a subpoena for his notes on Black Panther activities, *New York Times* reporter Earl Caldwell said that he got information no white could have obtained, because Panther officials confided in a fellow black.

Obviously, one reporter can sometimes get more information than another—not because of ability, but because of some personal characteristic. The effect of a journalist's race may be obvious today, but only within the past few years have news organizations assigned non-whites to cover the black ghetto or Chicano *barrio*. Behavioral scientists, on the other hand, have known for much longer how data is affected when interviewer and interviewee are closely matched. Chapter 5 summarizes some of this research on *social distance*.

While editors are increasingly aware of the way race can affect a story, they are much less conscious of other factors that should also be taken into account. Behavioral science shows that wide discrepancies—and sometimes even too perfect a match—between interviewer and interviewee on age, sex, religious background, income, or educational status can all influence survey results. Presumably the same holds true for newsgathering. When the interviewer and interviewee are optimally matched, rapport may be more easily established, fewer communication barriers may result, the source may feel fewer social pressures, a high degree of empathy is possible, and both parties to the interview may be put at ease.

Yet, every situation is unique, and matching reporter and source on salient characteristics is not always desirable or practical. Appropriate minority-group reporters are not always available. Sometimes minority-group sources will perceive a reporter of their own race as a "sell-out" to the establishment and be less cooperative as a result. Assigning a particular type of reporter may be dangerous. The *Detroit Free Press* assigned whites to night duty during that city's race riots, because police might otherwise have mistaken black reporters for rioters.

Sometimes there are distinct advantages when the reporter and the source are not matched on the social variables mentioned above.[7] When the interviewer has superior social status, for example, he might arrange and control the interview more easily, the interviewee might be motivated to please the interviewer, the interviewer might observe his subject under pressure, and he might reward the interviewee. Similarly, there are advantages when the reporter is in a subordinate position: the source might not feel threatened, might feel freer to speak, and might feel sorry for the reporter and want to help him.

Interview Error: The Reporter as Cause

When two people get together, there are two sources of human failing. An interview is just such an event: whenever a reporter and the source meet, each relies on the other to present undistorted information—the source gives the reporter accurate material, and the reporter transmits it accurately to the public. Unfortunately, both participants almost inevitably play havoc with the reporter's ultimate goal—to present an accurate picture of reality. Both can bias information. To some extent, reporters cannot correct the errors of the subject, but they can be aware of how they intrude and can minimize their impact. They can also be critical of their own performances—if they realize their weak spots. This section aims at suggesting first the sources of interviewer bias and then those of the interviewee.

Behavioral science research suggests that interviewers can affect the truthfulness and accuracy of the information they gather by their personal characteristics (appearance, manner, and attitudes) and by their data-collecting ability. We have already seen one example of the former—the race, sex, and similar characteristics of a reporter sometimes alter a story when they differ too

---

[7] Charles J. Stewart and William B. Cash, *Interviewing: Principles and Practices,* William C. Brown, Dubuque, Iowa, 1974, pp. 90–91.

sharply or match too perfectly those of the source. But other problems arise from the reporters' personal characteristics.

What of the reporter's manner? MacDougall writes that the best interviews are those that proceed in "a natural, friendly, informal way." [8] On the other hand, psychologists Eugene Webb and Jerry Salancik say, " 'Be Natural!' is the worst possible advice." [9] They take the view that in each interview, reporters must assume a certain role. Their roles differ from situation to situation and even within a single interview. To obtain the most useful information, interviewers must ask what role in what situation will help yield useful information.

Wise reporters will indeed adjust their manner to suit the occasion, but within limits. Reporters should not play roles in which they are uncomfortable. An observant interviewee can spot nervousness and exploit that nervousness to his or her advantage. But reporters should have a wide repertoire of techniques—friendliness, hostility, and neutrality—and be able to resort to each comfortably whenever necessary.

In addition to their manner, reporters' attitudes and expectations can also mislead them. Consider a study in which transients were asked the causes of their destitution. The principal researcher noticed that one interviewer's respondents consistently cited overindulgence of liquor, while a second interviewer seemed to find a high number of transients who blamed social and industrial conditions. After probing, the researcher was scarcely surprised that the first interviewer was a prohibitionist, the second a socialist! [10]

The journalist must skirt the same pitfall. Three traps, though, make that difficult. Social psychologists have called these *selective exposure, selective perception,* and *selective retention.* Selective exposure is the least common of the dangers so far as journalists are concerned. Studies have concluded that people tend to expose themselves to events or information that support strongly held beliefs, and they avoid that which challenges those beliefs. Re-

---

[8] MacDougall, *Interpretative Reporting,* p. 35.
[9] Eugene Webb and Jerry Salancik, "The Interview, or the Only Wheel in Town," *Journalism Monograph* No. 2 (1966), p. 11.
[10] Stuart A. Rice, "Contagious Bias in the Interview: A Methodological Note," *American Journal of Sociology* 35 (1929):420–423.

porters, however, are usually told what to cover. Moreover, they realize their professional obligations to search out a variety of views, and so it is unlikely that a Republican political reporter will selectively ignore pro-Democratic news.[11]

Selective perception and retention, however, *are* journalistic problems. Persons who somehow find themselves confronted with disagreeable information may misunderstand it so that it becomes palatable. A reporter can experience the same problem.

Finally, there is selective retention. If disagreeable information gets past the hurdles of exposure and perception, it may be forgotten. The anecdote by journalism professor William L. Rivers relates how this happened to one reporter.

Why do these processes take place? Psychologist Leon Festinger attributes them to *cognitive dissonance,* a psychological theory which suggests that individuals are driven to reduce the tension that results when two related cognitions, both important, are incompatible.[12] Frequently, the easiest way to reduce tension is to prevent it from happening in the first place. This can sometimes be done by ignoring new information that would tend to make us psychologically uncomfortable. It is also easier to distort or forget one little chunk of new information than it is to revamp a larger body of attitudes and beliefs that have been with us a long time and have provided the rationale for a whole range of past behavior.

Psychologists Edward Jones and Harold Gerard note that we do sometimes accept discrepant information, thus proving that dissonance does not always lead to the three selective processes outlined. But they suggest this occurs because an individual realizes the importance of being open to change, especially before he has undergone any changes in behavior deriving from the new information.[13]

The journalist's attitudes and expectations regarding the inter-

[11] A review of the literature on selective exposure, and an argument that it is not so widespread as behavioral scientists previously believed, can be found in David O. Sears and J. L. Freedman, "Selective Exposure to Information: A Critical Review," *Public Opinion Quarterly* 31 (1967):194–213.

[12] Leon Festinger, A *Theory of Cognitive Dissonance*, Row Peterson, Evanston, Ill., 1957.

[13] Edward E. Jones and Harold B. Gerard, *Foundations of Social Psychology*, John Wiley and Sons, New York, 1967, pp. 227–255.

Selective Retention on the Campaign Trail

When William L. Rivers was a Washington correspondent for *The Reporter,* he covered the 1960 Presidential campaign between John F. Kennedy and Richard M. Nixon. His coverage of a pre-election rally of the African Methodist Episcopal Church details the selective processes at work and illustrates what Rivers says was his "most grievous mistake as a reporter."

During the meeting, Pennsylvania Senator Hugh Scott claimed that Nixon had integrated a Missouri motel by refusing to stay there unless a black member of his entourage was allowed to put up with the others. Says Rivers: "Now I didn't like Mr. Nixon, and I didn't think he would do anything so forthright. . . . After taking detailed notes on the many other aspects of the convocation, I returned to my office that night and telephoned the motel." The manager acknowledged that Scott's story was true, adding that the motel was still integrated.

The next morning, Rivers wrote a 500-word report in which he linked the meeting to an overall Republican strategy of convincing blacks that Kennedy had two positions on civil rights, one for Northerners, another for Southerners. He reported that Scott's speech was devoted to variations on the theme. The article quoted Scott: "Kennedy has never even integrated a bathroom." Rivers went on to cite Kennedy speeches that disproved Scott's charge of silence on civil rights in the South:

> Perhaps most important, Senator Kennedy said in Jackson, Mississippi, in October 1957: "I have no hesitancy in saying the same thing that I have said in my own city of Boston: that I have accepted the Supreme Court decision as the supreme law of the land." This had apparently escaped Senator Scott's convenient memory, for he told the Negro churchmen, "Senator Kennedy has very suddenly, since he became a candidate, developed an interest in your problems."

Reflecting on this report, Rivers wrote several years later:

> The fact is, of course, that *my* memory was more convenient than Scott's. Nowhere did I point out that Richard Nixon integrated a motel, a fact which certainly would have helped win Negro votes to his cause. I did not omit this consciously. My prejudices did the work. . . .

SOURCE: William L. Rivers, "Appraising Press Coverage of Politics," in Richard W. Lee, ed., *Politics and the Press,* Acropolis Books, Washington, 1970, pp. 40–43.

viewee may affect in other ways what information is gathered. Webb and Salancik observe that even the reporter's physical behavior may be affected by expectations which, in turn, influence the source. All of this is unconscious but still very real.

Suppose the source makes a statement that the reporter expects. The reporter may nod, lean forward, or say "good," all of which reinforce the source to continue in that vein, rather than to go on to something new.[14] Frequently, reporters feel the need to express their own feelings. Indeed, research suggests a taciturn source says more when an interviewer agrees slightly. This tip is particularly handy for broadcast interviewers. But the reporter must understand the tradeoffs involved.

Cub reporters are unfailingly told to prepare themselves for interviews. Writes British journalist E. Frank Candlin: "It is a sound plan to decide what sort of response on the part of your 'subject' would make the best story and then to frame your questions toward that end." [15] Candlin advises the neophyte to know as much as possible beforehand about an interviewee's background, hobbies, and so on. This is not an invitation to decide in advance what stance the source should take and lead into it. It applies only to deciding the topics and subtopics likely worth exploring.

But if preparation permits reporters to form attitudes, should they forego preparation in order to keep an open mind? Probably not. In the first place, many people who are important enough to be interviewed are likely to be busy and will resent the journalist who asks trite questions, or questions for which answers are readily available elsewhere. Second, the unprepared reporter may understand so little about the subject at hand that he or she cannot ask a source to clarify ambiguous statements, to complete incomplete ones, or to reconcile contradictory ones. And third, reporters may be swept up by an enthusiastic interviewee. With no objective yardstick, they may thus attach more importance to the source and its opinions than they deserve, or be unable to weigh the comparative significance of various remarks by the source. This is not an open mind, but a vacuous one.

Reporters' expectations about their employers and audience also affect what is retained from the interview. Behavioral scien-

---

[14] Webb and Salancik, "The Interview," p. 35.
[15] E. Frank Candlin, *Journalism*, English Universities Press, London, 1951, p. 66.

tists Claire Zimmerman and Raymond Bauer conducted an experiment that demonstrates journalism students are less likely to remember information that would conflict with the audience's views than they are to remember that to which the audience would be hospitable.

Using working reporters rather than students, behavioral scientists Ithiel de Sola Pool and Irwin Shulman demonstrate how crime reporters differentially used facts of violence depending on their expectation of the audience and the effect of the story on that audience. Journalism researcher Jean Kerrick and her colleagues show that journalism students voluntarily bias news stories in the direction of a hypothetical newspaper's editorial policy and that those most in disagreement with the policy write the stories most one-sided in its favor. This conforms to sociologist Warren Breed's finding that reporters become socialized toward a paper's editorial policy through an elaborate system of rewards and punishments.[16]

Journalists also hold expectations arising from the nature of news itself. News cannot be defined concretely; it is really what reporters and editors say it is. And so, reporters are unsure that their evaluation of the importance of things is correct. This leads a reporter to seek "assurance from other reporters that his judgment is correct. He relies on other reporters to help him determine what is important, and believes that if his colleagues agree, then it really must be news." [17]

Because reporters form a consensus about what news is, the scope of what a reporter might independently seek in any given news situation is reduced. They come to learn over time what makes news. When news, then, derives from an interview, there may be many interesting or significant points, but reporters pick those that conform to their ideas of what news entails.

---

[16] Claire Zimmerman and Raymond A. Bauer, "The Effects of an Audience on What Is Remembered," *Public Opinion Quarterly* 20 (1956):238–248; Ithiel de Sola Pool and Irwin Shulman, "Newsmen's Fantasies, Audiences and Newswriting," *Public Opinion Quarterly* 23 (1959):145–158; Jean S. Kerrick, Thomas E. Anderson, and Luita B. Swales, "Balance and the Writer's Attitude in News Stories and Editorials," *Journalism Quarterly* 41 (1964):207–215; Warren Breed, "Social Control in the News Room: A Functional Analysis," *Social Forces* 33 (1955):326–335.

[17] Delmer D. Dunn, *Public Officials and the Press*, Addison-Wesley, Reading, Mass., 1969, p. 30.

An illustration may help. In 1968, there was a large demonstration against the Vietnam War in London. For two weeks before the event, the leading newspapers predicted violent clashes between police and demonstrators. In fact, the 20,000 marchers were peaceful, although a small group broke away from the crowd and tried to get through police barricades. This incident led the television news. All the coverage was in the context of the press predictions: the little violence there justified newspaper prophecies, but reporters were also able to write that violence had been prevented by the police.[18] The event itself was perceived through the expectations that the media had created.

There is reason to believe, then, that reporters' predispositions—about sources, audience, bosses, and news itself—all conspire to shape the information that comes from an interview. Findings from the Kerrick study suggest that a reporter, trying to compensate for personal biases, may bend too far in the opposite direction, although this evidence clearly arises from one laboratory situation and cannot be transferred to the field without caution.

At any rate, we feel that reporters should analyze their prejudices. Perhaps good practice would be to tape a few interviews, write stories in the usual way, and compare them with the tapes. Discerning reporters may come to recognize patterns in their selective processes.

Just as personal characteristics, manner, and expectations can mislead reporters, so, too, can the actual information-gathering performance. They may phrase or deliver their questions faultily; they may not probe fully; they may record the interview unfaithfully.

In the first place, many reporters are not sufficiently aware of proper question-wording. Survey researcher Stanley Payne observes that in public-opinion surveys slight (and seemingly unimportant) shifts in question-wording have created dramatic changes in the results. In a survey of recent visitors to a patents exposition, half the respondents replied negatively to the question, "Have you heard or read anything about patents lately?" Comments Payne, "Apparently the 'heard or read' phrase, as all-inclusive as it

---

[18] James D. Halloran, Philip Elliott, and Graham Murdock, *Demonstrations and Communications: A Case Study*, Penguin Books, Harmondsworth, 1970.

was meant to be, did not bring to mind what had been seen at the Exposition." [19] When even simple words can distort information, we can easily assume the significance of other problems with question-wording. And yet, as the Arbuckle findings noted earlier make clear, working journalists are not familiar with these problems.

Let us consider, then, a few of the precautions behavioral scientists have learned to take. Psychologists Eleanor and Nathan Maccoby give six tips for question clarity that are instructive for the journalist.[20]

1. Avoid words with double meaning. For example, the phrase "put up" may mean to nominate a candidate, stay for the night, endure an insult, or preserve fruits. Usually, the source will know which meaning the reporter has in mind, but not always.
2. Avoid long questions. The longer the question, the more elements it is apt to contain. The subject may find one part that is of interest and respond with a reply so lengthy that both reporter and subject forget the other elements involved. When a reporter wants an answer to each element of a question, each element deserves its own question.
3. Specify exactly the time, place, and context. Imagine a reporter researching a story on a local construction boom. Thirty minutes have been spent with a prominent building contractor. The discussion has skipped back and forth between residential and commercial development, but the last few questions have centered on the latter. Now, near the end of the session, the reporter asks, "How much more did your company build this year than last year?" Because the discussion has been most recently focused on commercial construction, the builder assumes that it is in this context that the question was framed and answers it accordingly. The contractor thinks the interview went well until the next day when he reads that his firm's *total* increase over the previous year was what only his commercial work had

---

[19] Stanley Payne, *The Art of Asking Questions*, Princeton University Press, Princeton, 1951, p. 28.
[20] Eleanor E. Maccoby and Nathan Maccoby, "The Interview: A Tool of Social Science," in Gardner Lindzey, ed., *Handbook of Social Psychology*, Addison-Wesley, Reading, Mass., 1954, vol. 1.

Avoiding Long Questions

During 1974, President Richard M. Nixon was embattled on all fronts by allegations that he had obstructed justice by covering up numerous illegal campaign practices in the 1972 Presidential election. In a March 1974, news conference, he was peppered with questions about the Watergate mess. Consider this one:

> Mr. President, I would like to ask two questions, if I may. You surprised a lot of us by calling a second news conference within eight days, and I'm wondering if that's the start of a new policy. Secondly, I would like to ask this question: It has always been the custom that foreign money from foreign citizens is permitted to be accepted and spent in American political campaigns on all levels, and in your campaign in '72 I think at least $150,000 came in from foreign citizens. Do you think that is right and if not, will your campaign financing reform bill include a prohibition of that kind of money?

The President's answer demonstrates the difficulty with long questions. He briefly announced that only domestic contributions would be permissible under his campaign financing reform bill. Fixing on that legislation, however, he went on for more than four hundred words to outline other items in the proposed bill, all only tangentially related to the reporter's question. He never said whether he thought foreign financing was right, nor did he respond to the question about a new news policy.

SOURCE: Question from "Transcript of the President's News Conference on Domestic and Foreign Affairs," *The New York Times*, March 7, 1974.

---

been. Clearly, the reporter did not make the context clear, and in this case was seriously misinterpreted.

4. Make explicit all alternatives. In providing alternative answers, reporters should be sure they have really listed them all. Arbuckle observes that the question, "Do you write with a pencil or pen?" can bias a response if the interviewee writes with a crayon or does not write at all.[21] Perhaps the best use to which alternatives can be put is in posing embarrassing questions. If the alternatives are extreme enough, then the source may feel

---

[21] Arbuckle, "The Incomplete Interviewer," p. 13.

that his or her behavior or attitude is not, in comparison, nearly so outrageous as he or she thought, and he or she will be forthright.

5. Unfamiliar topics should be prefaced with an explanation. Suppose that a number of school children have been struck by cars while crossing an intersection on the way to school. Suppose, too, that several parents have joined forces to demand city action that would decrease the danger. A city hall reporter seeking reaction from civic officials may have to summarize the situation for the mayor if the parents have only recently grouped together and have not yet formally approached him. (The need to explain the situation, of course, may also confirm the parents' charge that their weeks-long protest has fallen on deaf ears.)

6. Question in terms of immediate experience not generalities. "Has anything newsworthy happened in your department today?" is so general that it throws the burden of reporting and probing on the person questioned. In such circumstances, the source often may see no reason to unduly bother with a reply.

As a general rule, journalists should know and adhere to these rules. But practising them is not always easy. Typing out questions in advance of the interview may be one solution. Journalist Hugh Sherwood uses this procedure, claiming he can cover all important points, more easily keep the interview on topic, and prove to his interviewee he has thought about the topic.[22] But counterbalanced against these benefits are the twin dangers of reinforcing reporter expectations (and the biases just discussed in that connection) and encouraging the reporter to stick to prepared questions although other important paths suggest themselves during the interview.

Moreover, there are occasions when journalists, fully aware of the wisdom of these principles, will break them for good reason. They may ask obtuse questions designed to camouflage the true intent of the query; they may ask a general question to find out what aspect of a topic most interests the subject. But these are particular exceptions, for special purposes, and reporters embark upon them wisely only when they understand their limitations.

---

[22] Hugh C. Sherwood, *The Journalistic Interview*, rev. ed., Harper, New York, 1972, pp. 44–45.

Faulty question-wording can be a source of bias in the interview. So, too, can faulty probing. If editors drafted a list of common complaints about new reporters, reluctance to probe would surely rank high. Probing is important at two levels. Reporters must understand accurately the details they are being told, and they must also understand the meaning of those details. First, they must see whether the name is "John Smith" or "Jon Smyth." If they do not know, they must make sure—a simple, direct question is enough. More important, they must dig so that statements of complicated fact and interpretation are clear. If they do not understand, neither will their readers. Journalism professor David Grey writes that the reporter "must be an active interpreter of information and ideas. This means he cannot passively sit back and receive messages without thinking about and critically questioning them." [23] Reporters must push both themselves and their source, so that they understand completely what the source has said. This may mean asking the source to repeat statements, to provide examples when things are not clear, to search out inconsistencies in an interview and to have them cleared up, to ask the source to compare its statements with contradictory evidence.

Two studies on newspaper accuracy specifically urge reporters to routinely ask news sources such questions as "what is the significance of this event?" or "what should the public know about this event?" [24] In every assignment, the reporter's goal is to be so complete and clear that the reader is left with no questions unanswered.

Few reporters work for long before being charged with misquoting. Sometimes the accusation is a smokescreen because the source regrets what it said, and sometimes the reporter has deliberately twisted the meaning of a source's statement. But just as often, the reporter has unknowingly changed the source's statement. When this happens, the reporter has recorded the source's statements faultily during the interview or has reconstructed them incorrectly afterward. Let us see how such errors occur.

---

[23] David L. Grey, *The Writing Process*, Wadsworth Publishing Co., Belmont, Calif., 1972, p. 35.

[24] Gary C. Lawrence and David L. Grey, "Subjective Inacuracies in Local News Reporting," *Journalism Quarterly* 46 (1969):753–757; Phillip J. Tichenor, Clarice N. Olien, Annette Harrison, and George Donohue, "Mass Communication Systems and Communication Accuracy in Science News Reporting," *Journalism Quarterly* 47 (1970):673–683.

At the simplest level, each individual seems to have distinctive word patterns, preferring to use some words out of proportion to their average use. In a study of behavioral science interviewers, communication scientist Andrew Collins discovered that each interviewer idiosyncratically recorded supposedly verbatim answers, using their "favorite" words in place of those actually spoken. That is, according to the "verbatim" records of one recorder, the subjects frequently used the word "knowledge" and the subjects of another interviewer seemed to like the word "improvement." Moreover, some interviewers were more verbose than others in recording answers.[25] What this means for the reporter is obvious: he or she may literally put words in the mouths of the sources, by using *his or her* favorite words when transcribing *their* answers.

Often reporters are so worried about getting the "jazzy" quotes exactly right that they fail to grasp the significance of what the source has said. Too often, a story sparkles with precise quotes but, taken as a whole, the interviewee's full meaning is lacking. Conducting interviews with a tape recorder could reduce both problems. The reporter can double check quotes by replaying the relevant segment of tape. And the reporter, not concerned with the *way* ideas are worded, can reflect more fully on the *substance*.

Many reporters avoid tape recorders, seemingly for two reasons. First, they claim people freeze at the sight of a microphone. This argument is absurd when applied to those who are in the limelight regularly. They are accustomed to radio and television and probably feel somewhat "safer" when they are electronically recorded. It is true that some subjects, microphone-shy, may not be so frightened by a reporter's pad and pencil. The point, however, is that fright of a tape recorder is not so widespread as some reporters believe. *New York Times* reporter David Shipler, in fact, says that some print reporters have taken to carrying tape recorders because many people speak more openly when confronted by them! [26]

---

[25] W. Andrew Collins, "Idiosyncratic Verbal Behavior of Interviewers," A Report of the Institute for Communication Research, Stanford University (October 1968).

[26] "Interviewing Techniques," taped discussion by David Shipler, Judy Klemesrud, and Clifton Daniel (available from *The New York Times* public relations department).

Reporters also claim the tape recorder is unwieldy and slows down the writing of copy in a business where deadlines are crucial. But nothing stops the reporter from making a brief note of each different point and its location on the tape. Back at the office, they can zero in on relevant segments. In short, reporters can let a machine do mechanical work—recording every memorable turn of phrase—so that they can concentrate on understanding the source's general idea.

When they rely on note-taking, however, how much should reporters write? A study by journalism researcher Friedrich Abel shows that the answer is not clear. He gave a seven-minute taped interview to introductory reporting classes, who were instructed whether or not to take notes. Those who took no notes were more likely to omit factual elements, but note-takers were more apt to record facts incorrectly in their stories.[27]

Some reporters believe that note-taking may inhibit an interviewer's participation and that the reporter is more alert and retentive when forced to remember everything. These reporters believe that the wise journalist "keeps his notebook well out of sight, at least in the early stages of an interview, for many people are put off by the thought that anything they say is being taken down and may appear in tomorrow's newspaper for all to read."[28]

But, as Webb and Salancik point out, this is doubly error-prone: when the reporter *does* take notes, it tends to instruct the source about what is worth saying, and the reporter will selectively remember those statements he or she expected the source to make. At any rate, whatever the style and amount of note-taking, wise reporters will review their scribblings as quickly as possible. The rate of memory decay is phenomenal, and a brief phrase that made perfect sense when it was written down may be meaningless only a couple of hours after the interview has concluded.

Interviewer accuracy is also an issue in telephone interviews. The evidence is not unanimous, but most studies show that telephone interviews are less accurate than those conducted face to face.[29] A prime reason is that many channels of human com-

---

[27] Friedrich E. Abel, "Note-Takers vs. Non-Note-Takers: Who Makes More Errors?" *Journalism Quarterly* 46 (1969):811–814.

[28] Candlin, *Journalism*, pp. 68–69.

[29] Fred C. Berry, Jr., "A Study of Accuracy in Local News Stories of Three Dailies," *Journalism Quarterly* 44 (1967):482–490; Lawrence and Grey, "Subjective

munication are lost in telephone use. Albert Mehrabian suggests, for instance, that only 7 percent of human feeling is communicated verbally, while an additional 38 percent is carried by vocal qualities like intonation and stress. Fully 55 percent of feeling is communicated nonverbally through facial expressions, and all this is lost over the phone.[30]

Still, the telephone is indispensable in the harried world of journalism, and it would be foolhardy to recommend that it not be used. Reporters should simply restrict its use, when possible, preferably to obtaining factual information that does not depend on the entire communicative apparatus of an interviewee to give it meaning.

Interview Error: The News Source as Cause

Two people are involved in an interview, each with his or her own human failings, so it is no surprise that the interviewee, like the interviewer, is a source of bias. The latter, we have seen, cannot always control the errors created. Even more is he or she unable to control those of the interviewee. But, as with personal biases, reporters can minimize distortion if they understand the ways the source can distort and if they account for them in their own behavior.

Survey researchers Charles Cannell and Robert Kahn organize the behavioral science literature on respondent bias around three broad questions.[31]

1. Does the respondent have access to the information required?
2. Does he or she understand his or her role and what the interviewer wants?
3. Is he or she motivated to fulfill the requirements of that role?

Inaccuracies in Local News Reporting"; Tichenor et al., "Mass Communication Systems and Communication Accuracy in Science News Reporting"; T. Joseph Scanlon, "A New Approach to Study of Newspaper Accuracy," Journalism Quarterly 49 (1972):587–590.

[30] Albert Mehrabian, "Communication Without Words," Psychology Today, September 1968, p. 53.

[31] Charles F. Cannell and Robert L. Kahn, "Interviewing," in Gardner Lindzey and Elliot Aronson, eds., Handbook of Social Psychology, 2d ed., Addison-Wesley, Reading, Mass., 1968, vol. II.

Accessibility is a simple enough concept. People cannot tell a reporter things they do not know. Most journalists, for instance, can recall sources who were so thoroughly involved in events that they could not be aware of dimensions of the event that were apparent to a detached observer. Many people, too, are unaware of personal idiosyncracies, so these cannot be discussed in interviews.

Information may also be inaccessible because it is forgotten, distorted, or suppressed. We gradually forget unimportant information, and it may be for such a simple reason that reporters fail to get what they seek from a source. Reporters can sometimes frame questions to aid recall. They can ask the source to consult records; they can provide a context that helps the source reconstruct the past; they can pose questions that require recognition rather than recall. People recall simple, factual information, but even here there are quirks: people can remember more accurately their date of birth than their age in years.

As for other material, events that were important to the individual when they occurred are usually better recalled than minor events. Most of the time the reporter will not face a problem with simple forgetfulness. Occasionally, a source may fabricate answers so as not to appear stupid, but it is more likely that he or she will consider the embarrassment of appearing wrong in the public print and feel that admitting his or her forgetfulness is preferable.

More problematic for the reporter than an outright lie is the unconscious distortion. One study shows that the public, although it is accurate in reporting expenditures on gas, rent, and medical care, underreports liquor consumption. Mothers' reports on aspects of childrearing are incorrect and inconsistent, and they distort facts of a child's development in ways that make the child appear precocious.

The same occurs in journalistic interviews. Officers of an organization, for instance, may inflate the number of members who participate regularly in meetings. Government officials exaggerate the importance of their departments or projects because they have invested their time and energy in the program's well-being and they really believe in their work. The mild skepticism with which journalists greet political interviews could wisely be extended to all encounters. And, as we shall see later, simple observation frequently allows an independent cross-check on verbal statements.

Repression also makes material inaccessible. We noted that important events are generally more easily remembered than minor ones. Some of these events, however, are so unpleasant or involve such emotional stress that they have been pushed out of the conscious memory. Finally, the source may consciously know the information sought, but a problem in language, vocabulary, concepts, and so on may prevent its transmittal to the journalist.

ROLE OF THE SOURCE

A second element of successful interviewing is a good understanding by the source of his or her role. An illustration helps explain. When the author of this chapter was a daily newspaper reporter, he interviewed a scientist who was attending a spectroscopy convention. The reporter asked the scientist about the practical applications to which his research could be put, but the scientist discussed in technical language what his work *was,* rather than its ultimate uses. It was only after explaining carefully the paper's needs that a breakthrough was reached, and the scientist explained the many potential benefits of his work.

This interview initially failed because the scientist misconceived what was wanted of him. The reporter's introductory remarks were inadequate in preparing the spectroscopist to act, not as a scientist in the laboratory, but as an informed citizen who understood the advances this research could bring to people.

Every source needs to know what to do to fulfill the role satisfactorily. The reporter deals with many people who are so familiar with the press that they more or less understand their job. Through reporter reactions in each interview and through reports actually published or broadcast, these regular press sources learn to modify their behavior in the direction that reporters seem to want. But reporters should broaden their range of sources, and these new interviewees must be taught their role. As Cannell and Kahn put it:

> (F)ew of us are familiar with the role; still fewer of us have had much experience in it, and virtually none of us has been trained for it. The result is that the interviewer must define the role for the

When the Role Should
Not Be Clear

Although it is usually good to outline clearly to the source what role he or she should play in the interview, sometimes obscuring that information works to the reporter's benefit. Consider the ploy of one-time Denver drama critic Kap Monohan:

> There was a rumor around that (movie actress Clara Bow) was going to quit—at the height of her popularity—to marry and have a family. Of course the studio denied it. But Kap reasoned there must be a little fire when there was so much smoke, so when a Denver organization booked the head of Clara's studio for a dinner speech, Kap loaded his guns. He found out everything he could about the man, discovered he was very fond of a couple of little granddaughters—call them Pattie and Connie. He was also proud of his fine home, a swimming pool, and whatnot. He had produced some marvelous movie successes and made some wonderful talent discoveries, such as Clara.
>
> When the man came to town, Kap asked for a private interview, rather than one of those group affairs. It was granted, and Kap went to the movie mogul's room. First thing he said, when they shook hands was: "How are Pattie and Connie?" The mogul's face brightened, and they went on from there, talking about his home, swimming pool, etc. Then Kap mentioned the many stars this man had discovered. He named them, but purposely left Clara Bow out. "You forgot Clara Bow," the man said. "Oh, yes, I did," Kap said casually. One word and another about her and the movie mogul said: "You've heard about her retiring, I guess?" Kap said: "Oh, yes, but that's a lot of hooey—press agent stuff." Then he started to talk about something else, but the producer insisted on talking about Bow. Kap eventually made like the hell with Clara and the retirement stories. Whereupon the producer got himself all worked up, thus: "If you think she's not quitting, you're crazy. She is." Then he went on to tell him where, when, and how, with details about the home she and her intended were planning, their honeymoon, and whatnot. Kap almost broke a leg getting back to the office and had a world beat. He had used his knowledge of the man, along with a bit of flattery, to get his story. And he never asked a question about Bow.

SOURCE: From *Keys to Successful Interviewing*, by Stewart Harral. Copyright 1954 by the University of Oklahoma Press.

respondent, teach it to him, let him practice it, so to speak, and then instruct him as to his weak and strong points in performing it. There must be a continuous checking and communicating from interviewer to respondent, a kind of quality control which is undertaken to bring the respondent to a level of understanding which will produce valid data.[32]

The respondent needs to understand not only his or her role, but also the meaning of specific questions and the depth and level of specificity of the responses desired. Even a simply-worded question can be misunderstood, as we saw with Payne's example on patent expositions. The reporter must make sure the respondent understands what is asked. Sometimes the nature of the source's reply makes obvious a misunderstanding. As the anecdote about the building contractor illustrated, however, such confusion can sometimes escape notice. Careful phrasing of questions is the best antidote to such mistakes. When the respondent does not reply with sufficient precision, the reporter should probe until he or she *does* answer appropriately.

MOTIVATION

Motivation is the third of Cannell and Kahn's conditions for successful interviewing. A reporter must show a potential source why the interview would be a benefit, and the reporter must kindle that desire throughout the interview itself.

The reporter confronts many resistances. The source may lack time or may place higher priority on other activities. The source may be embarrassed at revealing its ignorance. He or she may dislike journalists in general or the particular organization for which the reporter works. He or she may fear the consequences that could arise from the interview.

Reporters cannot invariably overcome these objections, but they have weapons they can exploit. Appearance in the media still affords many with a great deal of personal prestige. Some sources so frequently enjoy media exposure that yet another appearance is meaningless, but many of the busiest sources relish all free publicity.

---

[32] *Ibid.*, p. 575.

The Self-Serving Interview

For several years a parliamentary writer for the *Toronto Telegram,* Peter Dempson, often got exclusive stories from the government of Canadian Prime Minister John Diefenbaker because the *Telegram* was a staunch supporter of Diefenbaker's party. In 1959, when Diefenbaker's Minister of External Affairs died suddenly, speculation was rife about the successor. The following anecdote from this period illustrates vividly how an interviewee can be motivated to grant an interview for self-serving reasons. Incidentally, "Jackson" refers to Richard Jackson, a reporter for the *Ottawa Journal,* another consistent Diefenbaker supporter.

> One morning, when Jackson and I were talking to Diefenbaker, he referred to the stories we had been writing about who might get the external affairs post. "Interesting speculation," he said, nodding his head, "very interesting. Nice bunch of candidates. But there's an obvious one you're overlooking."
> "Who's that?" snapped Jackson, somewhat excitedly. "I thought we had covered everyone."
> "Well," said Diefenbaker slowly, his gooseberry eyes smiling at us, "the Minister of Finance is doing a very good job in the cabinet. It's just possible he could do as well in some other portfolio."
> "You mean he's to get Smith's job?" I asked incredulously. No one in the Press Gallery had even considered Donald Fleming as a

Occasionally individuals harbor antipathy to the press in general, but do not hold the same sentiments against particular journalists with whom they have had previous dealings. Thus, Tichenor and associates found that scientists were more willing to help reporters they had already been in contact with than they were to help other reporters.[33] Lawrence and Grey suggest that news sources prefer personal contact with reporters, so when journalists have difficulty persuading a source to be interviewed, it may cement future relations if they establish face-to-face contact and check back with the source to assure the accuracy of facts.[34]

---

[33] Tichenor *et al.,* "Mass Communication Systems and Communication Accuracy in Science News Reporting."

[34] Lawrence and Grey, "Subjective Inaccuracies in Local News Reporting," p. 756.

potential successor to Smith. We didn't think that Diefenbaker could afford to move him from finance.

"I didn't say that," said Diefenbaker, turning up his lower lip in a teasing manner. "All I'm saying is that he is a very capable minister."

The Telegram and *The Journal* carried prominent front-page stories the following day that said Diefenbaker was considering appointing Fleming to External Affairs. The Prime Minister had told us that he would likely be making an announcement within two or three weeks.

. . . *The Telegram* questioned me about the report which the editors couldn't take very seriously. Fleming just didn't fit the pattern of a diplomat. . . . I wasn't convinced that Fleming was the man; but the tip had been strong.

Two weeks later Jackson and I were again in Diefenbaker's office. Before either of us could say anything, the Prime Minister pointed to a stack of letters on his desk, and said: "Forget about Fleming. I'd like to let you read these, but I can't. Anyway, they've given me my answer." He added that he had already reached a decision, had informed the person in question, and would be making the announcement in about another week. . . .

It . . . became apparent to Jackson and me that Diefenbaker had used us and our papers, to test public reaction about Fleming. When our stories evoked a prompt and negative reaction, he dropped the idea.

SOURCE: Peter Dempson, *Assignment Ottawa*, General Publishing Co., Toronto, 1968, pp. 103–104.

One technique designed to reduce hostility toward a specific journalist is worth reviewing. A beat reporter interviews an individual on a routine basis. When he or she discovers potentially explosive news, the editor is notified to send another reporter to do the job. The beat reporter can sympathize with the disgruntled source, plead for cooperation since the damage was created by "that other s.o.b., not me," and thus keep the channels of communication open.

A potential source, fearful of the consequences of being interviewed, may be won over if the reporter suggests that a "no comment" is more damaging than anything an interview could reveal. Again, though, the reporter must consider in what ways, if any, these ploys will affect the substance of the interview that has been granted.

An opposite problem of motivation is the source who is eager to cooperate with the press for a self-serving reason. Because of the obvious bias in such information, reporters prefer independent support of any claims or assertions from either documents or a second source. In their research on the 1972 Watergate break-in, for instance, reporters Bob Woodward and Carl Bernstein were careful to print *nothing* until it had been verified.

The interviewee may be motivated to grant an interview but must also be motivated to continue it. Motivation is likely to endure if the respondent can sustain self-esteem, show that he or she does not violate important social norms, and presents an image of consistency and worthiness. Thus, the politician who is interviewed as a prominent authority on auto safety is obviously more positively motivated than the colleague who is asked to explain participation in a kickback scheme.

Reporters can demonstrate their ongoing interest in a source's pronouncements by using encouragements—what the behavioral scientist calls *positive reinforcement* or *rewards*. Encouragements, such as "Uh-huh" or "That's interesting," show that the interviewer is listening and interested and would like the source to continue in that vein. Of thirty-eight studies made on the effects of such words, thirty show that responses can be lengthened significantly.

This sort of tool is helpful with a taciturn source. But the reporter must be aware of biasing effects. When reporters say "good," they influence the respondent to continue along the lines of previous answers. Using "uh-hum," does not. Reporters must carefully choose their encouragements. Short silences can elicit longer responses, although those lasting ten seconds or more may be dysfunctional. Nonetheless, reporters often find that lengthy, sustained silence on their part does force a reluctant source to start talking.

Also having an inhibiting effect on sources are "guggles"—interruptions by the reporter, like "ah" or the beginning of words, that indicate to the interviewee that the reporter wants to speak. Frequently, the respondent will stop to permit this.

A final tip: interviewees tend to talk twice as much as interviewers, so in general, the longer the question, the longer the answer. Again, the reporter may feel it worthwhile to sacrifice the safety of short questions in order to motivate an otherwise silent subject.

Observation and the Interview

Most discussions of journalistic interviewing focus solely on the verbal interaction between reporter and source. But communication involves much more than words, and the good reporter is always conscious of that fact. When Michael J. Connor of the *Wall Street Journal* wrote about Charles Kuralt, the newsman who reports *On the Road* features for the *CBS Evening News,* he began his story with a number of observations:

> *Gardnerville, Nev.*—As the big, white Cortez motorhome lumbers northward on Route 395, this quiet community's main street, and heads on out of town, CBS News correspondent Charles Kuralt sits back and takes a sip of his morning coffee. Mr. Kuralt and a three-man CBS News film crew have been here more than a day now, but, Mr. Kuralt concedes, the product of their work—a short story about diamonds, a master diamond cutter, and his diamond-cutting school—probably doesn't contain much news. As a matter of fact, Mr. Kuralt agrees, there probably isn't much news of national import in this entire town of some 3,000 people.
>
> "But you know," he muses, staring out the window, "I'm not sure it's news we're after. I'm not so sure what we do *is* news. But I do know this: There are at least two or three stories in this town. And, if we poked around a little, I bet we could find two or three more." [35]

So, journalists often use description during interview stories. But their observations are frequently haphazard rather than conscious and regularized. Descriptive passages sometimes seem to be used more as literary devices, designed to make a story sparkle, than as relevant bits of information that naturally expand upon points being made.

Reporters can make observation systematically when they realize that it can serve three uses during the interview situation. First, it can perform a check on a source's *life-style.* Second, observation can help test the *veracity* of a source's statements. And third, observation can help determine whether a source's *behavior* is what he or she claims.

The so-called "new journalists" seem to delight in describing an individual's way of life just by enumerating observations about appearance. One of Tom Wolfe's best articles is about Junior John-

---

[35] Michael J. Connor, "CBS' Charles Kuralt Roams Nation, Seeks the 'Old and Enduring'," *Wall Street Journal,* December 11, 1973. Reprinted with the permission of *The Wall Street Journal,* © Dow Jones & Company, Inc., 1973.

son, the fabled stock-car racer from the hills of North Carolina. Early in the piece, Wolfe makes the point that men from that area of the South do not fit the stereotypical image of the overalled hillbilly—but he does so by careful description:

> These good old boys in the airport, by the way, were in their twenties, except for one fellow who was a cabdriver and was about forty-five, I would say. Except for the cabdriver, they all wore neo-Brummellian wardrobing such as Lacoste tennis shirts, Slim Jim pants, windbreakers with the collars turned up, "fast" shoes of the winkle-picker genre, and so on. I mention these details just by way of pointing out that very few grits, Iron Boy overalls, clodhoppers, or hats with ventilation holes up near the crown enter into this story.[36]

Wolfe practices the same observational procedure as many journalists but, unlike most, he has routinized it as a regular part of his research. The possibilities open to the innovative reporter are endless. Is a politician's desk cluttered or neat, and does this give a clue to the efficiency in solving constituents' problems? What color is an executive's office furniture, and what does this say about his or her power within the hierarchy? In some organizations, decors are keyed to levels of executive responsibility.

How luxurious is a university professor's home, and does this indicate extensive outside income from book royalties and consultantships? Does the bachelor pro football player have needlepoint material around his home, and does this signal his attitudes toward masculine-feminine stereotypes? These are observations reporters should make constantly. At the same time, they must jump to conclusions with care: the rich professor may have married a wealthy woman, and the athlete may have a handicraft-loving girl friend. But without making these observations in the first place and then following them up, reporters can miss a lot—and so, unfortunately, can the audience.

Just as journalists must be conscious of the *physical artifacts* on and about their subject, so too should they be aware of the *nonverbal* aspects of their source's statements. Herb Lawson, of the *Wall Street Journal,* recalls an occasion when his attentiveness paid off. He had unverified information that a company was involved in stock manipulation and requested a meeting with its top officials. At the same time he created fear by advising them to

---

[36] Tom Wolfe, "The Last American Hero Is Junior Johnson. Yes!" *Esquire,* October 1973, p. 212.

have their counsel present. They denied any wrongdoing. But, Lawson says, "I kept picking up nonverbal cues that told me I had something. So I ran it out and left them with the impression that I was going ahead with what I had. They called the next day and asked for another hearing, and I knew I had a story." [37]

Best-selling books about "body language"—that is, the study of what is communicated by specific body movements—are glib popularizations that drastically overstate the findings of the young science of *kinesics*. We cannot interpret nonverbal vocalizations and body movements with the certainty these books suggest. However, there is some knowledge in the field, and journalists should be applying it daily.

We urge just one important cautionary word. Because nonverbal studies are still in their infancy, generalizations are difficult to make. For one interviewee, wiping the forehead may signal lying. But for another, it may simply mean he or she is hot or that it is a nervous habit done under a variety of emotional states.

Of many good points made by Webb and Salancik, none is more sound than this: only when reporters know a source well can they make safe assumptions from nonverbal cues, for it is then that they learn the repertoire of responses from which the source draws. Otherwise, nonverbal literature should be used as nothing more than a guide.

Observation can also help check the consistency between words and actions. The reporter smells more than a fish when billows of black smoke and a stench hover over a factory the same day the plant's public relations person says it does not pollute the air. The reporter must not assume automatically the PR person was lying. The smoke may have been accidental, different from normal plant emissions. But, by the same token, the reporter should not be blind to it, and should not let the discrepancy pass unresolved.

Ethical Issues

More than the other reporting methods discussed in this book, interviewing is a familiar tech-

---

[37] Leonard Seelers, "Investigative Reporting: Methods and Barriers," paper presented to Program on Communications and Society, Aspen Institute for Humanistic Studies, Aspen, Colorado (August 1973), pp. 19–20.

Observing Nonverbal Communication

Because we emphasize communicating with words, what we try to hide often comes out in our nonverbal acts. It is easy to disguise emotions and beliefs verbally but more difficult in other modes of communication.

The reporter can exploit this discrepancy by comparing verbal and nonverbal outputs when interviewing sources. We cannot catalogue, in this brief space, the research findings in nonverbal studies, but we can give a flavor of the sorts of ways a reporter can use them. A good, brief introduction to this research is Mark L. Knapp, *Nonverbal Communication in Human Interaction*, Holt, Rinehart and Winston, New York, 1972.

KINESICS

Kinesics includes gestures, body movements, facial expressions, eye behavior, and posture.

How much does the source like the reporter? When a male likes a fellow male, he will turn his body orientation slightly away from that person. With a female-to-female relationship, the most direct orientation is with neutral addressees, the least direct with those who are intensely disliked. When a source indicates that he or she dislikes the reporter, what is the reason? How might it affect willingness to provide information?

Is the source trying to persuade the reporter? The degree of liking communicated nonverbally correlates directly with his intended persuasiveness. Is there reason to suspect the persuasiveness of the source?

Is the source trying to deceive? Deception clues likely include tense leg positions, frequent shifts of leg posture, restless or repetitive leg and foot movements.

---

nique for most readers. It is a basic device learned early in either formal or on-the-job training. Because of that, readers should have been confronted with at least some of the major ethical questions surrounding the interview. This chapter has introduced little that will raise new ethical issues, and so we can quickly run down the concerns that are already familiar in checklist fashion.

Interviewing has an ethical impact at four key stages. First are

PARALANGUAGE

Dealing with the way something is said, paralanguage includes voice qualities (pitch, tempo, resonance) and vocalizations (sighs, whispering, drawls, half-words like "uh-huh").

Newsweek reports that State Department spokesman Robert J. McCloskey deliberately manipulated his voice, conveying to reporters various meanings:

> McCloskey has three distinct ways of saying "I would not speculate": spoken without accent, it means the department doesn't know for sure; emphasis on the "I" means "I wouldn't but you may—and with some assurance"; accent on "speculate" indicates that the questioner's premise is probably wrong.

Undeliberate vocalizations are also important clues for reporters. A source's dominance correlates positively with low pitch, loudness, and resonance. High introversion relates negatively to those qualities.

Speech errors—things like stuttering, incomplete sentences, slips of the tongue, changing sentences in mid-stream—seem to increase with anxiety or discomfort. Satisfaction seems to be associated with normal loudness, pitch, rate and rhythm of speaking, but also with a somewhat resonant timbre, slight upward inflection, and somewhat slurred enunciation.

PROXEMICS

Proxemics is the study of how people perceive and use physical space.

Under stress, a person appears to sit farther away from the individual causing the stress; the same occurs with general unfriendliness.

Status may be judged by the length of time it takes one individual to acknowledge the presence of another—the higher the status, the greater the length of time. When one person approaches another, the distance he or she maintains relates to his or her subordination. The reporter may get some clues to a source's position within a hierarchy if others in the hierarchy approach during the interview.

issues involved in arranging the interview. Does it constitute an *invasion of privacy?* Is there an overriding public interest that sometimes demands the interruption of private lives? Is it proper for the media to throw the spotlight on the spouse of a public fig-

The Ethics of Hassling Sources

During their research on the Watergate break-in, one of the *Washington Post*'s reporters, Carl Bernstein, who won a Pulitzer Prize for his role in unmasking the story, noticed that one of the employees of the Committee to Re-elect the President was an acquaintance of his. What happened when he called her for lunch illustrates the anguish a reporter can cause a source, and raises hard ethical questions.

He suggested half-a-dozen places where they could meet and not be seen, but she insisted on a sandwich shop where dozens of Nixon campaign workers were eating. When they sat down, she explained why: "I'm being followed. It's open here and doesn't look like I'm hiding anything. People won't talk on the phones; it's terrible."

Bernstein asked her to calm down and said he thought she was overdramatizing. "I wish I were," she said. "They know everything at the committee. They know that the indictments will be down in a week and that there will only be seven. [Along with the original five burglars and Howard Hunt, G. Gordon Liddy, finance counsel to CRP, was now a suspect.] Once, another person went back to the D. A. because the FBI didn't ask her the right questions. That night her boss knew about it. I always had one institution I believed in—the FBI. No more.

"I've done my duty as a good citizen. I went back to the D. A., too. But I'm a fatalist now. It'll never come out, the whole truth. You'll never get the truth. You can't get it by reporters' talking to just the good people. They know you've been out talking to people

ure, just because he or she *is* the spouse? Are there areas of a public figure's own life that are properly kept private? What are they?

Is *badgering* acceptable when a potential source initially refuses cooperation? Are repeated requests for an interview merely an irksome bother, or is there a point at which this behavior leads to ethical misconduct? If so, what is the dividing line? If there is no other way to obtain an interview, is it ever permissible for the reporter to pay a source for an interview? Would the exclusivity agreement that often accompanies such "checkbook journalism" conflict with the right of *all* the public to know?

Should the reporter's *identity* and *purpose* always be clear and at night. Somebody from the press office came up to our office today and said, 'I sure wish I knew who in this committee had a link to Carl Bernstein and Bob Woodward.' The FBI never even asked me if I was at the committee over the weekend of the break-in. I was there almost the whole time."

She asked Bernstein to walk back to the office with her to avoid any appearance of furtiveness. While they were waiting to cross the street at 17th Street and Pennsylvania Avenue, Maurice Stans, finance chairman for CRP, pulled up across the avenue in his limousine.

"He was an honest man before all this started," she said. "Now he's lying, too."

Bernstein studied Stans from across the street as the former Secretary of Commerce entered the building.

About five o'clock, the woman telephoned Bernstein. She sounded almost hysterical. "I'm in a phone booth. When I got back from lunch, I got called into somebody's office and confronted with the fact that I had been seen talking to a *Post* reporter. They wanted to know everything. It was high up; that's all you have to know. I told you they were following me. Please don't call me again or come to see me."

Later that night, Bernstein went to her apartment and knocked on the door.

"Go away," she said, and Bernstein went off to bang on other doors.

explicit? Or, is it sometimes permissible for him or her to ask questions of someone who thinks he or she is, say, an insurance adjuster? If journalists are upset when policemen pose as reporters, then can they think themselves blameless when behaving identically?

Part of the process of arranging an interview might be warning the naive source of *possible consequences* of the interview. If the source could face danger—physical, financial, mental, or legal—should a warning be given? Is the source's well-being more important or less important than the public's right to know information that the source alone may hold?

Even if assured anonymity in the news columns, is it possible that his or her role in the news can still be traced by those for whom there is a payoff in doing so? If reporters must promise anonymity, are they prepared to follow through on their pledge, even if it means going to jail? Should the journalist have ethical qualms about building innocent people into celebrities for a while, helping them get used to attention and its delightful benefits, and then ignoring them, perhaps for the rest of their lives?

A second series of ethical dilemmas arise out of *ground rules* often established at the start of an interview. Sometimes the reporter is invited to enter into a background or an off-the-record session, and is asked to respect the secrecy of information gathered under such circumstances. Journalists must have a clear idea of whether it is ever a good idea to participate in such interviews. If reporters are a party to a "backgrounder," they may have to keep under wraps information they think should be public; on the other hand, if they do not participate, they could miss a good deal of perspective on complicated issues.

Reporters who agree to off-the-record briefings must also determine whether they might properly break the agreement of secrecy for some greater good. Frequently, they can keep confidences while publishing the key information—through on-the-record confirmation by a second source, for instance. But this is rare and, in any case, simply skirts the question of whether reporters can ethically publish what they had promised not to.

Another ground rule may stipulate the way the interview is recorded. If the reporter is restricted to use of notes or to no record at all, deployment of concealed tape recorders or film cameras creates a thorny situation. On the face of it, it is not right to violate the ground rules set up at the start of an interview. Counterbalanced against this is the potentially damaging testimony a wrongdoing source may give, and which needs to be in a verbatim record if it is not to be denied later.

The reporter is confronted by a third set of ethical issues, these concerning the *ploys* sometimes used to obtain information. Is it proper, for instance, to put words in a source's mouth—to ask Councilman Jones, "Would you say that Mayor Smith is the wrong man in the wrong place at the wrong time," and then report that "Councilman Dan Jones said today that Mayor Cecil Smith is the wrong man in the wrong place at the wrong time." Jones did not say any such thing, of course, and likely would not have raised the topic himself. Does such interview reporting mislead the public, and does it do injustice to the source? Similarly, should the reporter fabricate statements, attribute them in the interview to a vague undisclosed source, and then ask for a reaction?

Should the reporter take advantage of the natural nervousness of some sources? Unlike public figures who are accustomed to the press and are not easily flustered during interviews, for many sources the situation is novel, and their mental state is agitated as a result. These conditions give rise to inadvertent statements that may not reflect what the source wanted to say. Should the reporter ignore these, especially if they are embarrassing or dangerous? Should the reporter ask the source specifically whether these statements may be quoted? Or, does the public have a right to know the source's innermost feelings, even if they were uttered by accident?

Similarly, should a journalist exploit a source's natural nervousness by badgering him or her with question after question until his or her resistance weakens, or by pretending to sympathize and win over his or her full confidence?

The last of the four stages is weighing the *competence of the information* gained. Although they knew that Senator Joseph McCarthy's charges of Communist affiliation were frequently baseless, reporters in the 1950s nevertheless dutifully recorded each fresh accusation. Was it unethical to thus aid McCarthy in ruining the careers of many innocent victims? Or, alternatively, would it have been ethical to try to balance the scales by either placing an embargo on unsupported charges or indicating they were unfounded? If readers are to establish the competence of sources for themselves, on the other hand, is the reporter behaving wrongly when cloaking information under the cover of anonymous attribution?

As long as interviewing remains a key weapon in the reporter's arsenal, the journalist must confront such ethical questions as these almost daily.

Conclusion

Gay Talese once wrote a profile for *Esquire* about popular singer Frank Sinatra.[38] When he

---

[38] Gay Talese, "Frank Sinatra Has a Cold," *Esquire*, April 1966. Reprinted in Talese, *Fame and Obscurity*, Bantam, New York, 1970, pp. 3–38.

reached California, Talese found his subject plagued by a bad cold, which put Sinatra into a mood so surly that he refused an interview.

Talese was undaunted. Used to breaking out of the conventional journalism mold—only convention says one must personally interview the subject of a profile—Talese attacked his research in other ways. He relied heavily on observation—watching Sinatra sit morosely in a private club, a band of underlings respecting his anti-sociality; watching two tapings of a Sinatra television special, the first cut short by the singer because he felt the cold ruined his voice; watching him and his buddies at a prize fight, in a casino, on a movie set.

Talese recorded other conversations, but he also conducted interviews—with Sinatra's parents, with his son, with his agent, and friends. Talese seized the cold, which might have turned back some reporters, and made it the theme of his piece. But, he knew that restricting himself to such a picture of Sinatra would be misleading, so the article alternates between Sinatra's querulous character of the moment and his generosity once the cold clears up.

Talese is a good wordsmith; his personal style makes the profile enjoyable. But he is also a good reporter. He knows that interviews need not be the sole source of information, even in a personality profile where they tend to be central. But Talese *did* interview, confirming and reconfirming facts and feelings culled from observations. It is this skillful combination of the interview with other techniques that makes the profile insightful, and insight is one of the reporter's main goals.

If the interview is to aid in insights, it must be as reliable as possible. This chapter has outlined ways in which the interview fails to live up to that infallibility demanded of it. Yet, the reporter must go on using it, embracing its strengths and weaknesses alike. The comforting thing is that the weaknesses can be minimized. And the interview's strengths can be magnified, when combined with the other methods in this book. One technique will help keep the others honest. After all, if checks and balances are a cleansing principle in government, then why not in journalism? Of course, if reporters exploit interviewing to its highest potential, journalism may not have to call upon Sherlock Holmes at all.

Chapter 9

Participant Observation

Peter Johansen and
David Grey

Can psychiatrists distinguish the sane from the insane in mental hospitals? Psychologist David L. Rosenhan set out to answer that question in a study that caught national media attention after it was published in the highly respected academic magazine *Science*.[1] Rosenhan and seven others feigned schizophrenia and gained admission to twelve psychiatric hospitals across the United States. None of the eight were initially judged sane by the medical staffs. Although they acted normally once they were admitted, Rosenhan's researchers were detained up to fifty-two days, with an average length of stay of nineteen days. They regularly wrote down their observations of patient-staff interaction (or, more accurately, lack of it), their conversations with fellow inmates, their feelings of personal powerlessness, and so on.

Rosenhan concludes that hospital staffs could *not* distinguish between sane and insane, and suggests why. Physicians "are more inclined to call a healthy person sick . . . than a sick person

---

[1] D. L. Rosenhan, "On Being Sane in Insane Places," *Science* 179 (1973):250–258. Also see: "Letters," *Science* 180 (1973):356–369. For examples of media coverage, see: Sandra Blakeslee, "8 Feign Insanity in Test and Are Termed Insane," *The New York Times*, January 21, 1973; David Perlman, "Social Sciences," *Saturday Review of the Sciences*, January 27, 1973, pp. 55–56.

healthy" because "it is clearly more dangerous to misdiagnose illness than health." [2]

Once saddled with a loose diagnostic label like "schizophrenic," a patient's personality and behavior are interpreted within the diagnosed framework. Rosenhan says the normal behaviors of his colleagues were distorted by the staff to be consistent with their diagnosis. ". . . There is nothing the pseudo-patient could do to overcome the tag," concluded Rosenhan.

What Rosenhan did was *participant observation*, a behavioral science methodology that has contributed richly to behavior theory. Journalists have occasionally borrowed the technique with varying success. Here we shall analyze the strengths and weaknesses of participant observation, suggest a few tactics that will maximize its utility, and look at some journalistic efforts in the participant observation field.

Some attention will be paid to specific decisions the reporter must make, but there is no step-by-step methodology here. Situations vary, and no checklist of steps could cover them all. Moreover, as behavioral scientists John Bollens and D. R. Marshall point out, making the procedures too explicit "may unintentionally make field work sound difficult" and make it sound "much more complicated than it actually is." [3]

If there are journalistic examples, why begin with a 200-word recap of an academic study? The choice was deliberate: Rosenhan's work paradoxically emphasizes the application of participant observation to journalism. Journalists, too, have exploited the tool to report on social institutions. And their attempts are not all recent. Nellie Bly, famed reporter for Pulitzer's *New York World*, feigned insanity in the 1880s to get into an asylum on Blackwell's Island. Her exposé of the shocking conditions there led to reform of the mental health system of the day. Nearly a century later, the *Chicago Tribune* published an investigative series on state nursing homes and a Sunday magazine feature on a rehabilitation center, both using participant observation.

As a participant observer, the journalist joins a group or organization, preferably for an extended period of time. He or she engages in intense social interaction with the other members in

---

[2] Rosenhan, "On Being Sane in Insane Places," p. 252.
[3] John C. Bollens and Dale Rogers Marshall, *A Guide to Participation*, Prentice-Hall, Englewood Cliffs, N.J., 1973, p. 43.

Participant Observation as a Partial Tool

Participant observation usually forms the cornerstone in newspaper articles that rely on it. But it need not be the principal research tool. When the *Ottawa Citizen* wanted to see how safe local school buses were, reporter Mike McDermott found that participant observation helped, but only as the first step of his investigation.

McDermott trained with a local bus line and then spent a week driving students to and from high schools for that company. For another bus company, he drove elementary-school children for several days. But the reporter was not himself trained to judge the safety of each bus. After dropping the students off each morning, he took the buses to a mechanic hired by the *Citizen* to inspect them before they were needed for the afternoon return trip.

Among the shoddy conditions found in the twelve buses studied:

—Nine had poor or no emergency brakes;

—Nine had defrosters incapable of keeping the drivers' front and side windows clear;

—Three had leaky exhaust systems, allowing fumes to seep into the passenger compartment;

—One bus, with no emergency brake, had a fourteen-pound stone beside the driver's seat to be used as a parking brake on hills;

—In two buses, heavy fire axes were lying loose near the driver's position;

—One bus had an emergency rear door with hinges so rusty it was impossible to open it from the outside.

McDermott reported that $1,000 could make an average school bus safe. Nonetheless, he cited statistics showing that most school bus accidents are the fault of the driver, not the bus. He also noted that most Ottawa drivers are part-time workers—a retired clerk or serviceman, a farmer's wife who needs a little extra money, or simply someone who wants to get off unemployment insurance rolls—who earn only $10 daily.

SOURCE: Mike McDermott, "Defects in Buses Show Up in Study," *Ottawa Citizen*, March 9, 1974.

their own milieu and collects information with a battery of tools, the most common of which are formal and informal interviewing, observation, and reflection upon his or her own thoughts and feelings as a pseudo-member of the group.

Activity of this sort seems natural for the journalist. In fact, one textbook on behavioral science methods suggests that "recording observation in a natural setting tends to take a journalistic form . . . ." [4] Despite that, and despite the fact that crusading reporter Nellie Bly understood the power of participant observation more than seventy years ago, it has been used too little. This is unfortunate for, as we shall see, participant observation offers exciting prospects in journalism as an aid in portraying accurately the complex world in which we live.

Advantages of Participant Observation

In what ways is participant observation useful to the journalist? Consider the question Rosenhan asked at the outset of his study: can psychiatric hospital staffs identify accurately the sane and the insane among those presenting themselves for admission? This is a proper subject for journalism. It is the sort of question a reporter should ask. Taxpayers have a right to know how effectively their taxes are spent in mental health care. (Mental health *did* make national headlines in 1972, in fact, when it was revealed that the Democratic vice-presidential nominee, Senator Thomas Eagleton, had undergone psychiatric care.)

Rosenhan's question, then, is both legitimate and plausible for the journalist. How might he or she find the answer? The journalist could interview authorities. Possibilities include medical personnel from a range of hospitals and in different types of psychiatric work; academics, who have an interest but are, perhaps, less ego-involved; and former patients, whose views will not be representative of patients at large insofar as they were able to get hospital discharges, but who have a unique perspective. The reporter might also consult reports on mental health care by universities, government, and research foundations. He or she can tour medical facilities, observe procedures, ask questions.

---

[4] Dennis P. Forcese and Stephen Richer, *Social Research Methods*, Prentice-Hall, Englewood Cliffs, N.J., 1973, pp. 150–151.

All of these methods would help draw an accurate picture of mental health care, but each is weighted in favor of the spokesman's own perspectives, and reporters could be influenced by their assessments. Questions would probably be answered affirmatively because most sources could justify their value only if it were affirmative.

Rosenhan's method tackles the subject from a different perspective, relying little on official sources, and so contributes a new piece to the jigsaw puzzle of mental health. Two advantages of this unique perspective are particularly worth noting.

1. The participant observer looks at human settings and individuals holistically.

The methodology's main strength is the comprehensiveness it affords for understanding the group under study. The reporter may focus on specific aspects of a group, but this is viewed within a setting of other points that impinge upon the main one.

In Rosenhan's study, the theme was the diagnostic ability of hospital staffs, but the participant observers were exposed to a range of activity that helped them understand how and why treatment of patients occurred as it did. Thus, they learned a good deal about diagnosis by observing the isolation of staff from patients, the ignoring of patients' conversations by staff, the violent physical attacks on patients by staff, the flushing down the toilet of medication, and so on.

As Howard Becker, a veteran participant observer, has noted, the methodology forces the researcher "to consider, however crudely, the multiple interrelations of the particular phenomena he observes." [5] By observing the group over time, the observer can see the dynamics of internal conflict, change, and stability "and thus see organizations, relationships, and group and individual definitions in process." [6]

2. The participant observer can discover natural behavior.

It was said earlier that interviewing might have given an inaccurate answer to Rosenhan's research question. Verbal descrip-

---

[5] Howard S. Becker, "Social Observation and Social Case Studies," in David L. Sills, ed., *International Encyclopedia of the Social Sciences*, Macmillan and the Free Press, New York, 1968, vol. II, p. 233.

[6] Robert Bogdan, *Participant Observation in Organizational Settings*, Syracuse University Press, Syracuse, 1972, p. 4.

tions of behavior, even for topics less ego-threatening than this one, can be misleading for reasons outlined in the previous chapter—among them, that interviewees are not always aware of their own behavior or ideas, that they do not want to discuss a topic, and that they are unable to put thoughts into words.

Observation helps overcome these difficulties. Especially when they are unaware of the observer's purpose, people will not alter their behavior for the public's benefit. Even if the journalist's goal is known, though, it is not possible to keep up a façade for long, and behavior approaches normal as time wears on. Since the reporter's task is to present as accurate a portrait of reality as possible, this feature of participant observation is appealing.

Disadvantages

There is no perfect reporting method, of course. If there were, this entire book would be about it. So, in addition to its very real strengths, participant observation is fraught with pitfalls the journalist must be careful of. Four of these deserve comment.

1. By simply being present, the observer becomes a new element in the situation.

Reporters can never be certain of the effects of their presence on those being observed. If they identify themselves as reporters, people will react to that bit of information. The spotlight of publicity causes a kind of human equivalent of Heisenberg's Rule of Indeterminacy, a physics principle stating that some particles can never be studied because the light that must be shone on them to see them alters them.[7]

When reporters masquerade as new members of the group they are studying, group behavior will still change. In the Rosenhan study, for instance, the patients commonly detected the pseudo-patients' sanity, with many citing the overt note-taking as

---

[7] A behavioral science example, although not from participant observation literature, is found in Kurt and Gladys Lang, "The Unique Perspective of Television and Its Effect: A Pilot Study," in Wilbur Schramm and Donald F. Roberts, eds., *The Process and Effects of Mass Communication*, rev. ed., University of Illinois Press, Urbana, 1971, pp. 169–188.

the work of a journalist or professor checking on the hospital. Given this, it is difficult to know to what extent their behavior was shaped for a journalist's benefit.

2. *The reporter is unable to witness all relevant aspects of the group.*

Because reporters cannot possibly see everything that happens, they must necessarily be selective. How this distorts is shown by reporting of the Washington, D.C. riots following the 1968 assassination of Martin Luther King, the civil rights leader. Reporters on the streets at that time witnessed blacks setting fires, breaking store windows, and looting from them, waging battle against the police. From their vantage point in the thick of the melee, reporters thought that blacks in general were milling about the streets. The image consequently given the public was of a massive black revolt.

There *were* riots, but the reporters stationed themselves in such a way that all they saw was violence. The fact that this was not universal did not seem to be a theme in the mass press. A Swedish social anthropologist, Ulf Hannerz, however, was studying a Washington ghetto at the time, and he reported that many blacks stayed home, turned on the television, and waited for the burning to begin.[8] That was Hannerz' perspective. Both the reporter on the street and the behavioral scientist in the home reported riots accurately (reliably), but because of the limitation of physical perspective, neither report was completely valid.

Perspective can be restricted by more than physical constraints. Journalists see most groups at particular points in time. They cannot determine from observation alone what any group's history has been. Many features of the organization cannot be fully observed—motives, intentions, and perceptions of its members, for example. The reporters' social position in the group will determine what they see. If he or she is a low-level member of the organization, he or she will not be privy to the private "pow-wows" of the group's elite. These all restrict the omniscient view of the organization for which the reporter should ideally strive.

3. *Observations are funneled through the twin distorting processes of selective perception and retention.*

---

[8] Ulf Hannerz, *Soulside: Inquiries into Ghetto Culture and Community,* Columbia University Press, New York, 1969.

Anthropologists, perhaps the foremost practitioners of participant observation, are subject to a special form of selective perception—they have a penchant for exotic data. That is, they tend to report that which is different from their own society and to ignore what is similar.[9] On the other hand, as an observer becomes familiar with the group, the unfamiliar becomes familiar and thus goes unreported. This occurs in any new situation. More than fifty years ago, Walter Lippmann noted that we all stereotype people and events.[10] The best antidote to this distortion, however, is a firm knowledge of how the process works. The brain is not physiologically capable of processing each discrete bit of information in a unique way.

Psychologists Gordon Allport and Leo Postman suggest that stereotyping occurs in three simultaneous steps—*leveling, sharpening,* and *assimilation.*[11] Over time, we retain fewer and fewer details of an event. What we remember is shorter, more concise, more easily grasped and told than when it first occurred. This is leveling. Sharpening is the opposite process: because leveling disposes with so many details, those retained assume great importance. Assimilation determines what is stored and what is lost. We absorb that new information not likely to disturb the habits, interests, and sentiments already in the mind.

4. The participant observer can never fully understand those being observed.

In 1959, white author John Howard Griffin, a specialist in race issues, set out to see what life in the South was like for a black man. A dermatologist darkened Griffin's skin with medication and ultraviolet rays, and the author shaved his head. For several weeks he traveled through four Southern states as a black, and recorded his experiences in a diary, *Black Like Me.*[12] In the preface, Griffin writes:

---

[9] Eugene Webb *et al., Unobtrusive Measures: Nonreactive Research in the Social Sciences,* Rand McNally, Chicago, 1966, p. 114.

[10] Walter Lippmann, *Public Opinion,* Macmillan, New York, 1922, chapter 1.

[11] Gordon W. Allport and Leo J. Postman, "The Basic Psychology of Rumor," in Daniel Katz, Dorwin Cartwright, Samuel Eldersveld, and Alfred McClung Lee, eds., *Public Opinion and Propaganda,* Holt, Rinehart and Winston, New York, 1954, pp. 394–404.

[12] John Howard Griffin, *Black Like Me,* Signet Books, Toronto, 1961.

(This book may not cover all the questions about race relations) but it is what it is like to be a Negro in a land where we keep the Negro down.

Some whites will say this is not really it. They will say this is the white man's experience as a Negro in the South, not the Negro's.

But this is picayunish, and we no longer have time for that.[13]

In that period of American history when black consciousness was expanding swiftly and the plight of blacks was in the forefront of political dialogue, Griffin was likely right when he said Americans had no time to quibble about whether or not his experiences were authentic. But here in *this* book, some fifteen years later, the question of whether Griffin reported a white man's experience as a black, rather than a black's own experience, is worthwhile.

In many respects, journalists are different from those they try to understand. If the group is a voluntary one, the journalist comes with a different purpose; for legitimate members, it serves needs that the reporter does not have. Journalists also have different personal histories. Griffin could compare the hostility against him as a black with his life as a white; a true black would have no such built-in yardstick. Similarly, Rosenhan's collaborators were never really mentally ill, so they could not comprehend exactly what it felt like to be a patient in a psychiatric hospital. The journalist also has a different personal future. They cannot escape the knowledge that they must experience the situation for only a short, definite time; as in the case of blacks, the situation may well stay with the reporter's subjects the rest of their lives. In many particulars, then, the reporters' total experience only *approximates* that of the people they hope to understand. This is a crucial limitation of participant observation, and yet to have it any other way, the reporter would deny the chance of objectivity.

These are the weaknesses that cannot be wholly eradicated, but the first three, at least, can be minimized if the researcher-journalist carefully chooses the tactics. Let us now consider some of the more obvious decision points.

---

[13] *Ibid.*, p. 6. We are grateful to our colleague, Marvin Schiff, for reminding us of this example.

Participating Is Not Experiencing

According to columnist Nicholas von Hoffman, the journalist can hope only for "a vicarious approximation" of another's life. Why that is so is explained in the following discussion, excerpted from a von Hoffman column. What prompted it was journalist Kate Coleman's experience in researching an article on prostitution for *Ramparts* magazine. Her article is solid, he writes,

> but prostitution is in journalistic vogue this year and there are other articles around that will give you the same information. What makes Kate's the most unusual offering of the season is the last section of her story.
>
> "During the course of my interviews a number of call girls generously offered me their 'John Book' (a John being the name that whores have for their customers), playfully urging me to gain first-hand knowledge of the subject. Certainly the idea of doing so had crossed my mind, but I rejected it. . . . I did not feel a serious lack of verisimilitude in my reporting. . . .
>
> "Furthermore, while harboring a commitment to involved journalism—as opposed to the great American myth of objective reporting—the idea of doing a George Plimpton-on-the-job-reportage number seemed absurd in the case of prostitution. . . . With all these thoughts firmly imprinted on my conscious mind, I nevertheless found myself turning a trick. . . ."
>
> But after Kate had exchanged sex for money in one of the bedrooms of a Manhattan call-girl establishment, she still hadn't tasted

Tactics

PARTICIPANT OBSERVATION OR NOT?

Let's assume that a medical reporter has been assigned to do a Sunday feature on the ability of psychiatric specialists to diagnose correctly sanity and insanity among patients—the familiar Rosenhan topic. In deciding whether to use participant observation, he or she must have a firm grasp of the goals of the assignment, in this case quite clear, and determine whether participant observation can help achieve them.

There seem to be two general areas in which this technique is helpful. First, participant observers typically look at a wide range of group behavior, considering myriad interrelationships. Single, simple problems are researched more efficiently through less in-of what she calls the private vision of those in this occupation. The John she took to bed was a handsome, sexy younger man who provided her with what she called a "stunning pleasure. . . ."

But then, after it was over and she was having coffee with the other girls, she writes, "Suddenly, I heard myself addressed by one of the (other) Johns. I looked up and saw a paunchy, shiny suit and horned-rimmed glasses on a doughy face. Omigod, he's asking me to go into the bedroom with him—with him! I stuttered my refusal . . . . The other hookers urged me to go with him, but I was adamant. . . . This man was flaccid, gross, and wore an American flag pin in his lapel—a complete turn-off. One of the hookers chided me, 'But you see, that's the point; your research is unreal . . . you don't have the right to refuse. You don't have that kind of choice.' "

Kate's experience shows that a journalist can never know, not completely, not as it is lived. When she does know, then she ceases to be a journalist and turns into a memoirist. It's as the hookers said, one trick with an exceptional John isn't enough; you have to be a hooker to share the hooker's private vision. But that private vision excludes you from so many others. How, as a hooker, are you next going to capture the private vision of a detective on the vice squad?

The best a journalist can hope for is a vicarious approximation, one that will not be exactly right, and which those readers who do know will see and object to, be they hookers, politicians, or pro football players, but it's given to each of us to have only one private vision and that of the journalist must be journalism.

SOURCE: Nicholas von Hoffman, "First Person Singular," *San Francisco Chronicle.*

volved procedures. For our medical reporter, interpersonal relationships *are* important. While he or she might answer the question by poring through medical reports and talking to a wide range of informed sources, the reporter wants to understand the problem fully and to report on the factors contributing to psychiatric diagnosis. A second major reason for choosing this technique is to ensure valid information. As outlined earlier, even a variety of interview sources might reasonably be expected to have a vested interest in the problem of diagnosing sanity and insanity. Their answers, though interesting, would not necessarily be valid.

THE QUESTION OF TIME

The reporter must also consider whether there is adequate time to carry out a participant observation study. Participant observers submit to a lengthy resocialization process, and may have to learn new jargon or behavior. Only gradually are they accepted by an organization, either as an observer or as a member with all the privileges of membership. For the reporter, acceptance is crucial. All groups have private and public behavior; if the reporter remains outside the group, only the public activity will be seen. Thus, the reporter must decide whether, in the amount of time the editor has allowed, the group's confidence can be won.

Consider, again, the newspaper story on mental health care. The reporter has two weeks to research the piece. Can it be done? If he or she wants to get an in-depth report on life in a psychiatric hospital, then this brief period will allow nothing more than a superficial glimpse of superficial behavior. Hospital patients do not form meaningful relationships in two weeks, and long-time patients will converse guardedly while a newcomer is present. Moreover, the reporter may find the time too brief to overcome personal apprehensions. Morris Schwartz, who spent five years on mental hospital research, recalls:

> My initial period at the hospital was one of disorientation, shock, and disequilibration. It lasted for about three or four weeks and was highlighted by my need and attempt to find firm ground upon which to stand and to reconstitute an integrated "self" with which to operate.
> Although I had previously done some research in mental hospitals, I was utterly unprepared for the impact of the hospital and especially the ward. . . .
> Life in the ward appeared at first as a continuous flow of confused transactions, eruptions of intense feelings, unpredictable behaviors, and obscure processes caught in some primitive mold with a contemporary façade. I simply could not sort it out. I did not know where to look, what to concentrate on, how to make some order out of the chaos. At this point I had not as yet acquired the confidence that the fog would lift in time, that directions for ordering and organizing myself and the research would emerge, and that I would develop some perspective on the situation. I felt that the experience was so complex, intense, confused, and disorienting that perhaps I should give up.[14]

Fourteen days may permit a reporter to answer the question about detecting the sane versus insane, however. In Rosenhan's

---

[14] Morris S. Schwartz, "The Mental Hospital: The Research Person in the Disturbed Ward," in Arthur J. Vidich, Joseph Bensman, and Maurice R. Stein, eds., *Reflections on Community Studies*, John Wiley and Sons, New York, 1964, p. 87.

Participant Observation Not Always Enough

When poorly used, participant observation produces stories as shallow as any. A report on a welfare hotel in Atlantic City, N. J. provides a case in point.

The reporter, Frank Lowe, stayed there only eight hours. After checking in, he left and walked along the city's famed Boardwalk, watching a "Bango" game, checking the popularity of local eating places, noting the Boardwalk tram which carried near-capacity crowds. The "thought of going back to my dismal room" kept Lowe out two hours. Returning to the hotel at midnight, he went to bed, though he lay awake until 4 AM. "pondering what it might be like to live permanently" in a hotel like that one. At 8 AM., en route to checking out, the reporter spied an "old friend," who seemed "reasonably content," although "like other residents [of the hotel], she is just marking time until she can find a better location."

Apart from this last observation, we have no sharp portrait of what life is like in the hotel. There is a one-paragraph description of Lowe's own room—is it typical?—and an indication of a small party in the mezzanine. Is there always one there or was it a special occasion?

What do the residents think about the accommodation? Do amenities improve as customers stay longer? Just how long *does* the average resident stay? In what ways is the hotel substandard, as was alleged? How many guests are pensioners, the group apparently taken advantage of by the hotel? Are the guests employed or unemployed? Are they whites or members of minority groups? Is there a sense of camaraderie or do the residents distrust one another?

Because Lowe apparently talked to no customer except his old friend and because he left the hotel from check-in at 10 P.M. until midnight, the story really leaves unsaid more than it reports.

SOURCE: Frank Lowe, "Reporter Inspects Hotel: 'Wouldn't Do It Again,'" *Philadelphia Inquirer,* August 28, 1973.

---

study, one pseudo-patient was released within seven days, and the average length of stay was nineteen days. The reporter would have to realize, however, that a single situation was hardly worthy of generalizing—that one patient in one hospital does not prove a theory. More time and more reporters would, of course, increase reliability and validity.

If the reporter has not been discouraged from participant observation by these considerations, a decision must be made about specifically what to search out. There is no hard-and-fast rulebook. Three sample checklists do, however, demonstrate the scope of what to look for and how to look for it.

Selltiz and her associates suggest five points worth examining: [15]

1. Who are the *participants?* What is their function in the group? How many are there? What are their relationships to each other?
2. In what *setting* does the group activity occur? What is its appearance? What behavior does it encourage and discourage?
3. What *purposes* does the group pursue? Are they official or not? What other goals are pursued? How do the participants react to them?
4. What *social behavior* occurs—by whom, and with what is it done? What initiated the behavior? What is its objective? What are its effects? What are the qualities of the behavior, including its intensity, duration, and unusualness?
5. What is the *frequency* and *duration* of the behavior? Is it recurring or unique? How typical is the observed behavior?

Selltiz and associates warn that the list will not cover every situation, but it can at least aid the reporter in planning observational activities.

Symbolic interaction theory leads to a second guide, proposed by sociologist Robert Bogdan. The theory, most comprehensively described by sociologist George Herbert Mead in *Mind, Self and Society*,[16] says that man constantly interprets or defines the situa-

---

[15] Claire Selltiz, Marie Jahoda, Morton Deutsch, and Stuart W. Cook, *Research Methods in Social Relations*, rev. ed., Holt, Rinehart and Winston, New York, 1959, pp. 209–210.

[16] George Herbert Mead, *Mind, Self and Society*, University of Chicago Press, Chicago, 1934.

tions in which he finds himself, and these definitions determine his personal meaning of each situation. A person's actions, in turn, are based on his definition of the relevant situation. Bogdan's list of questions are: [17]

1. How do various participants define the organization and its various aspects? This could involve both individual actors' definitions and also those shared by groups.
2. What is the process by which these definitions develop and change, and what factors contribute to the formation of the definitions?
3. How do the various definitions held relate to each other? Are they compatible, congruent, conflicting? What ramifications do they lead to in action? "This question leads to the building of an organizational model and to questions of organizational activities." [18]
4. How does the model, constructed in response to question three, relate to organizational effectiveness or to any other interest the journalist has?

Bruyn has devised still a different checklist. He asserts that the main element binding an organization is its communicative acts. Meanings that are important in people's lives are expressed through their *thinking, feeling,* and *acting,* the three behaviors found in any message within the group. The participant observer breaks down group communications into these three components, then, and studies each component along six dimensions—*time, place, circumstance, language, intimacy,* and *consensus.* The questions that can be asked for each of the three categories, along each of the six dimensions, are summarized in the following table.

We do not push the use of any of these checklists. Their presence here is to stimulate inquisitive reporters into thinking about the range of possibilities and problems in their own studies. Whatever checklist is used, it must be systematic. It must cover the whole range of relationships and behavior relevant to the reporter's goal. Such a list will be complete only when reporters think carefully about what they eventually hope to find.

---

[17] Bogdan, *Participant Observation in Organizational Settings,* pp. 67–68.
[18] *Ibid.,* p. 68.

BRUYN'S CHECKLIST FOR PARTICIPANT OBSERVATION

Categories of Data	Dimensions of Data					
	Time	Place	Circumstance	Language	Intimacy	Consensus
Cognition (How is the meaning made intelligible?)	How long has the meaning been intelligible?	Is it cognitively associated with the environs?	Is it associated with social roles and groups? How?	How is the meaning communicated?	Is it expressed in private? How is it conveyed intelligibly?	How is it confirmed?
Cathexis (What quality of feeling is associated with the meaning?)	How long has sentiment been associated, and does time change it?	Is the sentiment associated with environs? How?	Is it felt differently in different roles and events?	How is the sentiment communicated?	How is it experienced privately?	How is the sentiment confirmed?
Conduct (What kind of social action accompanies the meaning? How many people are involved?	How long have how many people participated?	In what places do how many people act accordingly?	How do people act in different groups?	How is it conveyed in action? (In sound or ritual?)	How do people behave behind the scenes?	How do people show agreement in action?

SOURCE: Severyn T. Bruyn, *The Human Perspective in Sociology: The Methodology of Participant Observation*, Prentice-Hall, Englewood Cliffs, N.J., 1966, p. 261.

The reporter must also decide how to gain entry to the group and just what role will be adopted. He or she must first decide whether or not the group, or at least members of it, are to know that he or she is a reporter. As we have said, anonymity has the advantage of doing away with the reactive effects of a known observer, although the reporter can never be sure how much he or she *as a member* has changed group performance. However, the reporter in this case runs great risk of feeling excessive loyalty and obligation to the group and becoming caught up in the private dramas of its members, thus losing the detachment that is still a hallmark of journalism.

Researcher Rosalie Wax notes, too, that "it is the group that defines the terms of acceptance or rejection of new members" [19] and that the observer may never meet the requirements of acceptance. Moreover, reporters will find that admitting their true purposes is often simpler. It is difficult to suddenly become a new member in some organizations: reporters have little choice but to inform *somebody* that they want to be admitted to prison, unless they are willing to commit a crime. Full disclosure also increases one's chances of getting information, since a journalist has reasons to ask questions that would not otherwise be posed by a group member.

When reporters admit their ties to journalism, they must be prepared to help their subjects accept them and define their role. After all, groups are not accustomed to being observed in this manner. They may suspect ulterior motives, such as a desire to ridicule them in public print. They do not know what benefits the reporter can offer them. They must, therefore, outline their role for the subjects as well as themselves. To do this, they should find out in advance something about the group. If they understand its structure, they can decide where within that structure they are best apt to fit. Choosing an appropriate role is extremely important, as researchers George McCall and J. L. Simmons stress:

> The role which he claims—or to which he is assigned by the subjects—is perhaps the single most important determinant of what

---

[19] Rosalie H. Wax, *Doing Fieldwork*, University of Chicago Press, Chicago, 1971, p. 45.

he will be able to learn. Every role is an avenue to certain types of information but is also an automatic barrier to certain other types. The role assumed by the observer largely determines where he can go, what he can do, whom he can interact with, what he can inquire about, what he can see, and what he can be told.[20]

Reporters also need to remember, however, that their individual characteristics—sex, age, socioeconomic status—will likely enter into the determination of their role; strategic concerns must usually give way, in some degree, to these.

Reporters must also take care in their personal relationships with the community; they cannot be aligned with any faction, because identity with one subgroup could curtail rapport with others. The best procedure is to "stage a simultaneous entry" [21] into all sides of the group.

Let us turn to a specific consideration of three disadvantages of participant observation mentioned earlier and consider how they might be minimized by careful behavior in the field.

MINIMIZING REACTIVE EFFECTS

Journalists cause their subjects to react to their presence in two ways—one, if they decide to identify themselves as journalists, and the other, if they try to fit in as members of the group.

Reporters who reveal their identity do not have to describe their aims too specifically. Knowing the project only in general terms, the group cannot know what specific behaviors to alter in order to be seen in the best light. Sociologist Herbert Gans, for example, told a suburban community that he was researching the history of their community organizations. This gave him an entree, but covered the fact that he was primarily interested in the suburbanites' everyday lives and relationships.[22]

Reporters can also spend enough time with the group to overcome the novelty of being watched. Many behaviors are so ingrained that it is too difficult for people to think about them all

---

[20] George J. McCall and J. L. Simmons, *Issues in Participant Observation: A Text and Reader,* Addison-Wesley, Reading, Mass., 1969, p. 29.

[21] Selltiz *et al., Research Methods in Social Relations,* p. 219.

[22] Herbert J. Gans, *Urban Villagers,* Free Press of Glencoe, New York, 1962. Also see Gans, *The Levittowners,* Random House, New York, 1967.

the time. This process was demonstrated in the 1973 public television series, *An American Family,* an intimate portrait of several months in the life of the Bill Loud family. According to *TV Guide:*

> The family members themselves say they were aware of the camera almost all the time, though they tried to be cooperative and ignore it. Alan and Susan Raymond [who did the camera and sound work] think there were many times when the ideal of "acting naturally" was nearly achieved. . . .
>
> "The Louds were jittery the first week or so," says Susan. "After that they got used to us being around the house, and the next few months were dynamite." [23]

In some cases, though, observing for *too* long can also be negative. Susan Raymond said that in the fifth month, the Loud family began "acting," and she concludes that seven months was too long for the project to carry on.

The reporter can also rely on informants to advise whether the group's behaviors are natural. Although not in this same context, sociologist Arthur Vidich advocates the use of the *socially marginal* informant—someone who is *of* the group, but who is also capable of viewing it as an outsider. An example of such a person is a small-town intellectual, Vidich suggests.[24] Such an individual may be able and willing to tell the reporter about the ways in which the group has changed.

When the journalist is under cover, he or she must stay on the periphery as much as possible. To become involved in group conflict, for example, is inadvisable. As Bogdan notes, by giving advice or acting as an arbitrator, the journalist would alter the very situation under observation.[25] In all situations, in fact, he or she must not "get involved" or "go native," and must "learn to control some normal participant feelings." [26]

Three other tactics can be adopted by journalists in any participant observation experience. First, they should write their notes inconspicuously. They should not write constantly, which they would not be likely to do if they were masquerading their true

---

[23] Max Gunther, "The Pain Wasn't Only the Louds'," *TV Guide,* May 19, 1973, pp. 8–10.

[24] Arthur J. Vidich, "Participant Observation and the Collection and Presentation of Data," *American Journal of Sociology* 60 (1955):357.

[25] Bogdan, *Participant Observation in Organizational Settings,* pp. 31–32.

[26] *Ibid.,* p. 22.

purpose, in any event. They should go off into some private place and jot down notes every hour or so. Circumstances are unique in every situation, however, and this may sometimes be disruptive. In all cases, the observer must decide what is most nonreactive and follow that course.

A second tip also concerns notes: reporters should record their own behavior and conversation. In rereading these notes, they can understand their findings better and learn in what ways they have affected them. Finally, the reporter can exploit unobtrusive observation. As earlier chapters asserted, reporters can profitably read Webb *et al. Unobtrusive Measures.* Its numerous examples of nonreactive research will give the creative reporter a score of ideas that can be applied to reporting, whether participant observation or not. Consider how the participant observer-reporter could use these:

> —The floor tiles around the hatching-chick exhibit at Chicago's Museum of Science and Industry must be replaced every six weeks. Tiles in other parts of the museum need not be replaced for years. The selective erosion of tiles, indexed by the replacement rate, is a measure of the relative popularity of exhibits.
> —One investigator wanted to learn the level of whiskey consumption in a town that was officially "dry" and did so by counting empty bottles in ashcans.
> —Library withdrawals were used to demonstrate the effect of the introduction of television into a community. Fiction titles dropped, nonfiction titles were unaffected.
> —The role of rate of interaction in managerial recruitment is shown by the overrepresentation of baseball managers who were in-fielders or catchers (high-interaction positions) during their playing days.[27]

The second principal danger of participant observation is *selective perception* and *retention* on the part of the observer. It, too, can be greatly reduced by noting a few precautions.

The reporter may approach his or her research with no specific hypotheses, merely wanting to grasp the new situation first. None-theless, there are inevitably some hunches or preconceived ideas

---

[27] Webb *et al., Unobtrusive Measures,* p. 2.

of what might be found. These might be recorded at the outset of the research. Then as the field work continues, the reporter can see what his or her initial biases were and perhaps assess how they have influenced subsequent work.

Related to this is allowing the group to define the situation as the group sees it. That is, although the journalist may eventually want to pose specific questions, he or she should first get people talking about what is on *their* minds. This can be done by engaging them in small talk or by asking very general questions, such as "How are things going?" In this way, the reporter will discover what they think is important, not their views on what the journalist considers significant.

Some observations can be "objective." If available and feasible, devices like tape recorders and cameras can record certain information easily. Another gadget is the mechanical hand-counter. Such instruments have limitations, however. For example, a camera has restricted visual scope, unable to focus on everything simultaneously, and what is omitted might be significant.

The journalist can also use other people to offset imbalances. Perhaps more than one reporter can be engaged in a given story. Their individual observations can be compared and discrepancies can be ironed out. The use of independent observers will not always be fruitful—both may share the same perceptual "blinders." Reliability does not guarantee validity. However, blatant distortion on the part of one reporter is likely to be detected. The reporter could relate his or her experiences regularly and frequently to someone outside the group. As the reporter's perceptions change, he or she begins to take for granted things that once appeared novel. By relating his or her experiences, especially if more than a week or two is spent in the group, queries can be asked about changes in perception, important points not reported, and so on.

The reporter may also interpret events improperly. For example, street-gang behavior that appears aggressive to a middle-class observer may really be good-natured horseplay. Interviews with the participants or other informants in the group might clear up some of these difficulties. Some group members may also be able to read the reporter's copy before publication; although this practice is rightly frowned upon in journalism, in some cases there may be sound justification.

Finally, the reporter can reduce distortions by diligent note-taking. This task will be examined later in more detail, but one point is worth mentioning here: reporters can try separating their interpretation of the situation from the factual information they gather and label each entry for what it is.

The restrictions on perspective will largely be minimized by tactics already discussed. The use of more than one observer, for instance, can expand perspective tremendously, especially if locations are consciously decided upon in order to maximize this. Thus, readers would have understood more fully the race riots in Washington, D.C., if reporters had covered the reactions of the blacks that anthropologist Ulf Hannerz was studying, as well as those blacks who were demonstrating in the streets. Similarly, the participant observer must infiltrate the group carefully; becoming attached to one subgroup will restrict observation of other subgroups.

Increased length of observation time minimizes distortion by permitting the reporter to sample a longer span of behavior. This reduces the probability of viewing only unusual or unique events. A particular shortcoming of limited research is the increased likelihood of being captured by "tour guides." These are people who take researchers in tow and, often for a price, relate stories they think outsiders want to hear.

Finally, the participant observer should rely on more than simple observation. Written materials record the history of the group, particularly of long-standing or formal organizations. Such sources include official documents, newspaper clippings, academic treatises, and so on. Here is another potential role for *content analysis*. But it is important for the journalist to remember that such documents are only as reliable as the people who wrote them.

Key informants can also be interviewed as checks on the observer's own perspective, and former members of the group can also be valuable sources of information. Former members may have unique perspectives and the freedom to be quite candid.

It may seem odd to discuss note-taking here since it is something the journalist does regardless of

Getting Others to Observe

Smaller newspapers and broadcast stations may not have the resources for large-scale participant observation studies, but that need not deter them from selecting topics that are manageable in both cost and time. Small operations can also exploit the resources of others doing participant observation, such as professors at a local college.

George Kirkham, a criminologist at Florida State University, for example, noted that most of his colleagues write about the police without having themselves been policemen. He decided to change that, and his experience makes unusual reading.

Taking a leave of absence from his duties, Kirkham attended a police academy and became a patrolman with the Jacksonville-Duval County, Florida, police force. After six months' duty and more than one hundred tours of duty as a patrolman, Kirkham learned that:

—People interpret a policeman's kindness as a sign of weakness that invites disrespect;

—There is a "world of difference" between confronting individuals as a patrolman "when they are violent, hysterical, or desperate," and facing them as a criminologist, "calmly discussing . . . the past problems which had led [them] into trouble with the law";

—Patrolmen experience fear regularly;

—Policemen should be allowed to carry shotguns—an attitude reached after he was confronted by an angry mob that endangered his life.

—His efforts to protect society and himself were menaced by lenient courts and patrol boards he had previously defended;

—Patrolmen face a complexity of tasks.

SOURCE: George L. Kirkham, "Bitter Lessons for a Scholar When He Dons a Police Uniform," *Toronto Globe and Mail*, May 15, 1974.

---

methods employed. But participant observation calls for a note-taking procedure somewhat different from that in most journalistic circumstances. First, one needs to take many more notes. The journalist must record not only the highlights of a speech, for instance, but must describe it completely. He or she needs to record not only a little descriptive material, but everything that can be recalled, because he or she does not know on the day of observation which trifle will later turn out to be revealing.

It is especially important to keep a journal on a daily basis. Bollens and Marshall caution:

> You can easily become deceived into thinking that you will re-
> member such details without a journal. But unfortunately impor-
> tant points fade from memory or are changed to fit with later
> perceptions.[28]

A daily record also permits comprehensive review, by which the
reporter can detect trends and gaps in the accumulated information.

The reporter should make notes as soon as possible after the
daily observation period. This means he or she should schedule
no commitments nor talk to others until the task is done. Notes are
not written in the familiar inverted pyramid form. Rather, they
should be chronological, completing a full account of one incident
before proceeding to an equally full description of the next. Aids
to this reconstruction might include diagrams of the physical
layout of a meeting area, seating plans, agendas of the topics in
lengthy conversations, brief notes scribbled unobtrusively during
the sessions, and so on. Gaps in the reporter's recall may be filled
in later but should be identified as such.

Consequences of Participant Observation

For many readers, Rosenhan's
study will raise nagging ethical questions. Some of these are representative of participant observation in general, and the reporter
must answer them before exploiting the technique. The sociological literature aids in understanding the concerns. Of course, what
is proper conduct for a sociologist is not necessarily proper for a
journalist. As sociologist Kai Erikson suggests, "the sociologist has
a different relationship to the rest of the community, operates
under a different warrant, and has a different set of professional
and scientific interests to protect" than the journalist.[29] Nonetheless, even if their resolution is different, the issues themselves are
the same for both professions.

---

[28] Bollens and Marshall, *A Guide to Participation*, p. 57.
[29] Kai T. Erikson, "A Comment on Disguised Observation in Sociology," *Social Problems* 14 (1966–67):367.

The most crucial ethical decision is whether or not reporters should identify themselves and their goals to their subjects at the outset. Apart from the question of whether better information can be obtained through disguise, reporters must judge whether this calculated attack on the privacy of the group is justified by the public's need for the information they expect to get. Although the courts have allowed the press to shine the spotlight of publicity over a wide swath of private life, legal right and moral right are not identical, and so the legal literature is only suggestive at best.

It is argued that in certain circumstances the greater good is served if the public knows the activities of certain groups. Thus, a journalist may be justified in infiltrating an extremist political group if he or she can publicize the group's plan to blow up a public building or assassinate political leaders. The question is more moot, however, when one asks whether Rosenhan's entry into mental hospitals is equally benign. Here, of course, there is no imminent danger to the public, although presumably benefits could derive to both the public and the medical staff from the publication of his findings. But it is at least debatable whether the potential embarrassment to staff and patients was worth the information gleaned.

The foregoing implies that judgments can be based on whether the groups themselves are "good" or "bad." That is, one may think it more ethical to infiltrate the Ku Klux Klan because it is pernicious than Alcoholics Anonymous because it is not. To justify this attitude, the journalist must first demonstrate that there is nothing wrong in holding a double standard. On the other hand, a professional rule allowing overt research alone

> would be an active violation of many people's moral standards who think that there are some groups, such as professional crime and fascist groups, that should be studied whether they are asked and give permission or not.[30]

Accepting the double standard also suggests that the reporter is capable of determining whether a group is "good" or "bad."

---

[30] John Lofland, "Reply to Davis," *Social Problems* 8 (1961):366.

The disguised observer can also injure the group "in ways [he] can neither anticipate in advance nor compensate for afterward." [31] In the very act of misleading people about their role, for instance, journalists may hurt them. Because they cannot know which actions are apt to be painful, the reporters must decide whether they have the right to inflict pain at all when they are aware of these risks and their subjects are not. If harm befalls people who know they are the focus of some journalistic enterprise, reporters have at least some defense: they knew something of what they were getting into and were willing to chance these dangers for the public's benefit. But no such defense is available when the group has no foreknowledge.

The reporter must also think about future relations between the press and the people scrutinized. The group may react so negatively to having been duped by a reporter that it will constrict future encounters with the media, including those that are fully aboveboard. This consequence for his or her colleagues and the public must certainly be considered.[32]

The reporter may face physical and psychological danger during participant observation research. Some conditions are obviously potentially injurious. If he or she joins a radical political group or a circus trapeze act, for example, the reporter will be well aware of the attendant hazards. But dangers, albeit of a different sort, also can arise in relatively innocuous settings, such as that reported by Rosenhan. He says that not all his confederates were familiar with psychiatric institutions, a revelation that raises the question of whether they fully comprehended what they were letting themselves in for. The inference is that they did not: "The psychological stresses associated with hospitalization were considerable, and all but one of the pseudopatients desired to be discharged almost immediately after being

---

[31] Erikson, "A Comment," p. 368.

[32] For behavioral science examples of research based on covert or overt participant observation see: Leon Festinger, Henry Riecken, and Stanley Schachter, *When Prophecy Fails*, University of Minnesota Press, Minneapolis, 1956; William F. Whyte, *Street Corner Society*, University of Chicago Press, Chicago, 1943.

admitted." [33] The participant observers were subject to the laws and practices governing psychiatric patients, including the extreme difficulty in being discharged on short notice.

Rosenhan admits, "I was not sensitive to these difficulties at the outset of the project, nor to the personal and situational emergencies that can arise," [34] and he had to go so far as to prepare writs of *habeas corpus* for each pseudo-patient. That a professor of both law and psychology did not appreciate the dangers he was creating for his associates dramatically underscores the fact that the less specialized journalist may expose himself to grave problems.

Not to be brushed off lightly either is the conflict a disguised reporter may experience. Such feelings are generated by both practical and moral considerations. The reporter may worry about being caught, unable to relax since he or she is constantly on guard against performing out of character. Or, as he or she cements relationships in the group, attraction or sympathy for its members may develop. This easily gives rise to doubts that the deception really does outweigh the need to publicize the group.

LOYALTY TO THE GROUP

Frequently reporters on a beat grow fond of their sources over time. Sometimes the result is a subtle shift from skepticism to boosterism by the journalist, who does not want to criticize his or her friends. Participant observation is similar. It permits intense interaction with people over time. The reporter may come to think of the subjects as friends and wish them no harm or embarrassment. After all, behaviors do not usually match beliefs. Disclosure of the discrepancy could hold up the group to ridicule or attack.

The reporter may choose to skirt the problem by keeping the group anonymous. Aside from the question of whether he or she will be successful, however, the reporter must decide if the public needs the group's identity to assess the validity of the findings or to allay its fears about the extent to which the group is a direct threat.

---

[33] Rosenhan, "On Being Sane in Insane Places," p. 252.
[34] *Ibid.*, fn. 8.

Conclusions

Many of the "new journalists" have written widely read books based on participant observation. George Plimpton joined the Detroit Lions training camp in the mid-1960s as their "last-string" rookie quarterback, went through the training program, and appeared in an intra-squad game. The result was a book-length piece of journalism, *Paper Lion*. For a while, Plimpton assumed the pose of just another rookie, although his identity soon became known. Plimpton originally set out to see how an amateur felt in that situation and then "write about my experience and enlighten those who had wondered as a sort of daydream what would happen to them if they actually became bonafide quarterbacks playing in a pro game." [35] But his book details training-camp life vividly and, in the process, assumes a much wider scope than its original aim.

What can be done in sports can be done in other areas. Joe McGinniss joined the campaign staff of Richard Nixon in 1968 and outlined the role of advertising in electing the president. John Sack talked the Army into letting him, as a reporter, join an infantry unit, go through basic training, and then accompany the unit on the battlefields of Vietnam. His own participation, observations, and interviews with the men gave him fine material for an article in *Esquire* magazine. Hunter S. Thompson rode off and on for eighteen months with the Hell's Angels—again, as a reporter— and survived a fierce beating in an Angels' encampment near Santa Rosa, California to write his book-length report.[36]

But what about daily journalism? Plimpton, McGinniss, Sack, Thompson—their work appears in magazines and books where time and money are relatively plentiful. Can the newspaper or broadcast station, with deadline pressures and frugal budgets, find these hints practical? The answer is a clear *yes* and *no.*

No, most newspapers and broadcast stations are unable to spare a man for several weeks to go through football training

---

[35] George Plimpton, *Paper Lion,* Pocket Books, New York, 1966.

[36] Joe McGinniss, *The Selling of the President 1968,* Trident Press, New York, 1969; John Sack, "M," *Esquire,* October 1966, pp. 79–86, 140–162; Hunter S. Thompson, *Hell's Angels: A Strange and Terrible Saga,* Random House, New York, 1967.

camp. All too many news operations still overwork their reporters. Professor Charnley's mythical reporter, Don Finnegan,[37] is burdened with a one-day assignment sheet that includes covering his county beat, reporting a doctor's convention, checking into a trial, interviewing a medical doctor and park officials on the unhealthy state of the city pool, finding out about the new bus depot, and doing a short feature about the official non-municipal departments in town. When editors stretch reporters so thin, there is little hope for deeper reports with more research.

But all newsrooms, regardless of resources, *could* adapt the precepts of this chapter. In the case of prestigious ones, like *The New York Times*, good journalists already know the value of participant observation.

When *The Times* decided to "beef up" its local human-interest reporting, veteran journalist John Corry was assigned to write about daily life on a city block on New York's upper west side. Corry actually moved into the block, considered a microcosm of Manhattan.[38]

The beauty of Corry's series lies in its range of subject matter and methods of reporting. It covers the gamut of big city life—the residents' shopping habits, unemployment, life for the aged, the problems of small landlords, and the precautions taken to prevent burglaries, rape, and murder.

Corry's research has equally wide scope. He was a participant observer, a resident of the area about which he wrote, sharing the same living conditions and neighborhood problems as his subjects. But like any good participant observer, Corry employed other research techniques. He followed two city housing inspectors on a tour of an old brownstone apartment and recorded their conversation with the proprietor. In an example of unobtrusive observation, he assessed the rate of unemployment on the block by asking the local mailman how many unemployment checks he delivered. Writing about crime in the area, he combed police records for historical data. For a piece on parking, Corry observed that most illegally parked cars were from out of state and that local res-

---

[37] Mitchell V. Charnley, *Reporting*, 2d ed., Holt, Rinehart and Winston, New York, 1966, p. 81.
[38] John Corry, series in *The New York Times*, September 3, September 24, October 4, October 14, October 27, and November 18, 1971.

idents stuck old traffic tickets under windshield wipers in order to fool the police.

We would not always have chosen Corry's methods to gather material, but that's not the point. What is noteworthy is his refusal to adhere to the rigid formulas of standard journalistic research. Still, not every newspaper can release one staffer to cover daily life in a city block. Corry's pieces appeared irregularly at two to three week intervals. Few dailies can (or will) afford to spend so much money for so little copy. Interviewing and observation can be used imaginatively, however, in more limited ways. The *Detroit News'* series on pollution in the life of a suburban family is a less expensive series. Even less staff time was needed for this example:

Science reporter Lydia Dotto used her one and one-half years' experience as a scuba diver "to get a feel for the stresses and challenges facing divers and scientists participating in Arctic IV, a two-month expedition to test diving equipment and human performance in northern waters." [39] In her first, short dive, Dotto's principal worry was the impact of the harsh environment on her personally. But, she reports, her "second dive was completely different from the first because the unknowns now had some boundaries. I was able to observe the environment, apart from a sole concern about its effects on me."

Pursuing a tip that there was illegal collusion between Chicago police and some ambulance companies, *Chicago Tribune* investigative reporter William Hugh Jones took a first-aid training course and found a job as an ambulance driver. In a six-part series that won a Pulitzer Prize in 1971, Jones outlined abuses that resulted in sixteen grand jury indictments, the barring of two companies from carrying welfare patients, and new laws regulating private ambulances.[40]

A four-part series detailed reporter Sheila Arnopoulos' two weeks as a factory worker in Montreal. Her goal was to find out what life was like for thousands of immigrant factory workers. Arnopoulos described her experiences in five factories and pointed

---

[39] Lydia Dotto, "Girl Under Arctic Ice Finds Cold, Danger," *Toronto Globe and Mail*, May 23, 1974.

[40] "Pulitzers Again Applaud Crusade for Environment," *Editor and Publisher*, May 8, 1971, p. 11.

The Earth and Eric Matus

The *Detroit News* tried to cut ecology down to size in 1971 with a series of articles on the environmental problems of the Eric Matus family who reside in a Detroit suburb. They were chosen after a computer determined they were a typical Detroit family.

The newspaper used a number of methods to determine the Matuses' relation to their environment:

Samples of the family's blood, hair, and fingernails were taken by the University of Michigan's School of Public Health to be tested for heavy metals.

The Michigan State Cooperative Extension Service dug up their lawn, looking for pesticides and herbicides.

The family recorded their eating habits for analysis by the Michigan State University School of Human Ecology.

The Michigan State Department of Public Health invaded their home, searching for sources of radiation and setting up an air-sampling station in their backyard.

Their cars were tested for exhaust emissions by the U.S. Environmental Protection Agency, tuned up, and retested.

The Wayne State University School of Pharmacy examined the contents of the Matuses' medicine chest.

Detroit Edison analyzed their use of electricity.

The industrial hygiene division of the Detroit Health Department examined their home for sources of mercury.

Observations were made by the newspaper of the Matuses' weekly garbage and of the number of small appliances in their home.

And the Matuses were interviewed on all aspects of ecology. They talked about privacy and their preference for swimming in the backyard pool to picnicking in an overcrowded public park.

Mr. Matus recalled the day the bomb fell on Hiroshima, and his wife was incredulous when she discovered radiation in her own home. They expressed surprise that there was more pollution now than when they were youngsters, because the window curtains were forever getting soiled back then.

Interviewing and observation could have, by themselves, produced a fairly interesting series. But, by using nearly every technique described in this book, the *News* came up with an exemplary series.

SOURCE: "The Earth and Eric Matus," nine-part series in the *Detroit News,* May 1971.

out deficiencies in the minimum wage act, the government inspection systems, and union organization of small shops.[41]

In a study of offshore oilman Joe Fry, *Wall Street Journal* reporter Danforth W. Austin describes drilling operations performed by Fry's crew for Mobil Oil Company. The story recounts the problems of drilling farther and farther offshore in order to slake the increasing world energy thirst. Austin also details working operations, living conditions aboard the crew's ship, and his subject's thoughts on handling possible disasters at sea.[42]

Broadcasting, too, is ripe for this kind of reporting. In the summer of 1973, on the heels of a U.S. Supreme Court decision which said that local communities could set standards on pornography, a number of cities raided adult book stores and "girlie" theaters. CBS television newsman Ike Pappas covered such a raid of a Chicago cinema for a network newscast. The cameras showed the arrival of the police; the theater manager closing up the theater, handing over his print of the objectionable film, and calling his lawyer, and the trip to police headquarters. There were also interviews with the theater owner and local law enforcement officials, and the legal background was sketched.

In radio, Marion Wylie underwent eight weeks' basic training in the women's branch of the Canadian armed forces and telephoned weekly reports to a magazine-format program on the CBC. Upon graduation, Wylie listened to excerpts from her first two reports and commented on the drastic changes in her thinking that had occurred during the course.[43]

These stories, all recent, demonstrate the breadth of topics and type of research some journalist-participant observers have thought appropriate. Jones and Arnopoulos assumed false identities, for instance; Dotto and Pappas identified themselves clearly as reporters on assignment. Arnopoulos based her stories on two weeks' work in five different factories, while Wylie underwent eight weeks of basic training.

A variety of methodologies other than participant observation

---

[41] Sheila Arnopoulos, series in *Montreal Star*, March 27–30, 1974.

[42] Danforth W. Austin, "Offshore Oilman: Joe Fry, Tool Pusher, Braves Wind and Wave to Drill Ocean Wells," *Wall Street Journal*, May 7, 1974.

[43] Marion Wylie, nine-part series on "This Country in the Morning," CBC radio, October, November, and December, 1973.

also characterize these stories. Arnopoulos turned to the history books to show that cheap immigrant labor is not a recent phenomenon in Canada. Dotto used government documents to provide background on the Arctic research. Pappas referred to judicial decisions on pornography to set his story in context.

Finally, the importance of spending time in research is underscored by both Dotto and Wylie. Dotto reports that her two dives were quite different; relying on only one would certainly have distorted the picture of Arctic research she was striving for. Wylie's surprise over the early tapes of her experiences drives home the need for observers to record their observations and attitudes on a regular basis.

Participant observation is a slippery methodology. It is not clear-cut in the sense, for example, that field experiments are. For some behavioral scientists, this raises serious problems about reliability and validity. Journalists should share that concern because they, too, are in the business of recording reality accurately, as Tankard makes clear in Chapter 3. But participant observation need not be so plagued as its detractors suggest. Its careful use, assured by sound decisions in the field, can produce insightful journalism.

Chapter 10

Journalistic Field Experiments

James W. Tankard, Jr.

Experimental observations are only experience carefully planned in advance.

Sir Ronald Fisher

In 1967, civil rights workers in Chicago claimed that blacks were being barred from purchasing housing in two neighborhoods.[1] The editors of the *Chicago Daily News* wanted to check out the charge. They could have used the journalist's standard tool—the interview—by having reporters call real-estate offices and asking if they would rent to blacks. The editors decided not to use this procedure. They knew that discrimination in housing was against the law, and real-estate agents were not likely to admit they were violating the law.

Instead, the editors sent a black reporter and a white reporter, separately and at different times, to a number of real-estate offices. The reporters did not identify themselves as reporters, but simply pretended to be trying to rent or buy a home. Then, still without identifying themselves as reporters, they observed and recorded how they were treated and whether or not they were offered the chance to buy or rent a home.

---

[1] Burleigh Hines, "No Prospects for Negro . . ." and Susan Pollock, ". . . Listings for White," *Chicago Daily News*, August 13, 1966, as reprinted in Curtis D. MacDougall, *Reporters Report Reporters*, The Iowa State University Press, Ames, Iowa, 1968, pp. 148–153.

The editors of the *Chicago Daily News* were attempting to answer the question: Are blacks and whites who are trying to obtain housing treated differently solely on the basis of race? Essentially they were trying to answer a question about *causality:* Does the variable of race have an effect on whether or not a person is shown a house? The technique they decided to use was one that scientists have developed as the most powerful means of demonstrating causality—the *controlled experiment.* An experiment, as the editors apparently realized, was probably the only sure way the question about racial discrimination could be answered.

The findings of the *Daily News* investigation were complex, but they did produce some evidence of discrimination. In at least three of the six real-estate offices visited, the white reporter was given a more encouraging reply than the black reporter.

The weakness of the other method the editors might have used—the traditional journalistic interview—is simply that a person's verbal report of his or her behavior sometimes does not correspond very closely to the actual behavior. Particularly when a person is questioned about a socially disapproved behavior or an illegal act, it is likely that the verbal report of the behavior will not correspond to the actual behavior.

In the behavioral sciences, the investigating technique used by the *Chicago Daily News* is called a *field experiment,* which can be extremely useful for certain types of reporting, particularly investigative reporting, by journalists. Because of practical or ethical limitations, it is not always possible for the journalist to conduct an experiment. Ethical considerations come into play when a particular investigation might involve deception, invasion of privacy, or physical or psychological harm for an individual. On some occasions, however, an experiment will be the only way to obtain a definite answer to a certain question and, furthermore, an experiment will be possible, practical, and ethical. The journalist should be prepared to take advantage of such opportunities.

The Controlled Experiment

The basis of the scientific experiment is that the investigator deliberately makes some change in natural events and then carefully observes to see what happens as a consequence of that change. In technical language, the factor that is deliberately changed is called the *independent variable.* The changing of this variable is referred to as manipulation of the independent variable. The phenomenon in which change is expected and looked for is called the *dependent variable.*

Behavioral scientists conduct experiments in the laboratory and in the field. Field experiments are likely to be of greater use to the journalist since they take place in natural settings and are more likely to deal with "real world" problems.

Many journalists are already conducting investigations that are essentially field experiments, although the experiments often have flaws. Many of these could be improved by using additional techniques or controls that are known to behavioral scientists.

Advantages of the Controlled Experiment

Numerous advantages make the controlled experiment a useful technique for the journalist. Three major features will be reviewed here.

DEMONSTRATING CAUSAL RELATIONS

The controlled experiment is the most powerful technique that has been discovered for demonstrating *cause* and *effect* relationships. The journalist is frequently interested in causes and effects. One of the five Ws the journalist is taught to answer in every story is Why.

Causal analysis is also fundamental to interpretative reporting. Journalism professor Curtis MacDougall writes:

> To interpret the news it is necessary to understand it, and understanding means more than just the ability to define the jargon used by persons in different walks of life. It involves recognizing the particular event as one of a series with both a cause and an effect.[2]

---

[2] Curtis D. MacDougall, *Interpretative Reporting*, 6th ed., Macmillan Co., New York, 1972, p. 12.

Mitchell Charnley, the author of another widely used newswriting and reporting text, states:

> Interpretive reporting is what Director Harold L. Nelson of the Wisconsin School of Journalism calls "the journalism of cause-and-effect relationship." As Nelson suggests, it may be the kind of reporting that says, "The causes that led to the news event were such and such . . ." Or, "The results of this news event may be expected to be such and such . . ." [3]

The experiment is a strong technique for demonstrating causality because it simultaneously gathers the three types of evidence that behavioral scientists say are necessary to show causality. Researcher Claire Selltiz and her colleagues describe these three types of evidence as:

1. evidence of *concomitant variation*—that is, evidence that the causal variable and the dependent variable are associated;
2. evidence on *time-order*, that the dependent variable did not occur before the causal variable;
3. evidence ruling out other factors as possible *determining conditions* of the dependent variable.[4]

Other kinds of information—the opinions of experts or correlational data—have little strength for showing causality. Experts can be wrong. And correlation alone can never prove causality since it provides only the first kind of evidence described by Selltiz.

Charles Darwin, in one of the first carefully controlled experiments ever conducted, investigated the effects of cross-fertilization and self-fertilization on plant growth. The example illustrates the logic of experimentation. Darwin used an experiment because he realized the opinions of experts were not based on careful, systematic observation.

The Associated Press wanted to determine whether using a zip code or mailing a letter by air mail really had an effect on the speed of delivery. They didn't look for the answer by asking postal authorities; they conducted their own experiment.

---

[3] Mitchell V. Charnley, *Reporting*, 2d ed., Holt, Rinehart and Winston, New York, 1966, p. 292.

[4] Claire Selltiz, Marie Jahoda, Morton Deutsch, and Stuart W. Cook, *Research Methods in Social Relations*, Holt, Rinehart and Winston, New York, 1966, p. 94.

A Classic Experiment

The logic of the experiment is well illustrated by Charles Darwin's study of the effects of self-fertilization and cross-fertilization on plants—a classic experiment from the physical sciences.

Darwin noticed some experts insisting that cross-fertilization had a superior effect on plant growth in comparison with self-fertilization, although no actual observations were reported to back up the claim.

Darwin conducted an experiment in which he took plants from the same parents and cross-fertilized some while self-fertilizing others. From these he grew fifteen pairs of plants. Each pair was made up of the offspring of a self-fertilized plant and the offspring of a cross-fertilized plant. He then measured the heights of the plants in eighths of an inch (apparently a conventional unit at the time). The cross-fertilized plants were taller than the self-fertilized plants by an average of 20.93 eighths of an inch (or about 2½ inches).

Darwin turned to the pioneer statistician Sir Francis Galton for help in analyzing his results. Galton concluded that cross-fertilization did have a superior effect on plant growth. Sir Ronald Fisher later re-analyzed the data by means of the *t* test and showed that Galton was correct.

The purpose of the Darwin experiment was the purpose of many scientific experiments—to demonstrate causality. It was to show that the type of fertilization—self-fertilization or cross-fertilization—has an effect on the growth of the plant.

The Darwin experiment was also apparently one of the first to be analyzed statistically. Darwin was studying a *sample* of plants; he had to use statistics to determine how likely it was that conclusions drawn from the sample would also apply to the larger *population* of plants of the same type.

SOURCE: Charles Darwin, *The Effects of Cross and Self Fertilization in the Vegetable Kingdom*, 2d ed., John Murray, London, 1900. Ronald A. Fisher, *The Design of Experiments*, 5th ed., Oliver and Boyd, Edinburgh, 1949.

Psychologist Elliot Aronson argues that the experimental method is the best way to understand a complex phenomenon. Aronson suggests that the only way to really know the world is to reconstruct it: that is, in order to truly understand what causes what, we must do more than simply observe—rather, we must be

The Associated Press
Mail Survey

Since 1971 the Associated Press has been conducting an annual investigation of the speed and efficiency of the U.S. mail service. Two parts of this broad study can be considered genuine experiments. These are the investigations of the effectiveness of zip codes and air mail.

The 1973 AP mail survey was conducted by AP bureaus in six cities—New York, Washington, Chicago, St. Louis, Houston, and Los Angeles. During the period of study, a staff member for each bureau went to an outside mail box six times. Each time he mailed twenty-two letters: two to his own bureau, one zipped, and one not zipped; and four to each of the other five bureaus, one first class with a zip code, one first class without a zip code, one air mail with a zip code, and one air mail without a zip code.

The effect of putting a zip code on a letter could then be determined by comparing the speed of delivery of the 396 zipped letters with that of the 396 unzipped letters mailed at the same time and places. The effect of air mail could be determined by comparing the speed of delivery of the 320 air-mailed letters with that of the 320 first-class letters mailed at the same times and places.

The 1973 results on the effects of using zip codes were reported this way in the summary AP story:

Zip-coded letters spent an average of 2¾ fewer hours less (sic) in the mail·than their nonzipped counterparts—49¼ hours vs. 52 hours—but there was no consistent pattern. Twelve percent of the zip-coded letters arrived later than their nonzipped counterparts, and 65 percent of the zip-coded letters arrived at the same time.

The 1973 findings on the effects of mailing air mail were:

In the latest survey, 62 percent of the air-mail letters arrived ahead of their first-class counterparts, compared with 46 percent in 1972 and 50 percent in 1971. But in all three surveys 9 percent of the air-mail letters spent more time in the mail than their first-class companions.

The article also reported that in 1973 air-mail letters spent an average of 1.8 days in the mail, while first-class letters spent an average of 2.4 days.

SOURCE: Howard Angione, "Delays Hurt Mail, Survey Shows," Associated Press, as printed in the *Austin Statesman*, April 26, 1973.

responsible for *producing* the first "what" so that we can be sure it really *caused* the second "what." [5]

The controlled experiment allows the inquirer to observe a person's behavior instead of relying on a person's verbal statement of what his or her behavior might be.

The interview, the journalist's standard technique, has one principal shortcoming. It is a verbal report and, therefore, may tell very little about a person's real behavior. An experiment overcomes this problem by putting a person in a situation and observing his or her actual behavior, rather than asking what might be done in such a situation. This may be particularly important when one is investigating unethical, illegal, or socially disapproved behaviors. Few people will admit in an interview that they would engage in such acts.

The experiment has an additional advantage over the interview: people are not very good at predicting their own behavior when they are asked verbally about a hypothetical situation. The fact that certain kinds of information can be obtained only through an experiment is illustrated by psychologist Stanley Milgram's experimental studies of obedience.[6] Milgram put subjects in a situation where an authority figure ordered them to deliver extremely intense electrical shocks to another person. Elliot Aronson has described the Milgram experiment to classes and *asked* students how many of them would deliver the most extreme shock of 450 volts.[7] He reports that only about one percent indicated they would. The scientific evidence from the Milgram experiment, however, indicates that 65 percent of them would deliver the full shock.

The discrepancy that can occur between people's verbal reports of their behavior and their actual behavior is also illustrated

---

[5] Elliot Aronson, *The Social Animal*, W. H. Freeman and Co., San Francisco, 1972, pp. xii–xiii.

[6] Stanley Milgram, "Behavioral Study of Obedience," *Journal of Abnormal and Social Psychology* 67 (1963):371–378.

[7] Aronson, *The Social Animal*, p. 283.

Purchasing Dynamite

One month after a fatal bombing at the University of Wisconsin, a reporter for the *Milwaukee Journal*, dressed like a student and wearing a "ROTC Must Go" button, walked into a hardware store and attempted to purchase dynamite. A short time later, another *Journal* reporter, older and dressed in work clothes, walked into the same hardware store and also attempted to buy dynamite.

The reporters were attempting to find out "whether it was easy to buy dynamite or whether the recent bombing at the University of Wisconsin and other violence had caused dealers to become cautious." One of the variables they thought might influence whether or not a person could buy dynamite was his appearance. They wanted to see if it was easier or more difficult for someone "who might be identified with radical youth" to buy dynamite than someone who might have a legitimate need for blasting materials.

The principal finding was that most of the hardware stores visited either didn't have dynamite or wouldn't sell it to either reporter. This finding answered their question of whether it was easy to buy dynamite. They failed to show that the appearance of the customer had an effect on whether he was sold dynamite, but this was largely because they were unable to find a large enough sample of stores selling dynamite at all. Despite this limitation, the story reported an attempt at a genuine field experiment.

SOURCE: Leon Hughes and John Carman, "Dynamite Becomes Too Hot to Handle," *Milwaukee Journal*, Sept. 27, 1970.

in a classic study by sociologist Robert LaPiere.[8] He traveled around the country in the 1930s with a Chinese couple, visiting hotels and restaurants. In only one of the 251 establishments was the Chinese couple refused service.

Some time later, LaPiere sent questionnaires to all the places they visited. One of his questions was, "Will you accept members

---

[8] Robert T. LaPiere, "Attitudes vs. Actions," *Social Forces* 13 (1934):230–237, as reprinted in Leonard Bickman and Thomas Henchy, eds., *Beyond the Laboratory: Field Research in Social Psychology*, McGraw-Hill Book Co., New York, 1972, pp. 122–127.

of the Chinese race as guests in your establishment?" He received replies from 128 of the businesses. Approximately 92 percent answered "No." Only one person answered with a definite "Yes."

Similarly, the *Milwaukee Journal* wanted to know if a person's appearance and clothing had an effect on whether he was sold dynamite. They did not rely on an interview, but used a field experiment to determine the actual behavior of hardware-store personnel.

The controlled experiment allows the investigator to observe events that would occur rarely or never by themselves. Suppose a journalistic team wanted to determine, as did a *60 Minutes* news team, whether garages make automobile repairs when they are not necessary. The best way to investigate this question is to take a car known to be in perfect working order to a number of garages to see if repairs are recommended. Yet, this is not something that would occur naturally in life—taking a car known to be in good repair to a service station for check-up. This kind of experiment is conducted, then, to observe a phenomenon that would not occur otherwise.

A similar technique to that of the *60 Minutes* investigators was used by the *Charlotte Observer* to check on inspection stations when the state of North Carolina began an automobile inspection program.

Or suppose an investigator wanted to study, as a team of reporters for WCKT-TV in Miami did, the reactions of bystanders in a public place to seeing a crime committed? An observer would have very poor luck in waiting around public places and hoping to see such an event occur naturally. One solution is to simulate a crime carefully in a public place and then observe the behavior of bystanders. This is an example of the use of an experimental technique to observe a phenomenon that occurs too rarely to be observed otherwise.

Allen Funt of *Candid Camera* used simple observation in the early years of his program, but found that a large amount of time was required to get a small amount of material. Funt then turned to introducing confederates who would intervene in the natural setting and direct attention to a contrived set-up.

The *60 Minutes*
Car Repair Story

A television news team for *60 Minutes* investigated fraud in the automobile repair business by taking a car in perfect repair to six garages to see to what extent repairs were recommended that were not needed.

"We chose the six garages at random, all of them near the nation's Capitol," correspondent Morley Safer said on the program.

The car was driven by a *60 Minutes* staff member, and a camera was hidden in a closed van parked nearby. A hidden microphone picked up the conversation between the mechanic and the staff member.

All six garages recommended that unnecessary work be done. The average (mean) of the unnecessary charges was $43.49.

Summary of Unnecessary Repair Work		
Garage A	Set of lower ball joints and realignment	$62.87
Garage B	Idler arm and alignment	31.61
Garage C	Lubrication	5.80
Garage D	Two wheel cylinders rebuilt	52.22
Garage E	Idler arm	19.71
Garage F	Brake drums refaced, brakes relined, new master cylinder	88.75
		$260.96

SOURCE: *60 Minutes* CBS telecast, Oct. 21, 1971.

Planning the Experiment

At least six aspects of an experiment are important and deserve some advance thought by the investigator.

EXPERIMENTAL DESIGN

The basis of an experiment is the manipulation of an independent variable and the observation of its

Inspecting the State Automobile Inspectors

The *Charlotte Observer* began checking on the new North Carolina automobile inspection program soon after it began in 1966. The investigative technique was simply for a dozen reporters to take their cars to different service stations, ask for an inspection (without identifying themselves as reporters), and then observe how the inspection was conducted. The stations were picked randomly from a master list. The reporters found that in a large number of cases, the inspections were haphazard, incomplete, carelessly done, and not up to requirements outlined by the state. Only four complete and proper inspections were done in visits to twenty-five stations.

The story got results. Within a couple of days, the administrator of the auto inspection program, R. B. Parker, was on his way to Charlotte to investigate the *Observer*'s findings, Parker said his department was "lucky to get this information. It has saved us a lot of time and trouble and you can be certain we will look further into it."

The investigation drew this reaction from the state president of the North Carolina Service Station Association: "This last weekend, we have been dealt a mighty black eye. It was not a low punch. It was a direct, honest punch. We shouldn't criticize the news media because they have pointed out a problem. We would be remiss if we allowed ourselves to continue inspecting cars as they were apparently inspected last week." Governor Dan K. Moore was quoted the same day as saying, "Those inspection stations that start chiseling will be removed."

The final result of the investigation begun by the *Observer* was citing one station for violations of inspection procedures and sending warning letters to fourteen others.

SOURCE: "Car Inspections: Pay Your Money, Take Your Chances," *Charlotte Observer*, February 20, 1966. "Auto Check Chief Begins Local Probe," *Charlotte Observer*, February 22, 1966. "State Cracks Down on Car-Check Units in Charlotte Probe," *Charlotte Observer*, February 26, 1966.

---

effect on a dependent variable. Experimental designs can become extremely complicated, but the journalist will probably find simple designs more useful for his or her purposes.[9]

---

[9] Two introductions to experimental method aimed at the beginner are Barry F. Anderson, *The Psychology Experiment*, Wadsworth Publishing Co., Belmont,

The WCKT-TV Crime
Witness Story

Newsmen from television station WCKT in Miami, with the cooperation of police, simulated a number of holdups, break-ins, kidnappings, and other crimes in public places. The purpose was "to film public reaction to what, for the most part, is common everyday crime, and to determine with some finality whether you and I . . . and our neighbors . . . are morally, if not legally, partners in crime."

In general, persons who found themselves witnessing the simulated crimes did nothing, and station news director Gene Strul concluded, "A majority of citizens apparently stand four square behind apathy."

The resulting documentary, "Partners in Crime," was later shown in part on the NBC *Huntley-Brinkley Report.*

SOURCE: Gene Strul, "Partners in Crime . . . A TV Station Proves Public Apathy," *The Quill,* March 1968.

For the journalist, two types of experiments appear to be useful:

1. The type in which the independent variable appears in only one condition and which is aimed at demonstrating that some phenomenon of interest does or does not occur. (For example, the *60 Minutes* car-repair story or the WCKT-TV crime-witness story.)
2. The type that has an independent variable appearing in two or more different conditions in order to see if the change in conditions produces a corresponding change in effect (the *Chicago Daily News* discrimination story, the *Milwaukee Journal* dynamite purchase story).

In the first type of experiment, the investigator focuses on creating *one* condition and then observing its effects. In these cases, the one condition is usually an event that would happen rarely, if ever, outside the experimental situation. An example of

Calif., 1971 and Robert Plutchik, *Foundations of Experimental Research,* Harper and Row, New York, 1968. More sophisticated problems of design are discussed in Donald T. Campbell and Julian C. Stanley, *Experimental and Quasi-Experimental Designs for Research,* Rand McNally & Co., Chicago, 1966.

this kind of experiment is Milgram's first investigations of obedience, in which he was initially interested in determining whether or not obedience would take place when subjects are ordered to deliver intense electrical shocks. These first experiments showed that about 65 percent of a cross-section of the public would deliver shocks they thought to be of lethal intensity.[10] Milgram can generalize these findings to a cross-section of the public because he has repeated the studies with men and women, people of different ages, and people from different occupational levels (working-class, white-collar, and professional).

In later studies, Milgram turned to the second type of experiment, in which an independent variable appears in two or more different conditions to determine if the change in conditions produces a corresponding change in effect.[11] He had demonstrated in the first studies that a phenomenon would occur—that many people would obey. In the later experiments, he was interested in studying the causes of that phenomenon. At this point, he began manipulating independent variables, such as proximity to the victim, to see whether they had an effect on whether or not a person obeyed.

FORMULATING THE HYPOTHESIS

Hypotheses are important because they focus an investigation. They force an investigator to be very precise about what he or she is studying. Typically, a hypothesis is a statement of a relationship between two or more variables. In an experimental inquiry, formulation of the hypothesis forces investigators to think very carefully about the factor they think may be a cause (the independent variable) and how it can be manipulated, and the factor they think may be affected by the cause (the dependent variable) and how it can be measured.

Formulating the hypothesis for an experiment requires that the independent variable be defined very carefully and that it be something that can be practically and ethically manipulated by the experimenter. How, for instance, could investigators who were in-

---

[10] Milgram, "Behavioral Study of Obedience."
[11] Stanley Milgram, "Some Conditions of Obedience and Disobedience to Authority," *Human Relations* 18 (1965):57–76.

terested in the effects of race, length of hair, or style of dress, manipulate each of these? Style of dress would obviously be the easiest. The investigator, serving as the stimulus object in the experiment, could simply change clothes, wearing casual clothes in one condition and more formal clothes in another condition.

A graduate student at Brigham Young University manipulated his hair length appropriately for a study of the effects of appearance on success in hitchhiking.[12] David Alcorn let his hair grow out for a year, then put on sloppy jeans and sandals and hitchhiked around Arizona and Utah. After hitching 3,000 miles, he cut his hair short, put on more conservative clothes, and hitchhiked the same route to see if appearance made a difference. He found the average wait for a ride was eleven minutes as a "straight," but thirty-three minutes as a "hippie."

Race is even more difficult to manipulate in an experiment than hair length. There is no easy way to make the same individual appear to belong to two different racial groups, although white journalist Ray Sprigle considered a number of ways of dyeing his skin black when he was planning to tour the South as a black man. He finally resorted to getting a good suntan.[13]

A more feasible method for manipulating race in an experimental study is to use black individuals in one condition and white individuals in the other condition. This is what the *Chicago Daily News* did in its investigation of discrimination. This procedure works even better when *several* blacks are used in one condition and *several* whites are used in the other. Then it will be less likely that some other factor, such as personality differences, is also contributing to a difference between conditions.

The dependent variable in an experiment must also be clearly specified. It must be made quite clear how the dependent variable will be observed, recognized, or measured. What is the observer, if there is one, to look for? Is it whether or not the real-estate salesman tells a customer that a house is available? Is it whether or not the real-estate salesman asks for the customer's phone number and says he will call when something becomes available?

One of the problems with some of the journalistic field experi-

---

[12] Parry D. Sorensen, "Freaks Stop for Freaks, But Not for 'Straights,'" *National Observer*, Oct. 13, 1973.
[13] Ray Sprigle, *In the Land of Jim Crow*, Simon and Schuster, New York, 1949.

ments described in this chapter is that apparently no hypothesis was specified. Reporters who went into real-estate offices or hardware stores had a "rough" idea of what they were looking for, but they did not have a precise idea. Consequently, in some of these stories, it appears that different reporters observed different things.

CONTROL

The *control* in a controlled experiment refers to the effort to make everything equivalent in the two conditions being compared except for the variable being manipulated, the independent variable.

Charles Darwin introduced control in his study of cross- and self-fertilization in plants by growing the two types of seeds from the same parent plant, by planting the seeds in the same pot, by giving them the same amounts of water and sunlight, and so forth.

The *Chicago Daily News* and the *Milwaukee Journal* were using some elements of control when they sent reporters under *different* conditions to the *same* real-estate offices and hardware stores. One important element of control in this type of experiment is to make sure that the reporters act the same way except for the factor being studied. For instance, they should use exactly the same question-wording in both conditions.

Overall, the principle of control requires that, as much as possible, all factors are equivalent in the two conditions being studied except for the variable being manipulated.

RANDOMIZATION

Randomization can serve two important functions in experimental design. First, if investigators desire to generalize about some universe or population on the basis of their experiment, they need to select the subjects *randomly* for their experiments from that universe or population.

As an example, suppose one wanted to study the honesty of automobile repair garages in the Washington, D.C. area. The universe would be *all* automobile repair garages in the Washington area, and the sample should be prepared from a complete list of these stations. It will not be random if a reporter picks all the garages near the office. The details of drawing a random sample were discussed in Chapter 6.

The second function randomization can serve in experimental design is to make two different treatment groups equivalent. An example from medical research might make this function clear. Suppose investigators wanted to determine the effect of a new drug for treating hypertension (high blood pressure). They want to give the new drug to half of their sample of patients and a placebo to the other half. But they want the two groups to be equivalent prior to the introduction of the independent variable, the administration of the drug. Then, any differences found in the dependent variable (blood-pressure reading) can be attributed to the independent variable alone. The best way to make the groups equivalent is randomly to assign subjects to the two groups. By using random assignment, any variables that have not been controlled will be distributed randomly across the various conditions. Matching is sometimes used to make two experimental groups equivalent, but it is not as effective as random assignment of subjects to groups. Random assignment makes the two groups equivalent even on variables the experimenter has not thought of but that might affect the dependent variable.

STATISTICS

Many journalistic field experiments do not require statistical analysis. If three out of six real-estate offices in an area offer houses to white customers but not to black customers, that speaks for itself.

Or, consider an experimental investigation by behavioral scientist Frances K. Heussenstamm of whether Black Panthers were being harassed by police.[14] After hearing complaints from Panthers that they had received so many traffic tickets that they were in danger of losing their licenses, Heussenstamm discovered that all had Black Panther stickers on their automobile bumpers. She then conducted an experimental test by having fifteen drivers with no traffic violations for the preceding twelve months attach Pan-

---

[14] Frances K. Heussenstamm, "Bumper Stickers and the Cops," *Transaction* 8 (1971):32–33, as reprinted in Paul G. Swingle, ed., *Social Psychology in Natural Settings*, Aldine Publishing Co., Chicago, 1973, pp. 27–31.

ther stickers to their cars. After attaching the stickers, these drivers received thirty-three citations in seventeen days. Clearly no statistical test is necessary in this case to support the conclusion that people were being given tickets because of the Black Panther stickers.

But in other cases it is not so clear that an experimental variable is having an effect, and a statistical test will be necessary before a conclusion can be drawn. For example, behavioral scientists James Bryan and Mary Ann Test were interested in determining if altruistic behavior is influenced by modeling, that is, witnessing another person engage in the same altruistic act first.[15] They conducted a field experiment in which the dependent variable was whether or not a car stopped to render assistance to a woman with a flat tire. In the model condition, another car with a flat tire was located about one-quarter mile before the test vehicle and a woman was watching a male change a tire on the car. In the no-model condition, there was no earlier car.

This table shows the number of cars out of 2,000 that stopped to render aid in each condition:

	Model	No Model
Car stopped	58	35
Car failed to stop	1,942	1,965
	2,000	2,000

Of the 2,000 cars in the model condition, fifty-eight stopped to help the woman with the flat tire. In the condition with no model present, thirty-five of the 2,000 cars stopped. Bryan and Test wanted to know if modeling had an effect on whether or not the cars stopped. But it is not possible to determine this simply by looking at the numbers.

There is a difference in stopping rate between the two conditions, but it could be due simply to *chance fluctuations*. This is where a statistical test becomes useful. A statistical test—in this

---

[15] James H. Bryan and Mary Ann Test, "Models and Helping: Naturalistic Studies in Aiding Behavior," *Journal of Personality and Social Psychology* 6 (1967):400–407, as reprinted in Bickman and Henchy, *Beyond the Laboratory,* pp. 11–17.

case, a chi-square test is appropriate—will let you compute *the probability that the empirical difference found is due to chance alone.*

The chi-square test indicates that this difference in frequencies would happen by chance alone with a probability of .02, only two times in a hundred. This is less than .05, the general level of acceptance for a hypothesis in the behavioral sciences. So the investigators accepted the conclusion that the two conditions really were different and that modeling had an effect on this kind of altruistic behavior.

The Associated Press mail survey story also seems to be a case in which statistical analysis would have allowed the reporter to come to more definite conclusions. (This will be elaborated on a little later.)

Many simple experiments of the kinds that journalists are likely to conduct can be analyzed with one of three simple statistical tests: the t test, the chi-square test, and the sign test. The journalistic investigator should consult some of the standard statistics texts for the logic of these tests and the procedures used to compute them.[16]

ETHICS

Field experiments raise at least potential ethical questions because they are almost always conducted without the subjects' awareness that an experiment is taking place. One of the primary reasons for conducting field experiments, in fact, is to observe people's reactions without their awareness that they are being observed.

A behavioral scientist or a journalist conducting a field experiment needs to weigh carefully, then, whether it involves potential loss of dignity, psychological harm, or physical harm to the individuals involved in the experiment.

---

[16] Explanations of the t test can be found in Hubert M. Blalock, Jr., *Social Statistics*, McGraw-Hill, New York, 1960, or Wilfrid J. Dixon and Frank M. Massey, Jr., *Introduction to Statistical Analysis*, McGraw-Hill, New York, 1957. Explanations of the chi-square test and the sign test can be found in Sidney Siegel, *Nonparametric Statistics for the Behavioral Sciences*, McGraw-Hill, New York, 1956.

A useful test to consider is whether the planned field experiment will cause a person to do something he would not be doing ordinarily. Social psychologists Leonard Bickman and Thomas Henchy suggest that the well-designed field experiment should not be a disruptive force in the subject's environment, but should be a "simple acceleration of natural events." [17] By this test, there would seem to be no ethical problem with the *60 Minutes* car story, the *Milwaukee Journal* dynamite story, the Associated Press mail story, or the *Chicago Daily News* discrimination story. In all of these cases, reporters were simply dealing with businesses and other institutions in the same way that any member of the public does.

By the same test, one might raise some ethical questions about the WCKT-TV crime witness story. For this report, bystanders in public places were deceived into thinking they were witnessing crimes, including jewelry store robberies, kidnappings, and prisoner escapes. What if some bystander had attempted to prevent one of these apparent crimes and had been hurt in the process? There seems little question that the television station would have been legally liable for the harm the individual received.

Field experiments differ from laboratory experiments in that in field experiments the subjects have not consented to participate in an experiment. For this reason, behavioral scientists are usually especially concerned to make sure subjects are not harmed in field experiments. The journalist planning a field experiment should show a similar concern.

Critiques of Selected Journalistic Experiments

Journalists are already using the experimental method, perhaps out of an intuitive understanding of its advantages for demonstrating causality and investigating actual behavior rather than verbal reports of behavior. Some of these attempts, however, could have been strengthened with refinements from behavioral science methodology. Let us examine several

---

[17] Bickman and Henchy, *Beyond the Laboratory*, p. 5.

field experiments actually conducted by journalists to see how they could have been improved.

One weakness of the *Chicago Daily News* story from the point of view of experimental design was that the black reporter was a man and the white reporter was a woman. This meant the investigators were manipulating two independent variables simultaneously instead of just one. In behavioral science terminology, the variable of race was confounded with the variable of sex. Because of this confounding, it is not really possible to draw strong conclusions about the effect of race alone. The difference might be due solely to race; it might be due solely to sex; or it might be due to a combination of the two. A second weakness was that the dependent variable was not specified very clearly. Each reporter should have been looking for exactly the same thing when he or she visited the real-estate office. He or she should have asked the same crucial question or looked for the same crucial behavior. Only in this way could comparisons be made accurately. Apparently the two reporters did not make sure they obtained the same information.

The table constructed from information in the *Daily News* stories shows that in some cases the information obtained by the two reporters was not comparable. Was the dependent variable whether or not the reporter was told that a home was available? Was it whether or not the reporter was told he or she would be called if something became available? Was it something else entirely? Unless the dependent variable is clearly specified beforehand, one is likely to come up with results that are not strictly comparable. It is not that the effort is wasted; it is just that a little careful planning would make it more useful.

A third problem is that two of the cells in the table contain no useful information because one reporter did not succeed in talking to someone at two of the real-estate offices. For Wojciechowski Realty and Soltes Realty, the table lacks information on the treatment of a white customer. This removes two of the six possible comparisons from consideration.

The story also would have been strengthened if a summary table of the type shown here had been printed in the newspaper.

Reactions of Real-Estate Offices to Requests for Housing

	Reactions to Black Reporter	Reactions to White Reporter
Wojciechowski Realty	"I don't have homes in Gage Park."	Not mentioned in story
Pech-Suski	No listings—"If something pops up, I'll let you know."	"Yes, I've got some listings."
Soltes Realty	Secretary said all the managers were on vacation.	Story said the door was locked.
Ernest Geissler Co.	"We closed our real-estate business about a month ago."	Not a "single listing," but took the number in case something came up.
Stevens & Sons	Only three homes available, one which hadn't cleared and the others which the manager thought the reporter wouldn't like.	Said there was a bungalow that hadn't been cleared and some higher listings.
Heineman Realty	"We haven't had anything for the last two months."	"I don't have a thing right now," but offered to take number.

SOURCE: Compiled from *Chicago Daily News.*

Such a table lets the reader get the total picture more clearly than the detailed report on each real-estate office contained in the stories.

DYNAMITE PURCHASE STORY

The *Milwaukee Journal* story would have been improved by giving a clear indication of how many hardware stores were visited and what the results were at each. This could have been done simply and effectively with a summary table similar to the one compiled from the information in the *Chicago Daily News* discrimination stories.

The *Journal* experiment also had the weakness that the variable of age was confounded with the variable of clothing. One reporter was dressed like a student and wore a "ROTC Must Go" button; the other wore work clothes to look like a farmer or construction worker. However, the one wearing student clothes was twenty-three years old, while the one dressed like a farmer was forty-four years old. If a difference had been found in whether or not they were sold dynamite, it would be impossible to determine if it were because of clothing alone, age alone, or a combination of the two.

CAR REPAIR STORY

The *60 Minutes* news team found impressive evidence that many service stations defraud the public since all six stations they visited recommended unnecessary work.

The major problem is that we do not know how the sample of garages was drawn and what population the sample was drawn from. Correspondent Morley Safer said on the program that the six garages were chosen at random. But from what population? The population is only vaguely specified in the phrase "all of them near the nation's Capitol." What were the exact geographical boundaries from which garages were selected? What was considered to be a "garage"? What kinds of places were included in the list of garages from which the sample was drawn? Was the sample truly random?

These points are not just technicalities. The question of how generally the *60 Minutes* findings apply, and thus the question of how widespread is the defrauding, depends on the care with which the population being studied was specified and the random sample was drawn.

POSTAL SURVEY

Two parts of this Associated Press survey can be considered genuine field experiments—the investigations of the effectiveness of zip codes and air mail. The analysis of each of these and the attempt to reach some conclusions would have been improved by the use of statistical tests. The zip-code analysis will be discussed, although the same general points apply to the air-mail analysis.

It appears doubtful that the AP statement "there was no consistent pattern" is an adequate summary of these results. When these figures are analyzed statistically, using the sign test, it becomes clear that zip-coded letters arrived significantly ahead of non-zipped letters.

Converting the percentages back to numbers of letters indicates there were ninety-one cases in which the zip-coded letter arrived ahead of the non-zipped letter, 257 cases in which they arrived together, and forty-eight cases in which the non-zipped letter arrived ahead of the zipped letter. The sign test indicates that the probability of finding this much difference between arrival patterns of zipped and non-zipped letters due to chance alone is less than .01, one time in a hundred. A t test could also be computed to see if the difference in average arrival times is significant, although the information reported in the news article is not sufficient to compute a t test.

Statistical tests, then, permit a more definite conclusion about whether or not zip-coding has an effect on the speed with which mail arrives than is possible from merely staring at the figures and trying to decide what they mean.

CRIME WITNESS STORY

One problem with the WCKT-TV report may be that it tried to deal with too many different types of crime. The events staged were a jewelry store break-in, some purse snatching, an act of resisting arrest, several shopliftings, four kidnappings, and the boarding of a bus near the jail by a man wearing handcuffs.

The description of the documentary by news director Gene Strul does not make clear how many stagings of each crime occurred, and of that number, how many resulted in bystander intervention. The overall impression is that no one intervened, but the article itself reported that a supermarket employee chased a man apparently resisting arrest, and that another bystander made "a weak effort" to chase a purse snatcher. Apparently some bystanders attempted to intervene and some did not. The reader or viewer should be given, then, an accurate count for each crime that was staged of how many attempted to intervene and how many did not. This might have required that some crimes be simulated more times than they were. Some were apparently staged only once.

Another refinement that other journalists studying this topic might consider is some causal analysis of the bystander non-intervention. Are there factors that make a difference in whether or not a bystander attempts to intervene? The WCKT documentary did not attempt a causal investigation other than to blame the non-intervention on apathy. But "apathy" is not an explanation of non-intervention. It is just basically a synonym.

A causal investigation would involve identifying variables that might have an effect on bystander intervention and then manipulating these variables in a field experiment. Examples of such variables would be modeling (Is a bystander more likely to intervene when he has just seen others intervene?) and perceived threat (Is a bystander less likely to intervene when it appears he himself will be harmed?). This is the approach that behavioral scientists have taken to studying citizen action in public places. Examples are Bryan and Test's study of the effects of modeling on helping behavior discussed earlier and Harvey Allen's study of the effects of perceived threat on helping behavior in the subway.[18]

In a close parallel to the WCKT-TV documentary, behavioral scientists Bibb Latané and Donald Elman simulated the robbery of a case of beer from a store while the cashier was in the back of the store.[19] This field experiment was repeated ninety-six times. The dependent variable was whether or not customers in the store would report the theft. The researchers also looked at three independent variables to see if they had any effect on whether or not bystanders reported the theft. These were the number of robbers (one or two), the sex of the bystander, and the number of bystanders. The only variable that made a significant difference was the number of bystanders. Bystanders were more likely to report the theft when they were alone: 65 percent of the single cus-

---

[18] Harvey Allen, "Bystander Intervention and Helping on the Subway," in Bickman and Henchy, *Beyond the Laboratory*, pp. 22–33.

[19] Bibb Latané and Donald Elman, "The Bystander and the Thief," as reprinted in Swingle, *Social Psychology in Natural Settings*, pp. 61–70.

tomers reported the theft, while in only 56 percent of the two-person groups did even one person report the theft.

The Need for Creative Thinking

The creative journalist will be able to think of many ideas for stories based on field experiments. Here are a few others that journalists have tried. Sam Adams, a black reporter for the *St. Petersburg Times*, conducted a field experiment using himself and his wife as the experimental stimuli when he did a series of articles on compliance in the South with the Civil Rights Act of 1964. Traveling through the South without revealing he was a reporter, Adams was able to observe the actual behavior of restaurant and hotel owners toward a black traveler.

How honest are television repairmen? Do they replace parts in a television set that don't need replacing? The *Ottawa* (Canada) *Citizen* conducted an investigation of these questions by taking a brand new television set, in perfect condition except for one burned-out tube, to a number of repair shops.[20] The paper found wide differences in the shops' diagnoses of the trouble and in their charges. Apparently as a result of this investigation, the television repair shop owners began forming an association and drawing up a television-repair code.

The *Citizen* also conducted a similar investigation of Ottawa area pharmacies to see if they were overcharging.[21] Many pharmacies in Ottawa had signed an agreement to participate in the PARCOST program, designed to insure "Prescriptions at Reasonable Cost." Two *Citizen* reporters had a cooperating physician write them ten prescriptions for penicillin and ten for Diazepam, a tranquilizer. They then presented the prescriptions at ten PARCOST pharmacies. Seven of the pharmacies charged more than they should under the program. The resulting article led to an investigation by the Ontario College of Pharmacy, the body responsible for licensing pharmacists, and resulted in disciplinary action against some pharmacists.

---

[20] "TV Repairs: A New Code," *Ottawa Citizen*, April 1, 1971.
[21] "Some Ottawa Area Pharmacies Overcharging Public for Drugs," *Ottawa Citizen*, Nov. 27, 1971.

How much fuel can be saved by lowering the thermostat? Reporter Benjamin P. Burtt of the *Syracuse Herald-Journal* answered the question by conducting experiments in his home.[22] He tried the thermostat at different settings and recorded the number of hours the oil burner ran per day. He did the experiment on a number of different days to account for differences in outside temperature. He found that lowering his thermostat from 75 degrees to 65 degrees would save 22 percent of his fuel bill.

A different twist was given to the bystander intervention story idea by Judith Neilson, a journalism student at San Francisco State University. She had herself tied to a telephone pole on a busy residential street in San Francisco and waited to see how much time elapsed before someone helped her. She waited sixteen minutes and watched 110 cars pass before one stopped and a man asked if she were all right.

Summary

Field experiments can be useful to the journalist for identifying causes and effects, for observing people's actual behavior instead of their verbal statements about their behavior, and for observing events that happen infrequently in everyday life.

Many journalists are already attempting field experiments, perhaps out of an intuitive understanding of their advantages. Journalists can improve their experiments if they keep in mind a few principles that the behavioral scientist uses to make experiments sounder. These principles include specifying both the independent and dependent variables clearly, drawing a careful sample, controlling other variables, using statistics to interpret results, using tables to display results, and considering the ethics of experiments that might result in loss of dignity or harm to a person.

---

[22] Benjamin P. Burtt, "Tests Prove You Can Save Fuel, Electricity," *Syracuse Herald-Journal*, Nov. 26, 1973.

Part 3

Nature of News

Chapter 11

Translating Data into Community Information

Steven Chaffee
Donald Lewis Shaw

Even if journalists gather their evidence in the same ways a behavioral scientist might, their approach to the knotty problems of presenting that data should be different. A scientist reports to other scientists, and they will want to see enough of the data so they can check the conclusions. A reporter, on the other hand, writes mainly for people whose primary interest extends only so far as knowledge conclusions. The journalist presents precise data sparingly, if at all. Audiences read or listen for the general story, so the reporter gives them only as much detail as is needed to tell that story accurately, concisely, and clearly. To say this is not to bestow approval on common journalistic practice, but simply to acknowledge that it has become an institutionalized procedure that reporters follow and that editors and audiences expect. It is not likely to be replaced, but it certainly can be improved upon.

Within the general traditions of journalistic presentation of quantifications and scientific inferences can be found examples ranging from the skilled to the abysmal. The difference can often be traced to the reporter's knowledge of the available options and when to use one instead of another. The difference also comes from the thought and care given to the details of presentation. In

273

this chapter we shall survey some of the most useful forms of presentation and compare various options within each form.

Numbers, Words, or Graphics?

Numbers do not speak for themselves in science or in journalism. They need context, and they benefit greatly from interpretation. But quantitative values in some form lie at the heart of any empirical presentation—a category that, hopefully, includes journalistic reporting. A critical decision for the writer is the mode of presentation. Generally speaking, there are three options. Numbers themselves can be used or they can be replaced by verbal interpretations or by graphic presentations.

Scientists routinely use precise numbers to describe quantities, and this might seem to be a reasonable procedure for non-scientists as well. But journalists observe solemn taboos against the profligate use of raw numbers. Most newspapers, for instance, either prohibit the use of a number at the beginning of a sentence, or discourage it by requiring that the figure be spelled out in word form. Numbers are studiously avoided in television news broadcasts, and when they are necessary, they are likely to be repeated or shown simultaneously on the video track in some fashion. Temperature forecasts in weather broadcasts are a good example.

One reason for the sparse use of numbers is that print and broadcast media are designed for quick reading or casual listening. It takes unusual mental effort to swallow a number of any size. But perhaps a better reason is that it is too easy to substitute a meaningless numerical statement for thoughtful reporting. A good test of the value of a number is to delete it or replace it by another figure and ask whether it makes any difference. For example, the statement, "There are —— miles of railroad track in Afghanistan" is likely to be equally uninteresting whatever number appears in the blank. This is a good sign that the figure—and probably the whole sentence—can safely be omitted.

Another sensible reason for avoiding precise numbers in reporting is that measurement of socially significant events is notoriously imprecise. Suppose a pollster asks a national random sample of 1,500 adults, "In politics, do you usually consider yourself a Republican, a Democrat, or something else?" If 640 of them say "Democrat," the pollster is scientifically correct in reporting that 42.7 percent gave that response. But this hardly means that exactly 42.7 percent of the nation's voters are Democrats. As we know from Chapters 4, 5, and 6, that figure is subject to many sources of distortion—sampling error, biases in the framing of the question, the appearance and voice of the interviewer, news events of the moment, and so on. A more sensible statement might be that "40 to 45 percent" or even "some four out of ten" consider themselves Democrats.

An even better method would be to compare this result with those of other polls, voting returns, and other kinds of evidence, and develop a general conclusion such as, "Recent surveys show that Democrats, the majority party since the New Deal era, have become a minority party again, but they still outnumber Republicans and Independents." In this example, numbers do not appear at all, although exact survey and statistical data lie behind the terms "majority" and "minority," which indicate that the democratically magical 50-percent line has been crossed.

Most journalistic use of quantitative data takes this sort of general, somewhat vague, verbal form. Readers and journalists, themselves, are often unaware of the extent to which quantitative concepts permeate news reporting. A major section of this chapter will be devoted to a review of some popular (and often loosely used) terms that represent quantifications and inferences based on data.

Graphic presentations also are highly prized in journalism. On television, the map or simple graph provides welcome relief from the constant image of the newscaster, who is on camera more of the time than either viewers or program directors like. Even more so, newspapers and magazines are in constant need of "art" to break up the grayness of their pages of print. Photographs are the most common form of art, but only because they are so plentiful. If more graphic material were available to accompany news stories, it would quite likely be used. Planning and preparation of various graphic devices for clarity and emphasis will often justify the extra effort required.

Integral or Separate Presentation?

Another set of options for reporters concerns the integration of quantitative data into an article or story versus the alternative of segregating this material into an entirely separate piece. When a major story is connected with a fairly complex body of data that can stand alone as an independent presentation, the *sidebar* is often used in newspapers and magazines. This is less common in broadcast news if only because quantitative information itself is less commonly used.

A sidebar can be devoted entirely to analysis of data or it might simply include more detail of several kinds, including numerical data. (Of course, there are many totally non-quantitative sidebars, too, such as the "human interest angle" piece that tells personal background or interesting anecdotes about people in the news.) The main purpose of the sidebar is to present information that would interest a sizeable subsegment of the audience but that would intrude too much on the telling of the main story. For example, when a government budget is proposed or enacted, it is a major piece of news. The main story must report such angles as the political forces and arrangements surrounding the budget compromises, the reactions of various officials, and the overall dollar figures. Important details, such as programs that have been eliminated or expanded and the particular kinds of tax increases that citizens should expect, can be handled better in a separate story. A sidebar article, or better yet a graph, explaining where the money will come from and will go would be at least as important as the story on the budget, although perhaps not as newsworthy by common journalistic standards.

To sum up, the reporter can think of the choices for data presentation as falling into four general categories, depending on whether verbal or graphic materials are used and whether the information is integrated into the main story or presented separately:

	Words	Art
Part of main story	Quantitative terms or figures in text or in caption for art connected to text.	Graphic display of data, accompanying text; may be noted in text also.
Separate item	Sidebar story that appears near main story or is located elsewhere, but noted with main story.	Graphic sidebar display that stands alone with caption and is self-explanatory.

These descriptions obviously refer to the print media. For television, words and art can be more easily integrated with one another by using superimposed visual information or by presenting general elements of the story orally and quantitative elements visually, or vice versa.

While the concept of a sidebar is not so widely recognized in broadcast journalism, it is common to have pieces by different reporters presented one after another. One reporter might, for example, broadcast from the capitol where the budget has just been approved by a legislative conference committee; then, another reporter appears from a studio to give a run-down on what elements comprise that budget. Broadcast journalists probably have more difficulty integrating the fragments of their news stories into a single presentation than do their print media counterparts. With skillful editing, however, these separate reports can be combined to give the listener a coherent picture of what has happened.

Quantitative Concepts

Thus far, quantitative data have been discussed from the viewpoint of the reporter as the producer or "outputer" of information. Other chapters in this book deal with different aspects of quantitative *inputs*. To tie these activities together, we need to think of the reporter mostly as a *processor* of information. That is, the key activity for which a reporter is responsible is to translate technical material into a form that can be understood readily by a general audience. To accomplish this, the reporter needs to know a great deal more information than will actually be presented. More important to our immediate purposes here, the reporter needs to understand some technical and scientific concepts that may never surface directly in the reporting output. These are the rudimentary concepts and terms of behavioral science. Although they may sound like so many "buzz words" at first, they are necessary tools. Without them, no journalist can assume a reliable footing for interpreting data and processing it into a form appropriate for general audience consumption.

VARIABLES

Both behavioral science reporting and journalistic reporting consist, in large measure, of the observation and systematic description of *differences*—differences in the same thing from one time to another, differences between two things at the same time, differences between one thing and an objective standard of judgment, and so forth. This vague term *thing* refers to what a scientist would call a *unit of analysis*. In a budget, the units of analysis are such things as dollars, departments and programs, cities and counties, months, and so forth. In an election, the units of analysis might be candidates, voters, aldermanic districts, or referenda. While a physicist, who is studying such subtle phenomena as light, photosynthesis, or gravity, must be quite careful in defining the units of analysis, the journalist usually assumes that this is straightforward and obvious. Most of the time it is, but sometimes a reporter's attempt to analyze a story quantitatively becomes fouled up simply because the reporter failed to define the subject and failed to stick to it.

Neither the scientist nor the reporter observes everything about any unit of analysis. It would be impossible, for example, to describe *totally* one person, much less one city or neighborhood. What we do instead is define *dimensions of observation*. When we describe a person, it is usually in terms of a few commonly used dimensions or attributes such as height, age, sex, hair color, and so on. Cities can be described along such dimensions as size, geographic region, or predominant occupations among the residents. Chapter 2 on *social indicators* suggested many other attributes of cities and neighborhoods for description.

A dimension or attribute on which different units of analysis have different values is called a *variable*. Quantitative descriptions consist of differences observed on one or more variables. Thus, length is a very useful variable for describing many physical objects such as streets, lists, noses, and sticks, although it is obviously not applicable to everything. The key fact to remember about a variable is that it is a dimension for *comparing* things and identifying differences among them.

Almost all descriptions that a journalist will find meaningful are comparative. For instance, the dimension *small–large* might be used to describe a baby as "small" and a railroad spike as "large." Obviously the comparisons implied in those descriptions are different. A baby is smaller than other people and a spike is larger than a nail or a pin. Journalists are also occasionally careless about the comparisons their descriptions imply. But as professional reporters, they should hold themselves to a higher standard than other people. To describe a six-foot man as "tall" is accurate enough perhaps in most comparative contexts, but not if he is a member of a basketball team.

AVERAGES

To most people, *average* means you and me. To a baseball player, *average* means life or death. To scientists it means one thing *and* another, for which they use various terms. These differences can be quite confusing to the layman, and it is the reporter's responsibility to clarify them.

If a variable can be broken up into several categories, the *mode* is the category in which there is the greatest number of units. For instance, if voters are divided into the categories Democrat, Republican, and Independent, the mode is the category that has the greatest number of people in it, which could be as few as 34 percent of the people, if things were very evenly divided. The mode might be very useful for describing the *average* value on some variables, particularly if the categories cannot be put in any certain order. For example, we are not certain whether Independent voters are to the left of Democrats, to the right of Republicans, or in between the two major parties. Probably the label "Independent" covers all three of these political types, and so it cannot be put in any certain order with the two party labels.

On the other hand, the mode can present a very innaccurate picture of average in some cases. For instance, the modal age of all persons in the world is probably less than one year. That is, there are more babies in their first year of life than there are one-year-olds, more one-year-olds than two-year-olds, and so forth. But it would hardly be sensible to say that the average person is a child less than a year in age. For *ordered variables*, either the *median* or the *mean* usually comes much closer to what we intend to indicate by the idea of average.

If a series of units are arranged in order on a dimension, from smallest to largest in terms of that variable, then the middle unit in that series is the *median*. Put another way, the median is the unit that divides the upper half of the distribution from the lower half. For instance, if a family has five children whose ages are 1, 5, 8, 10, and 13, the median age of the children is 8. If the parents are added to this distribution, then the median age in the family as a whole is 10. Why? If another child is born, the median age in the family would be calculated as halfway between the two ages in the middle, which in this case would make the family's median age 9 years, even though there is no one in the family who is 9 years old; 9 is the number between 8 and 10. It is the middle, or median, number.

The *mean* is the concept most often intended by the term average. If a series of quantitative values on a dimension are added and divided by the number of units, the result is the *arithmetic mean*. In the case of the ages of the five children just mentioned, the mean is 7.4 years:

$$[(1 + 5 + 8 + 10 + 13) \div 5 = 37 \div 5 = 7.4].$$

However, the careful reader should have noticed that this is an underestimate unless all five children are having their birthdays today. On the average (that is, the assumed mean case), we should expect the children to be about halfway between birthdays; so we should add half a year to each of their ages. For purposes of calculating the mean age, it comes to the same thing if we add half a year to the mean, which we would then *estimate* at 7.4 + .5, or 7.9 years.

As even this seemingly simple example demonstrates, the precision of the arithmetic mean is often lost because we do not have data precise enough to calculate it accurately. It does not make sense, then, to report a highly precise mean (for example, 7.9 years) when it is based on raw data that are in fact really less precise than that. Let us call this practice *overprecision* and identify it as a cardinal sin of reporting. It is overly precise to report the mean age of those children as 7.9 years. Since the original data were reported in years, we should estimate the mean no more precisely than that. The average age of those children, for reporting purposes, is 8 years.

In the preceding example, both the median and the mean (corrected for overprecision) were the same—8 years. Often this will not be the case. But other times, the mean and the median will be close enough together that either is sufficiently accurate. It is especially important to note that they will be quite different in cases where there are many extreme cases at one end of the continuum but not at the other.

A good example of a variable where the mode, median, and mean differ substantially is in the distribution of personal income. Because most people's incomes are clustered near the lower end of the distribution (between zero and $10,000 or so in the United States), the mode will be fairly low. But, because there are quite a few people with very high incomes (above $100,000), the mean will be a lot higher than the mode. The median income usually falls in between the mode and the mean and is the average that is most often reported. It describes precisely the income earned by the middle person—the one who makes less money than half the people and more money than the other half.

To take a more extreme example, consider an oil-rich sheikdom in the Middle East that is ruled by one man whose income is, say, $100,000,000 a year. If there are 50,000 other inhabitants, none of them earning more than $1,000 a year, the mean income would be about three (or more) times as much as the median, but it would not be an accurate description. The median or the mode obviously gives a more accurate idea of the average income in such a country than does the mean.

It has often been remarked that Republicans like to talk about mean income, while Democrats prefer to discuss the median. Socialists, of course, dwell more on the mode. These are not just different ways of saying the same thing, but are different ways of viewing reality. Different concepts of average refer to different things, and it *does* matter which you choose to report.

RATIOS

A highly useful technique for describing a mean is in terms of a *ratio*. For example, the average number of students *per* school, or the average income *per* family, or the average inches of rainfall in a locale *per* year, are all ratios. One kind of unit of analysis (students, income, or inches of rainfall) is being divided by another (school, family, or year).

The most important point to remember about ratios is that they cannot themselves be averaged unless they are converted to the original units and recalculated. For example, if the average annual income in Los Angeles is $10,000 and in San Francisco it is $12,000, the average for the two cities is *not* $11,000 because Los Angeles has many more people than San Francisco. To calculate a mean for the two cities, the total dollar amounts for both must be combined and then divided by the total population of the two cities. The mean will be considerably less than $11,000.

Perhaps this point can be demonstrated more vividly by a classical riddle. Suppose a driver is approaching a hill. The distance from the bottom to the top is one mile and from the top to the bottom on the other side is also one mile. She drives up the hill from the bottom at thirty miles an hour. When she reaches the top, she decides that she wants to average 60 miles per hour for the entire hill. How fast would she have to drive down the hill to achieve this (mean) average? The answer is *not* ninety miles per hour. In fact, it is impossible for her to average sixty miles per hour for the whole distance. In order to do that, she would have had to drive the two miles in two minutes. But in driving the first mile at thirty miles per hour she had *already* used up two minutes. Once the ratio (miles per hour) has been broken down into its original units of distance and time, it appears simple. And yet few people can solve this simple riddle when asked, because they try to calculate the mean of a ratio to find an answer.

STATISTICS

A single observation of the value of one item on a variable dimension is technically called a *datum;* the plural is *data.* The term datum, for instance, is used in antisubmarine warfare to refer to the last known location of the submarine that is being tracked by a sub-killer ship. Since quantitative observations usually make sense only in comparison with one another, we almost always deal with data rather than with a single datum. Since this is a plural noun, it is appropriate to say "these data are" rather than "this data is."

When data are grouped or organized into summary forms, they are often called *statistics.* This term is used very broadly in journalism, but it has a somewhat more specific meaning in science. As has been explained in Chapter 6, data may be gathered either from an entire universe or population (a *census*) or from a *random sample* that represents that population in all respects—within the probabilistic range of sampling error, of course.

When data from a census are available, the variables that have been measured are called *parameters.* That is, a parameter is one dimension of variation on which all the units in the universe under study can be compared. When a random sample from the universe has been taken, rather than a full census, the data on these same variables are called *statistics*. A statistic is, then, a probabilistic estimate of a parameter.

The word statistics is often inaccurately applied to other kinds of data besides random sample estimates of parameters. (Even more careless are those who use it to refer to the boundaries or limits of a body of data. They usually have the word *perimeter* in mind.) Parameter is one of many technical terms that have come to be increasingly used as "buzz words" by some journalists who want to sound more erudite than they are. But, if we assume that the purpose of reporting is to communicate information, such words have no legitimate place in journalism, except in the occasional cases where they are important enough to be explained *and* used properly.

Buzz words can be thought of as the extreme opposite of over-precision. They constitute a combination of imprecision and overwriting. Among other quantitative buzz words in current vogue are *significant difference, normal curve, skewed distribution, reliability, probable range of error, standard deviation,* and *validity.* All of these have important technical meanings that can only be eroded by thoughtless misuse. Any introductory statistics textbook explains them.

CORRELATION AND CAUSATION

There are three general levels of scientific activity. The first is measurement by *classification* of units on a single variable. The second is the measurement of *association* between two variables. The third is the inference of *causation* between one variable and another. A key concept for the second and third levels is *correlation,* which is a statistical measure of association and is also one of three key elements of causation. When two variables tend to change together, they are said to be correlated. Tall persons tend to weigh more than short persons; in other words, height is correlated with weight.

If two variables are *not* correlated with one another, then it would be hard to argue that one might be causing the other. But the reverse is not necessarily true. The fact that two variables have been found to be correlated does *not* mean that one of them *must* be the cause of the other. Other kinds of scientific evidence, in addition to correlation, are needed before it would be reasonable to conclude that there is evidence of a causal relationship. Correlation is simply the first element. For example, to choose between the conclusions "height causes weight" and "weight causes height," you would need *time-order* evidence—does an increase in height tend to come before an increase in weight or vice versa? Even more, a scientist in pursuit of causation tries to determine the nature of the causal relationship. If, as evidence indicates, an increase in height does tend to precede an increase in weight, why does it?

It is especially important to avoid describing a correlation between two variables in a way that would suggest that the relationship is causal unless there were additional evidence of causation. Two variables could be, and often are, correlated statistically although they are not really connected in any direct causal way at all. For instance, there is a correlation between skin cancer and the age at which a person quit school. There is no causal connection (going to school does not prevent skin cancer). It just happens that older persons, who are more prone to skin cancer, went to school at a time when it was common to drop out at a much younger age than is normal today. Scientists call this kind of noncausal association a *spurious* or *artifactual* correlation. The alert reporter especially should be chronically suspicious of correlations when they are offered as the major evidence for a conclusion of causation.

Choosing the Right Word, Avoiding the Wrong One

Since the most common method of presenting quantitative and scientific information is in narrative form, we need to review some of the terms that are in common journalistic use. Some examples have already been given. Here is a more systematic run-down, with italics indicating words to watch.

ABSOLUTES

There are very few *absolutely definitive* statements that can be made about anything of continuing importance in human affairs. This, of course, does not discourage people from saying such things, but it should discourage reporters from repeating them. Two favored terms to indicate absolute statements these days are *categorically* and *unequivocally*. Some people prefer to quantify this sort of fiction, as in the phrase *one hundred percent* or the cliché *every single time*. The superlative versions go one step better, as in *one thousand* percent and the over-worn redundant phrase *each and every*.

Occasionally there is a need to claim that something is absolutely different from everything else, for which purpose the terms *singular* and *unique* are used. (Note that it is a contradiction in terms to be *somewhat unique*.) Those who are aware of our lack of absolute knowledge are apt to *question the validity* of almost any statement. Since all statements are of questionable validity, that is a *truism*. Journalists would do well to heed the advice marital counselors often give: *"Never say always."*

FREQUENCY

Events that occur only once are accorded much more dignity by journalists than by behavioral scientists. Our news values require this attention. But a thorough behavioral scientist would account also for all significant events, not just the frequent ones. So journalists need scarcely apologize for concentrating on singular happenings. But when they deal with more frequently occurring things, they should not be overwhelmed by highly abstract claims from behavioral scientists. The main trick is to distinguish between the *example* of a recurrent event and the *instance* of a rare or inexplicable one.

There is a rich, though fuzzy, lexicon for dealing with frequency. The ordering *always/often/sometimes/rarely/never* seems to be fairly well agreed upon. The seemingly clear-cut *more than half of the time* unfortunately is too cumbersome to have entered the common language, but its meaning is tolerably well served by *mostly, normally, usually, commonly,* and *typi-*

cally. All these terms indicate more than *occasionally* and less than the melodic *almost always.*

There is some terminological overlap between statements about events that have been observed fairly frequently in the past and predictions about the future. This is because our best guide to what might happen is what has been happening. So, statements of the *more-often-than-not* variety take on the crystal-ball aura of *probably, likely,* and *chances are,* plus the smug *expectably* and *predictably.*

In a class by itself is the oft-invoked *vast majority.* To a politician, though not to others, a slight majority is at the least *substantial* or *clear.* Even a non-majority, properly called a *plurality* when it is the largest of several minority percentages in a field, has a way of becoming a *mandate* to politicians. The rhetoric of politics tends to obscure the size of a proportion, and the reporter should be able to cut through it to the less flowery facts even if the politician is not.

Unanticipated events are too often ascribed to *luck* or *chance* or are dismissed as *random* or an *aberration.* The reporter should assume that there are reasons for all the things people do and should try to uncover them. What seems to be a chance event might turn out to be an important news lead, precisely because it was not expected to happen.

If there is a lot of something but it does not occur very frequently, the term *many* and its near-synonyms *manifold, multifarious, myriad,* and *ubiquitous* can be popular obscurers. A clever ploy for inflating the trivial is the ominous *already,* as in "He has *already* taken to drinking beer." At any rate, let us stop a minute and consider our readers or viewers more closely.

Using Fires as a Community Example

In the end, your responsibility is to explain your story to the readers or viewers. How can you best enable them to understand what you are saying? Often some visual will help, but which visual? And what should we show anyway? Let us look at a simple community example. Suppose you are writing a story about how well your fire department performed last year in putting out fires and holding down property damage. You interview officials in the fire department and also obtain data from their records. Last year, the fire department answered 143 real calls. (There were seventy-two false alarms.) The total estimated property damage was $2,608,400. Of this, home fires accounted for 101 of the calls and $518,000 in estimated property damage; business fires accounted for the balance. There were no deaths or serious injuries. Month by month, if you charted the information obtained, it would look something like the information in Table 1.

ANALYZING THE DATA

What do all those figures in Table 1 really mean and what data should be selected for the

TABLE 1 *Monthly Record of Fires*

Month	Number of homes	Estimated damage	Number of businesses	Estimated damage	Total number both	Total estimated damage
January	11	$62,300	4	$199,100	15	$261,400
February	15	93,100	6	298,000	21	391,100
March	8	35,200	2	90,000	10	125,200
April	7	52,000	3	106,000	10	158,000
May	6	22,400	5	250,000	11	272,400
June	8	18,300	2	55,000	10	73,300
July	10	39,900	2	35,000	12	74,900
August	7	32,000	1	105,000	8	137,000
September	5	25,400	0	—	5	25,400
October	9	45,000	6	300,000	15	345,000
November	4	27,000	8	432,300	12	459,300
December	11	65,400	3	220,000	14	285,400
Totals	101	$518,000	42	$2,090,400	143	$2,608,400

reader? How should it be presented? Take a minute and examine these numbers more closely. One fact is prominent. There were far more fires in homes than in businesses—101 versus 42. You know that there are many more homes in a community than there are businesses, so that is not surprising. But you might make a note to yourself to ask whether the *proportion* of homes in which there was a serious fire was greater than the *proportion* of businesses. You might also make a note to ask the fire chief and the fire insurance experts which proportion is normally higher—homes or businesses. Maybe this community is different. Here, businesses may be more careful about observing fire safety precautions. Maybe the fire department is slow in answering calls to residential areas. Is there sufficient equipment? Perhaps the fire reporting system is inadequate in a growing community.

What about *means, medians,* or *modes?* A few simple calculations will show you that the mean residential damage amounted to $5,128, while the average for businesses was $49,771, considerably higher, as one might expect. Or should one? Ask your sources. Careful attention to data can lead to more effective use of other journalistic techniques such as personal interviews.

Examination for modes reveals that some months are much more likely to result in damage than are other months. February was the worst month for home fires and November the worst for business fires. Perhaps this has something to do with the winter months when heating systems are in action. That is a *hypothesis* that can be checked out (and perhaps it will suggest a convenient way to show your information to the reader). Certainly now you have a point of view for further information gathering and analysis.

Table 2 shows what we have when the twelve months of Table 1 are divided seasonally. The separation into residential versus business fires is kept since there are different problems in preventing fires in each category. Our hypothesis that fires may be worse during winter months is confirmed by Table 2 for both homes and businesses. For homes, there were *more* fires in these months, and the average fire resulted in *more* estimated damage. For businesses, there was actually one less fire in the winter than fall (thirteen versus fourteen), although the average damage was somewhat greater in the winter. Here you might make another note to ask during follow-up interviews if this has anything to do with heating systems being in operation. Ask why are there fewer summer fires and are they put out more quickly? They do result in less damage. You can think of other questions raised by these simple figures that can be pursued when you go to *other sources* in an attempt to explain the trends. You might, for instance, look at the records of local fire insurance companies. With what you know now, you can look for more specific information than you might have originally.

What will you show the reader or viewer? You could just use the figures in Table 1, the month-by-month run-down. Or, you could use Table 2 in which the same information is shown broken down into seasons. This would be easier for your audience than Table 1. But most likely you will want to use a combination of text plus a graphic presentation of what you regard as the most important information.

The annual number of home and business fires is easily handled in the text, as is the yearly *range* of fires—the month with the most fires and the month with the least fires. But, in order to emphasize that the winter months are the ones in which you need to be most cautious, months in which you are in most danger from

TABLE 2 *Seasonal Record of Fires*

Season	Number of homes	Estimated damages	Average damage	Number of businesses	Estimated damage	Average damage
Spring (Mar.–May)	21	$109,600	$5,219	10	$446,000	$44,600
Summer (June–Aug.)	25	90,200	3,608	5	195,000	39,000
Fall (Sept.–Nov.)	18	97,400	5,411	14	732,300	52,307
Winter (Dec.–Feb.)	37	220,800	5,967	13	717,100	55,161
Totals	101	$518,000	$5,128	42	$2,090,400	$49,771

a fire, you can use a pie chart, line graph, or bar graph. In general, pie charts and bar graphs are best for showing overviews of the big picture. Tables are best for presenting detailed information, as we have done here. Figure 1 shows the main information from Table 2, presented in the form of a bar graph. Notice how well the bar graph illustrates the seasonal variations in business and home fires. This conveys the substance of the findings *and* is visually attractive. The message can be detailed in the story or a caption that accompanies the graph.

Of course, you could do other things. You might show the *mean* or *modal* or *median* number of fires per month by seasons

FIGURE 1   *Danger, Fire! In Your Homes and Businesses Average Fire Damage by Seasons*

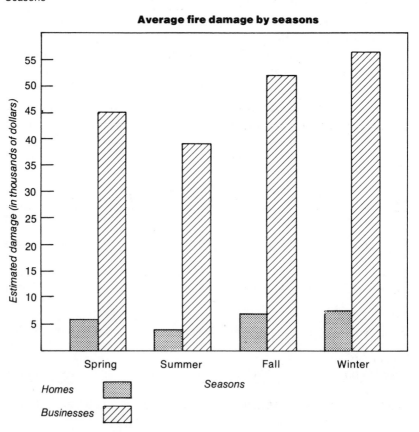

(or by any other logical grouping). You could obtain and show the average fire loss that was covered by insurance. You could compare losses against those of other years or other communities. There are many ways to translate such data into graphic information.

But don't bury your reader or viewer in pie charts, tables, or bar graphs. Use visuals sparingly to highlight the most important trends that will help the audience understand community issues. Solid reporting deserves excellent presentation, and your job is not done when you give your story to the copy desk. It is finished when the reader or viewer understands.

DATA FOREVER

There are many more ways we could consider data. We could discuss concepts of *central tendency* in more detail as well as *variation, time trends,* and claims of *causality.* For journalists seeking to explain very complex issues, these will prove important topics.

In coming years, many journalists will be digging into data gathering and analysis more deeply, especially as computer technology enables us to store and retrieve large amounts of information and as we develop more sophisticated techniques for gathering community information. But, of course, we cannot forget that our task, like that of John Campbell and Benjamin Franklin two centuries ago, is informing our audience about their communities. Our methods may be a bit more sophisticated and our audience enlarged, but our mission as journalists has not changed.

Chapter 12

The Nature of News
—Traditional Concepts

Richard Cole and
David Grey

At the end of each weekday *CBS Evening News* telecast, Walter Cronkite declares, "And that's the way it is." At the top left of its front page every day, the *New York Times* proclaims, "All the News That's Fit to Print."

Cronkite and *The Times* are two of the most respected news voices in the United States. At least one national poll has ranked Cronkite as one of the most trusted persons in the country. *The Times* is included among the most prestigious newspapers not only in America but in the world. Yet Cronkite's sign-off and *The Times'* slogan can be construed as oversimplifications at best and as lies at worst. For the *CBS Evening News*, which devotes only slightly more than twenty minutes of air time to actual news and the rest to commercials, cannot possibly present enough news, or convey the news it does show thoroughly enough, to justify the "as it is" phrase. No news broadcast could. And no matter how many columns of news *The Times* runs daily or how many pounds the Sunday edition weighs, it simply cannot publish all the news that's fit to print. No newspaper could.

Time and space alone are two basic limitations of the news media that preclude any such absolute statements, to say nothing about the limitations of the printed word in conveying news or the second-hand reality of the television medium.

These observations are aimed not at Cronkite or *The Times*, however, for those news outlets would rank high on virtually any list of the best in the United States. And their slogans are, after all, relatively harmless. The observations are directed at the idea that news is a simple, easily defined thing. On the contrary, news is a highly complex phenomenon that depends on a number of psychological and social variables in the news-gathering and news-dissemination process and on basic physical limitations of the media.

Of course, this discussion of news is, itself, limited by space and the same variables that apply to news. Nevertheless, an attempt is made to illuminate that elusive thing called news by discussing the overall phenomenon generally and by dissecting the phenomenon according to some of its most important component parts.

Classification of News

Journalists use a jargon to classify news. Both broadcasting and newspaper reporters and editors refer to some news as *hard* and to other news as *soft*. Those terms, used rather casually, vary in precise meaning from journalist to journalist, yet they have practical value as a broad distinction. *Hard* generally means news that is, for the most part, a factual account, usually with a time element. *Soft* refers to human interest or news in a lighter vein, often with less immediacy involved. A related classification is *straight* news and *feature* news; straight being more like hard, and feature being more like soft. Straight news offers a more straightforward and impersonal factual account. Feature news tends to exhibit more flavor, color, and human interest, often achieved through anecdotes, description, and other writing techniques.

In recent years, communication scholars have classified news in a variety of ways. One way concerns the reward a news item has for its audience. Communication scientist Wilbur Schramm reasoned that two basic motivations exist for information seeking:

immediate reward, which is related to Freud's pleasure principle; and *delayed reward,* related to Freud's reality principle.[1]

The first offers immediate gratification or a vicarious experience to the audience. Newspaper readers may get a great deal of enjoyment from the comics or sports stories; other examples include crime, accident, and human-interest stories. A television news viewer may smile at one of Charles Kuralt's *On the Road* episodes or cringe as the camera shows a man leaping to his death from a burning building.

Delayed-reward items offer information the audience may use later, such as stories on economics, public affairs, social problems, and health. An in-depth story on an economic principle might possibly help a reader vote in a future election. A television news special on the pet industry could help a viewer choose a breed of dog to purchase later on.

This immediate-delayed classification is complicated because some news items reward some members of the audience immediately and others later. A stockholder may get a kick out of a story describing how the market is turning bullish, yet the story may mean little to the non-stockholder until later, when and if it affects his or her pocketbook. Another complication arises when one considers the overall content of different media, not just the news. Most daily television fare is immediate reward, whereas the print media tend to offer more of a balance between immediate and delayed reward.

The oldest and most fundamental classification of news, of course, is *good* versus *bad.* Today, many newspaper readers and television viewers may think that a large proportion of the news is bad. That is true if one considers that 999 safe airplane landings are not news but one airplane crash is. News often constitutes what goes against the prevailing situation in society. Thus, the unusual often constitutes the news. The important point here is that the news media are in business not to disseminate good or bad news but to disseminate the news, whatever it may be. Incidentally, several studies show that more good news is published than bad.[2]

---

[1] Wilbur Schramm, "The Nature of News," *Journalism Quarterly* 26 (1949):259–269.

[2] See, for example, "You Print Only the Bad News About Youths," in *News Research for Better Newspapers,* vol. 5, Chilton R. Bush, ed., American Newspaper

Beyond these and other similar classifications, the news phenomenon from the reporter's viewpoint can be approached according to two major perspectives: constraints on the reporter and the newsroom situation.

Constraints on the Reporter

Initially, reporters and editors should be aware of the various *elements of news*. Reporting textbooks usually delineate a number of news elements, the number varying with the particular textbook. Here, four elements of news, especially accuracy and objectivity, are discussed individually in addition to some other elements.

ACCURACY

Noted press critic A. J. Liebling once proposed that the American Society of Newspaper Editors sponsor an annual award to a United States newspaper for lying. He suggested that it would inspire far more interest than the Pulitzer Prizes.[3] Liebling's critical jest aside, everyone knows that the news media should attempt to report news truthfully and accurately. Yet, everyone also knows that one does not necessarily believe everything one reads in a newspaper, hears on radio, or sees on television. On the whole, journalists strive diligently to be as accurate as possible, yet how accurate are all the media?

A number of studies have investigated that question for newspaper stories. The pioneer study, published in 1936, reported that 54 percent of the stories analyzed were accurate. The average number of errors per story was less than one.[4] Three investigations in the 1960s and 1970s found much the same results; approximately half the stories were labeled accurate, with the average number of errors per story ranging from .86 to 1.52.[5] Together,

---

Publishers Association Foundation, New York, 1971, p. 143; and Walter Gieber, "Do Newspapers Overplay 'Negative' News?" *Journalism Quarterly* 32 (1955):311–318.

[3] A. J. Liebling, *The Press*, Ballantine Books, New York, 1971, p. 218.

[4] Mitchell V. Charnley, "Preliminary Notes on a Study of Newspaper Accuracy," *Journalism Quarterly* 13 (1936):394–401.

[5] Charles H. Brown, "Majority of Readers Give Papers an A for Accuracy," *Editor and Publisher*, February 13, 1965, pp. 13, 63; Fred C. Berry, Jr., "A Study of Ac-

these four studies considered more than 1,300 newspaper stories, nearly all from daily newspapers published in various parts of the United States. Only half the stories were totally accurate. The most frequent inaccuracies included errors of meaning, a variety of factual errors including incorrect names and titles, misquotations, omissions, and typographical errors.

In these investigations, the judges of accuracy were the persons cited in the stories, people who usually knew more of the facts than the reporters did and perhaps more facts than the reporters thought newsworthy enough to include in the stories. It is possible to rationalize some of the inaccuracy by saying that those news sources or newsmakers have an obvious vested interest in a story and thus could label it deficient, if not inaccurate, merely because not every fact, no matter how trivial, is presented. The newsmaker's involvement could well influence his or her judgment, especially if depicted unfavorably. The large percentage of inaccurate stories, however, makes clear that such reasoning is part rationalization.

A 1969 study checked not only how the news sources in stories judged accuracy, but also the judgments of reporters who wrote the items. The study focused on subjective inaccuracies, defined as errors of meaning, omission, and under- or overemphasis. Both the news sources and the reporters mentioned insufficient background information on the reporter's part as the chief cause of many such errors. And both groups placed part of the blame at the hands of news desk and other editing personnel who changed the original version of the story. News sources stressed sensationalism and lack of personal contact with reporters as the cause of many errors. Reporters emphasized their lack of time to work on the stories.[6]

Several studies have suggested that the reporter should routinely ask the news source "What is the significance of this

curacy in Local News Stories of Three Dailies," *Journalism Quarterly* 44 (1967):482–490; William B. Blankenburg, "News Accuracy: Some Findings on the Meaning of Errors," *Journal of Communication* 20 (1970):375–386. Brown considered 143 news stories in 42 Oklahoma weeklies; Berry considered 270 items in three San Francisco area dailies; Blankenburg considered 332 items in two West Coast dailies.

[6] Gary C. Lawrence and David L. Grey, "Subjective Inaccuracies in Local News Reporting," *Journalism Quarterly* 46 (1969):753–759.

event?" or "What should the public know about this event?" in order to obtain the source's overall perception of the event's importance and thus reduce subjective error.[7] That appears to be worth trying.

A 1970 study of science reporting added another dimension—an audience. The audience was composed of respondents who read articles and then, without looking at them, told interviewers what the articles said. Accuracy was defined as the extent to which a message produced agreement between source (the person quoted) and receiver (the audience). Scientists quoted in the articles judged the accuracy of the statements made by the audience; 64.5 percent of the statements were called accurate.

In their criticisms, scientists singled out overemphasis on the unique as the greatest problem. Mentioned second was omission of relevant information, followed by misleading headlines. Reporters were interviewed to analyze, among other things, whether the stories originated with the reporters, were assigned by editors, or initiated by press releases or journal articles. The articles judged most accurate were those specifically assigned by editors, which is logical since some reporters attempt to produce accurate and understandable stories in order to please their editors and gain a promotion or a raise. In this study, reporters who originated articles on their own did not produce especially understandable stories.[8]

What about the number of inaccuracies in a news item? Does a cumulative effect build up with the number of errors so that the reader begins to distrust the entire story? An experiment tested that idea by comparing an error-free message with messages that included spelling, punctuation, and grammatical errors. Although the investigators warned that a large number of errors had to be present before the accumulation would affect the readers, they found that the readers perceived the error-free message as more favorable. Readers considered its source as better, and they actually learned more information from it. In messages with more er-

---

[7] Berry, "A Study of Accuracy," p. 490; Lawrence and Grey, "Subjective Inaccuracies," p. 757.

[8] Phillip J. Tichenor, Clarice N. Olien, Annette Harrison, and George Donohue, "Mass Communication Systems and Communication Accuracy in Science Reporting," *Journalism Quarterly* 47 (1970):673–683.

rors, the readers viewed the writing as less clear, and when the message contained a substantial number of errors, the source was seen as less competent and less trustworthy.[9]

What about the method used to obtain the information for the news story? Do personal interviews, for example, produce more accurate stories than telephone interviews? One researcher concluded that personal interviews produced approximately one and one-half times as many accurate stories as telephone interviews did.[10] Personal interviews do involve a more intimate relationship with the news source—observation of facial expressions, gestures, and the like.

Yet a 1972 study reported that telephone interviews produced a 40 percent accuracy rate, and personal interviews only a 33 percent accuracy rate. In an attempt to clarify this inconsistency, the 1972 study grouped information-obtaining methods into (1) passive—when the reporter is merely an editor, writer, or observer, as in rewriting a press release or being present at an event and not interacting with the source, and (2) active—when the reporter is involved in the flow of news. Finding that passive-reporter stories were 71 percent accurate and active-reporter stories were only 37 percent accurate, the investigator noted that accuracy could be best achieved by reproducing press releases and by restraining reporters. The fastest route to an error is to allow a reporter to get involved in an interview or dialogue.[11]

Do these rather disappointing findings mean that reporters should sit in newsrooms and wait until publicity-minded public relations agents drop by with releases? Obviously not. The mass media cannot get the news by depending on hand-outs. The findings really mean that it is simply much easier to rewrite a press release accurately than it is to write an original version of a personal interview accurately. Remember, also, that serious inaccuracies are most likely to occur when there is no personal contact between the reporter and the source.[12]

Does one wire service make fewer errors than another?

---

[9] Bradley S. Greenberg and Edward L. Razinsky, "Some Effects of Variations in Message Quality," *Journalism Quarterly* 43 (1966):486–492.

[10] Berry, "A Study of Accuracy," p. 489.

[11] T. Joseph Scanlon, "A New Approach to Study of Newspaper Accuracy," *Journalism Quarterly* 49 (1972):587–590.

[12] Lawrence and Grey, "Subjective Inaccuracies," pp. 755–756.

Newsroom lore often has it that the Associated Press is known for its reliability and United Press International for its lively writing.[13] The impression that AP is more dependable and accurate than UPI has been documented several times,[14] yet a 1970 study that paired AP and UPI stories on the same topics and quoted the same sources found no meaningful differences in accuracy.[15]

On the whole, too little time is the bane of mass media accuracy. While a book publisher often takes from six months to a year to publish a completed manuscript, a daily newspaper prints the equivalent of a book a day. A broadcast station airs a similar amount of rushed information daily. Thus, limitations on time makes some errors inevitable.

Other error sources include carelessness, poor listening practices on the part of reporters and editors, lack of attention to detail, failure to check facts, and misinformed news sources. Because no two observers ever see precisely the same thing in any one situation or event, and because of the necessity to check controversial information with more than one source, the *Washington Post* attempted to construct a fail-safe system for its stories on the Watergate affair. The stories came from anonymous sources and dealt with sensitive government material which, if incorrect, might have damaged the *Post* seriously. The editors adopted the rule of never carrying any set of significant facts unless it came from at least two independent sources.[16] Another accuracy truism is that the longer the news chain and the more people who handle the news and change it along that chain, the greater the likelihood that inaccuracy will result.

OBJECTIVITY

The fifth canon of journalism declares, among other things, that news reports should be free from

---

[13] Gene Gilmore and Robert Root, *Modern Newspaper Editing*, The Glendessary Press, Berkeley, Calif., 1971, p. 126.

[14] See, for example, B. H. Liebes, "Decision-Making by Telegraph Editors—AP or UPI?" *Journalism Quarterly* 43 (1966):434–442; and Walter Gieber, "Across the Desk: A Study of 16 Telegraph Editors," *Journalism Quarterly* 33 (1956):423–432.

[15] J. Richard Cote, "A Study of Accuracy of Two Wire Services," *Journalism Quarterly* 47 (1970):660–666.

[16] Remarks by Howard Simons, managing editor of the *Washington Post*, to the North Carolina Press Association at Duke University, January 1974.

opinion or bias of any kind. The canon concerns the notion of objectivity—one of the most hallowed journalistic goals—which holds that news should be presented objectively, impartially, and without prejudice. Yet anyone who thinks seriously about the subject realizes that absolute objectivity is an impossible goal for any journalist to attain, if for no other reason than because journalists are human beings, each of whom has built-in prejudices, biases, and limited capabilities. No reporter can overcome those things completely.

An eminently practical reason rules out absolute objectivity. That reason is the process of *selection* that exists throughout news gathering and dissemination. The selection process is fundamental and necessary. Assuming that all the news could be gathered, which it cannot, it could not be printed or broadcast because there is not enough space or time. Thus, what is reported is selected.

The reporter and editor select what material to include in a story and what to omit. They judge some material important enough for the lead and other material important enough only for the end. In newspapers, some stories are judged important enough to print and are then selected for the front page. Others are selected for the bottom of a column on page forty-four. Some important stories are illustrated with photographs or other art. Some have large headlines and prominent play. Decision and selection enter into each story's length and position in all the news media. These few selections merely typify the many options that exist. They show that news is not absolutely objective because so many selections and judgments are built into its existence.

Journalist-novelist John Hersey remarked:

> There is no such thing as objective reportage. Human life is far too trembling-swift to be reported in whole; the moment the recorder chooses nine facts out of ten he colors the information with his views.[17]

Yet professional journalists, according to one sociologist, sometimes invoke their objectivity almost the way a Mediterranean peasant might wear a clove of garlic around the neck to ward off evil spirits.[18] The sociologist reasons that objectivity is a strategic ritual through which journalists protect themselves from the risks

---

[17] John Hersey, *The Algiers Motel Incident*, Bantam, New York, 1968, p. 27.
[18] Gaye Tuchman, "Objectivity as Strategic Ritual: An Examination of Newsmen's Notions of Objectivity," *American Journal of Sociology* 77 (1972):660–679.

of their trade. Two of those risks are libel suits and audience criticisms aimed at distortion.

How do the media measure up on the goal of objectivity? In general, research has shown that the esteem in which a newspaper is held by its readers appears to be highly related to the readers' perceptions of its fairness and accuracy.[19] In a 1970 national survey, 51 percent of the respondents said they believed that newspapers did not confine their opinions to editorials; 49 percent said they believed that the newspaper's stand on politics affected the news stories.[20] And it has been documented several times that a considerable number of blacks distrust what they term the "whitey" press because of its lack of attention to black people and their problems.

Often government spokesmen have criticized news subjectivity. In what has become known, at least among many journalists, as that notorious news conference in October 1973, President Nixon lambasted the U.S. press, particularly the broadcast media. The news conference came a year after the Watergate scandal began to break in the press. "I have never heard or seen such outrageous, vicious, distorted reporting in twenty-seven years of public life," he said. Nixon's other adjectives for media coverage included "unfair," "frantic," and "hysterical." *New York Times* columnist James Reston later wrote that there has seldom been a more savage attack on the integrity of American journalism.

On the positive side for the media, however, stands the first opinion poll ever commissioned by the United States Congress. Pollster Louis Harris conducted the national survey for a United States Senate committee in September 1973, the month before President Nixon spoke. Respondents were asked, among other things, how much confidence they had in the leadership of key U.S. institutions. Only two institutions, television news and the press, improved in ratings over 1966, when Harris asked the same general question. Respondents in 1973 expressed more confidence in both television news and the press than they did in the executive branch of the federal government.

Some objectivity research has been conducted on college stu-

---

[19] "Fairness and Accuracy," in Bush, *News Research for Better Newspapers*, vol. 1 (1966), pp. 125–126.

[20] "How Skeptical Are Readers and Why?" in Bush, *News Research for Better Newspapers*, vol. 5 (1971), pp. 76–77.

dents. One study asked student readers to judge whether thirty-six news headlines, stories, and the combination of headlines and stories were biased for or against the subjects of the stories. The study found a considerable amount of bias.[21]

In an experiment, journalism students were told to write a news story about the second Nixon-Kennedy debate in 1960 for a newspaper with a pro-Nixon editorial policy. The students who were anti-Nixon themselves tended to write stories more favorable to Nixon than did the students who were pro-Nixon. They tended to follow the newspaper's known editorial policy and be less objective.[22]

The specific words the reporter uses obviously affect objectivity. One study investigated different ways in which quotations in news stories were attributed to the person speaking. The study focused on attributive verbs, the commonly used *said* versus stronger verbs such as *contended.* Another variable was the use of such "body-language" statements as "gesturing with his left hand" in sentences containing quotations. The study found that the readers, a group of college students, believed that *said* was more objective than such verbs as *contended,* and that "body-language" statements were least objective.[23]

What makes a reader decide that one story is biased and that another is more or less objective? Clearly the reader's knowledge and his or her own bias toward the topic of the story and the persons in it have some bearing. Another factor is the reader's feeling toward the newspaper, broadcast station, or individual reporter. And perhaps the word *objectivity* itself causes some of the trouble. Like so many other things, it is an unattainable ideal. Perhaps *conscious objectivity* is more appropriate. Even though one knows that journalists can never be completely objective, one knows that journalists should not be consciously subjective in news stories. Journalists must strive to be as consciously objective

---

[21] David B. Sachsman, "A Test of 'Loading': New Measure of Bias," *Journalism Quarterly* 47 (1970):759–762.

[22] Jean S. Kerrick, Thomas E. Anderson, and Luita B. Swales, "Balance and the Writer's Attitude in News Stories and Editorials," *Journalism Quarterly* 41 (1964):207–215.

[23] Richard R. Cole and Donald L. Shaw, "Using 'Powerful' Verbs and 'Body Language' Statements: Does the Reader Notice?" *Journalism Quarterly* 51 (1974):62–66.

as possible in order to present to their audiences the least biased stories.

PROXIMITY

Distance is obviously an element of news, for local news is basic to the newspaper and broadcasting industries. An old saw in newsrooms holds that, all other things being equal, news from close to home is more important than news from a far-away land—the reason being that more readers and viewers would be interested in the local news. The United States on the whole is a nation of local newspapers, in contrast with such countries as England and Japan, where large national newspapers can almost cover the nation and be shipped throughout the country in time to be read at the breakfast table.

Proximity, however, is much more than physical distance. *Psychological proximity* can be a paramount element of news interest within a country when one considers subgroups of the audience classified by ethnic, racial, religious, or other characteristics. One study, for example, showed that a group of students from a North Carolina university perceived Southern cities as being closer in actual miles than Northern cities that were equidistant.[24] Internationally, psychological distance in the news depends on a number of variables including social, political, economic, and cultural characteristics.

TIMELINESS

Every news item in newspapers and in broadcasts does not have to be timely or new, but most news stories have a time element. In the past, news in both print and broadcast media has tended to be event oriented. Now, more stories are becoming situation oriented. Erwin D. Canham, editor of the *Christian Science Monitor,* declared: "We have been the slave of the event, the servant of time alone, and we have wasted a lot of time just waiting around for things to happen." [25] Today,

---

[24] Roy E. Carter, Jr. and Warren J. Mitofsky, "Actual and Perceived Distances in the News," *Journalism Quarterly* 38 (1961):223–225.

[25] Erwin D. Canham, "Definition of News Offered," *Headlines 1972,* American Newspaper Publisher Association, December 1972.

radio and television have the advantage in immediacy—in disseminating the latest news developments—and newspapers should concentrate less on on-the-spot coverage of single events and provide more emphasis on in-depth explanation and analysis.

A number of other news elements exist. *Clarity* is one of the most important of these, for unless the reporter writes the story clearly the audience cannot understand it. Without clarity the rest of the news elements are of little value.

Because of time and space limitations, *conciseness* is basic in presenting news. Even though complicated stories may require considerable time and space, each unnecessary word in the story makes the audience's task of reading or viewing it last that much longer. Other news elements include *oddity, rarity, pathos, irony, conflict, sex, drama, emotion, surprise* and several that you could add to the list. Instead of concentrating on such a list of news elements, communication scientist Bruce Westley has declared that *identification* is the best measure of the worth of a news story to an individual member of the audience. He defined identification as the degree to which the viewer or reader identifies with places, persons, and events in the story.[26]

What do all these news elements mean? Will the reporter who carefully observes them write better news stories than one who does not? Although the quality of each story depends on the individual writer's talent and expertise, the general answer is definitely yes. An interesting study conducted by a professor of English and a graduate student is pertinent to this point. They investigated two groups of prominent authors, one group with journalistic training and the other without it. One journalist-novelist and one non-journalist-novelist were selected from each of four time periods from 1880 to 1960. Those with journalistic training were Stephen Crane, Theodore Dreiser, Ernest Hemingway, and John Hersey. Those without the training were Henry James, Edith Wharton, Thomas Wolfe, and Truman Capote. The journalistic group used more compressed syntax, clear and active word choice, and concrete, objective detail. They used shorter sentences and more active-voice sentence construction. The in-

---

[26] Bruce Westley, *News Editing*, Houghton Mifflin, Boston, 1953, p. 336.

vestigators in the study concluded that journalistic prose is well adapted to its purpose, appropriate and lean:

> It is objective; it seizes the highlights and paints strongly. There is no room for circumlocution or redundancy, but space for wit, humor, and drama. The journalist interprets life, not by commentary, but by selection of detail. He leaves out sentimentality, but appeals to human interest and sympathy.[27]

The Newsroom Situation

From the viewpoint of the people who produce it, news could be defined broadly as what journalists make it to be. And what they make it to be depends on the newsroom situation because a number of people are involved in putting out a newspaper or in preparing a newscast for radio or television. The news that results depends to a great degree on the complex organizational, social, psychological, and mechanical processes involved in the newsroom setting.

Consider the case of a new reporter at work who knows first that he or she cannot possibly reproduce for the audience the exact event, issue, or situation on which he or she is writing. Thus the news written cannot be the event itself, but must be an account of it, and therefore becomes second-hand reality.

In addition, beginning reporters are not normally told in any formal manner what the news organization's policy is on specific topics. Thus they may try to develop a feeling for what policy is. By viewing/reading the final edited product, they can see how stories are handled. By talking with colleagues, they may attempt to learn what to avoid and what to pursue in writing stories. Reporters may attempt to follow their feelings of what policy is whether or not the feelings are correct, because they fear sanctions if they do not. They may feel management looking over their shoulders. If reporters think they know the general manager or publisher looks with disfavor on women's liberation, for example, they may consciously or unconsciously allow that to affect the story.

And the reporter is merely one person. Numerous *gatekeepers*—persons who have authority to exercise judgment in al-

---

[27] Donald A. Sears and Margaret Bourland, "Journalism Makes the Style," *Journalism Quarterly* 47 (1970):504–509.

lowing some news to be disseminated and other news not to be—work on newspapers and in broadcast stations. They are decision makers in the flow of news. The wire or telegraph editor is one such gatekeeper. Numerous studies have investigated that editor's working situation and why one story is chosen over another. One paramount factor in the choice is which stories are available at various deadlines. Other factors include a judgment of the story's importance; the length of the story; the byline, if any; the amount of space available; the perception of the amount of local interest in a story; and, perhaps, a perception of the bosses' opinions on the story topic. Another factor is the wire services' national digests or budgets, which list the stories judged most important by the AP and UPI editors in New York City. Those digests undoubtedly influence many wire editors and therefore many stories that are played prominently across the nation.

On a newspaper, the copyeditor can be a gatekeeper also. If he or she questions whether a sentence in a story is in good taste and cannot locate the reporter to discuss it, he or she may simply delete it. It may be deleted without attempting to discuss it with the reporter. The copyeditor, if dissatisfied with the lead on a story, may rewrite it and perhaps change its emphasis. He or she may cut the bottom of a story because of length limitations or may make numerous other changes in it. He or she may even give an incorrect impression in the headline written. An excellent copyeditor, of course, improves stories significantly and composes meaningful and accurate headlines.

Consider the decision making of all the reporters and editors in the chain of command and flow of news at any broadcasting station or newspaper. Add in the fact that most reporters are Democrats and most general managers/publishers Republicans. Also consider the fact that the general manager is often more of a businessman than a journalist and can act not only in policy matters but also on particular stories. Very probably, the publisher is more likely to influence stories that will affect the organization's financial situation. This is the top decision maker in the organizational structure who sets news policy, and the policy is usually followed by members of the news staff.[28]

With all these decision makers involved in the news presenta-

---

[28] Warren Breed, "Social Control in the Newsroom: A Functional Analysis," *Social Forces* 33 (1955):326–335.

tion, news may be seen as more of a personal process, with each person who handles the news having the possibility of making personal decisions on it. News is seen more as a product of organizational, social and psychological processes and forces in the newsroom bureaucracy.

Then consider news outside the newsroom bureaucracy of any one newspaper or broadcast station. Think in terms of competing individual journalists and competing media. Although there is less emphasis on scooping one's competitors now than there once was, AP and UPI, for example, still try to best each other on coverage. The same is true for competing newspapers and broadcast stations in the same city, and sometimes even between the staffs of morning and afternoon newspapers owned by the same company. Competition, often keen among different media in a city, exists to some degree among reporters working on the same newspaper or broadcast station. It exists throughout the newsgathering and disseminating process and has an effect on what news is.

On the other hand, concentration of ownership of the mass media in the United States has been growing in recent years, as well as in a number of other countries with privately owned media. Government commissions in England and Canada, for example, have criticized the situation in which fewer and fewer owners control larger and larger media enterprises. In the United States, newspaper chains continue to grow; more than half of all daily newspapers are owned by chains. This means that fewer individual owners wield ultimate decision-making control over the press.

In addition, newsmen sometimes create news by their very presence. What is called "herd reporting," when numerous reporters gather to cover an event, by necessity changes the event, even if the change is only slight. On occasion unethical reporters have even brought signs that photograph well for protesters to carry in demonstrations that are to be filmed. Television cameras, of course, may lend excitement to an event and thus change its nature.

Consider technological factors. Throughout history, mechanical and technological advances have exerted tremendous influence on news: from before the invention of printing down through carrier pigeons, semaphores, undersea cables, the telegraph, all the way to today's laser-beam photographic transmission, cathode ray tubes, and computers. The future will bring more such developments. Besides increasing the speed of news transmission and production, these technological developments enable more news to be gathered and disseminated. Each development, however, brings its own characteristics into the news process and thus conditions in some manner the news that results. The telegraph, to cite only one example, gave impetus to the inverted-pyramid form of newswriting in which the most important facts of a story came first. That inverted-pyramid form has in turn produced enormous standardization in newswriting structure.

What Is News?

Not a scientific term with one precise definition, news is a four-letter word with multifaceted meaning and as many meanings as there are people to define it. People make and are most of the news. News is a communication product of cultural, social, psychological, physical, mechanical, and other variables in society. By necessity not 100 percent objective, news is selective content that exists in the minds of human beings and in the mass media. News is information, entertainment, and influence. It is dissemination, reaction, and feedback among news sources and reporters, for news is not news until it is learned and reported. It can be considered a depletable consumer product made every day,[29] for what is news one day is not necessarily news the next. News is a commodity that is sold for public consumption, sold by professionals throughout the world in newspapers, news magazines, newscasts, newsreels, and newsletters. Because news in the United States media system is supported chiefly by advertising, that advertising affects the news content and presentation, even if to no greater degree than the time or space that is allocated for news. In the first place, privately owned news organizations in free-enterprise nations must make at least enough money to stay in business. In the sense of staying in business, money is perhaps the primary goal.

Yet, in democracies, news is much more. The public must know the facts before it can reach informed decisions and focus its

---

[29] Tuchman, "Objectivity as Strategic Ritual," p. 662.

opinions into actions. Thus news is vital to democratic survival and to one's view of reality. Because news is so important, governments in all countries attempt to manage it, for knowledge is power. What news is results largely from the interplay of government and mass media.

Journalism, unlike such professions as the law and medicine, has no formal code of ethics that binds its practitioners. There is no license to practice and no board to disbar unethical members. No special educational background or training is required to become a journalist in many instances; yet more and more journalists today receive specialized training in journalism schools. In addition, more press councils—organizations often composed of both public and media representatives—are being formed as buffers between government and the public to serve, in part, as self-critical apparatuses for the journalism field. For the most part, news is produced by professional journalists who attempt to attain the highest standards and give the best quality performance they can.

Any one-sentence definition of news is inadequate. To understand the phenomenon, one must consider all the component parts and the processes that come together into making news what it is. All these things come together for each individual news consumer, making news a phenomenon that exists inside each person's mind, existing only as that person perceives it. As Alice in Wonderland could have said, news is anything at all, but not always, and sometimes it is more important than other times. Whatever it is, news is as alive, changeable, and complex as the people, events, and situations that make it, and as the institutions and people who report, edit, and disseminate it.

News Beats

How newsroom staffs are organized and assigned has a major influence on what is regarded as news. Consider the reporters assigned to the traditional news beats: city hall, police, courts, schools. Each has had an aspect of the local community carved out for him or her because this is the way newspapers and broadcasting stations have historically chopped up their communities.

As Chapter 2 pointed out, the news-beat system has persisted in large measure because police stations, courthouses, and similar vantage points are efficient ways of allocating observers. But while productivity per observer is high, it does mean a major constraint on the total package of news gathered by a staff of reporters.

There are clear implications here for what is or is not covered. For instance, before the Watts area of Los Angeles exploded in riots and racial strife, who was around to report what was happening and about to happen? Or, when there are massive thefts of bicycles from schools to support drug habits, is it the police reporter, the education writer, or the general assignment reporter who will write an in-depth feature on the drug problem?

Each reporter enters with his or her own news sources and definitions of what the beat is. There generally is a tendency in newsrooms to avoid straying into someone else's beat. It is little wonder that some younger staff members with fresher views toward local issues are frustrated by exposure to the hierarchy of the newsroom, where seniority often decides who does what.[30]

But there are ongoing signs of change as news editors realize they have been missing stories that fall between the beats. Often there are decisions to team up or separate the story into parts so that it is reported. And specialists have had to broaden the definitions of their beats—for example, the science writer must also be able to cover stories on the economics and politics of science and medical research. The university or college reporter must adapt to the potentially endless issues hidden and flowing out from the campus.

Other venturesome organizations have completely redefined the beat system of gathering news. Instead of organizing news beats *geographically*, they have defined beats *functionally*. In the past, news beats generally corresponded to a particular geographic location, usually a public building such as the city hall or county courthouse. Sometimes a beat covered several unrelated agencies—state court of appeals and state board of health, for example—simply because of their physical proximity.

Under a functional beat arrangement all, or at least many, of

---

[30] Warren Breed, "Social Control in the Newsroom"; Rodney Stark, "Policy and the Pros: An Organizational Analysis of a Metropolitan Newspaper," *Berkeley Journal of Sociology* 7 (1962):11–31; Lewis Donohew, "Publishers and Their Influence Groups," *Journalism Quarterly* 42 (1965):112–113.

the agencies dealing with health, for example, would fall on a single beat. So the city hall or other public office building is no longer the exclusive province of one reporter. Different offices fall on different beats according to the social function or service performed. Defining beats functionally also marks a movement away from an event orientation and toward a situation orientation of what news is and how it is reported.

Perhaps one of the most dramatic examples of bold thinking about news beats and approaches and philosophies comes from the breaking open of the Watergate story by the *Washington Post*, which used revealing and important different approaches that worked.

The *Washington Post* offers only one of many models of reporting behavior. It is a prestigious publication with extensive financial resources, which enables it to make international and national issues part of its local coverage. It also covers the District of Columbia and nearby Maryland and Virginia communities as any large metropolitan paper might. The same can be said for the *New York Times*, which perceives itself as even more of an international paper, with the mandate of trying to record daily history. The point is that each medium—local television news, for example—works under a self-perception of purpose and audiences. This is the model or self-image that defines for journalists what news is, what they can and cannot report.

Serving all major news organizations, of course, are the wire services, Associated Press and United Press International, which tend to concentrate on hard news—the more factual treatment of public events, hearings, speeches, and disasters for clients and subscribers around the world. The news syndicates, such as the *New York Times* and *Washington Post-Los Angeles Times*, also stress hard news, but tend to be more interpretative and deal more in features and in-depth series. The point is that each news organization has boundaries—roles and functions often defined by market economics and other demands—that determine greatly what kinds of news operations will be at work.

Within these structures and constraints are the important individual variations in reporting: aggressive and active versus passive, mostly mirroring; cautious versus bold and innovative. Within each news organization there may be several types permitted or even encouraged. The individual reporter can usually de-

How Two Davids Slew Goliath

The crucial point about Watergate is that it was the lowly metropolitan staff—not the prestigious national staff—that lifted the lid. None of the key figures who pursued and developed the story day by day—neither the working editors nor the reporters—had had a day of experience on the national staff of the *Post,* or any other paper. . . .

[Bob] Woodward and [Carl] Bernstein were both thrown into the Watergate story on the day of the burglary; Woodward, because he was on the District staff; Bernstein, because he sensed there was a big story and kept hanging around Barry Sussman [District Editor], pestering him for an assignment. . . .

"When we got into this thing," says Carl Bernstein, "we had to find out how the White House worked and how the Committee for the Reelection of the President worked. We found that nobody really knew. Oh, they knew generally that there was a 'Berlin Wall,' and all that, but there was really very little expertise around about the White House, especially at the middle and lower levels. It was obvious to me and to Bob [Woodward] from the beginning that you weren't going to find anybody to tell you what this was all about."

Ben Bradlee [Executive Editor] put it another way: "A reporter who

fine some of his or her own limits or non-limits. Yet the firm and its philosophy can still mean a great deal in what the reporter can cover and how.

Just as the reporter is constrained by the firm and its philosophy, so the firm in turn is constrained by the economics of the marketplace and the perspective of its audience. The success and failure stories within the magazine industry are perhaps the most obvious illustrations: *Playboy, Reader's Digest,* and *Sunset* find their niches and produce to fill them. As times change, *Life, Look, Saturday Evening Post,* and *Saturday Review* struggle for their identities and usually go through a series of self-image changes before finally folding or redesigning under market forces. The underlying point is that the news medium of today is evolving and is unable to remain stagnant during times of rising cost and audience demands and pressures. The journalist, even the free-lancer for print or broadcast media, must understand audiences and their needs and wants.

could call Henry Kissinger by his first name wasn't worth a damn on the Watergate story."

When the Watergate story broke last June [1972], Carl Bernstein had never attended one of Ronald Ziegler's White House briefings. He has been in the pressroom twice since. Bob Woodward had never attended a briefing, and hasn't yet . . . [as of summer 1973].

Woodward and Bernstein did not make a direct assault on the 'Berlin Wall' at the White House. They went around the wall, and then began to work their way up from the bottom. . . .

"It's like working on a murder story. You go to the people next door and ask them what they know about their neighbors, who the people were. If you call somebody at the White House on the telephone and ask for an appointment, they'll tell you no. But if you're standing out there on their front porch, facing them, they may let you in. . . ."

The old approach—but fresh for much of Washington political coverage—got between the lines and connected many of them. There is no guarantee that such tactics would always work or work again; but it is dramatic how redefining the beat system (and talent to be used) worked its way up to the point that other forces—governmental, legal, and political— could take over where the *Post* had only made its great beginnings. . . .

SOURCE: Reprinted from the *Columbia Journalism Review*, July/August 1973.

Trends in the "new journalism" and other alternative forms of news writing and news documentaries demonstrate the modifications, themes-and-variations, and even rebellions underway. Although newsrooms of the mid-1970s are showing signs of change, most indicators are that the evolution may not be quick enough to meet future demands.

While there will be fads and temporary successes, the longer-term revolution in journalism has already started on a no-stop course. The flood of information and images increases. The journalist simply must be better prepared to try to sort out our world and to help it with important problem-solving issues. This means not only being able to look in the right places and go to the right sources for possible answers and help, but also being able to "get into them" and to carry away the best of possible facts, knowledge, and insights. This is the nature of news, news beats, and models of reporting behavior of the future.

Chapter 13

The Nature of News
—New Concepts

Keith R. Stamm

A familiar procedure in reporting is to go out and talk to a lot of people or take a lot of pictures and then, after all the notes and pictures are collected, try to impose some order on all that was observed. This "seat-of-the-pants" approach illustrates what is often lacking in journalistic procedures. Too little thought is given beforehand to the range of observations that could potentially be made. Instead, journalists pull their questions out of their hats.

Of course, deference to the ethic of objectivity does not preclude the use of hypotheses or systematic planning. A major shortcoming of the traditional practice is that we rarely see any more than we prepare ourselves to see. We see what our questions allow us to see. That is why we must have some basis for generating new questions if we are to observe anything beyond the realm of previous experience.

A behavioral scientist planning a research project and an imaginative reporter have a lot in common. Ideally, each identifies a number of focal questions that could be asked in a given situation. This procedure allows both the behavioral scientist and the journalist to decide which focal questions would generate the most useful insights. It is only after the focal questions have been selected that the appropriate techniques of observation can be selected.

A Basic News Model

Recognizing that reporters must have some formal idea of what they're looking for *before* they begin to gather information, most journalism texts suggest the five W's and H technique. This technique, which emphasizes the questioning procedure rather than the information the questions are designed to obtain, can stifle the reporter's creativity. It provides no real framework for inventing new tactics. One way to overcome that restrictiveness is to see the elements of the five W's model as general *concepts* from which *specific questions* can be generated.

Figure 1 presents a translation of the five W's and H framework in which any given news situation is described in terms of its *boundaries, elements,* and *relationships.* The boundary concept corresponds roughly to the "where" and "when" of the traditional model, the elements to "who" and "what," and the relationships to "why" and "how."

In using this model, however, keep in mind that "where" and "when" do not always refer to time and space boundaries. You will not always report on events in terms of their location in space and time. For example, you might want to locate two people within the boundary of an idea or even use a third man as a boundary (for example, a spokesman for two other men).

The new model also suggests different questions to be derived from the "why" and "how" in a news situation. How are the two elements related to each another? Questions are needed in this case to establish the location of each of these two elements relative to a common boundary.

Using the Basic News Model

Journalists exercise considerable freedom in deciding how to picture news situations. They identify the elements to be included and determine the context, or boundaries, within which they are viewed. This power to manipulate the dimensions of news situations also generates many observational problems for reporters. Here is an example from the *National Observer.*

FIGURE 1 *Basic News Model*

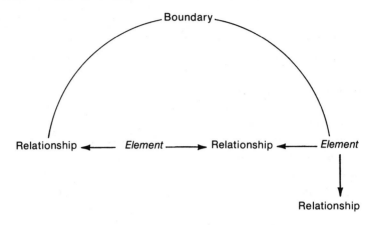

In April 1973, the *Observer* described a problem of alleged incompetence among vast numbers of technicians being trained for the United States medical system. The picture the writer had in mind was one of medical incompetence as a common characteristic shared by numerous institutions within the medical system. Thus, the story's entire claim of significance—its news value—was based on the commonness of incompetence across a large number of institutions. In the terminology of the basic news model, the boundaries of this picture are very wide and include the entire medical system. The elements are the medical units within that system, many of which are supposed to display the characteristic "incompetence of technical personnel."

You should ask two questions about this story: First, what evidence did the reporter present to fill in this picture? Second, is this the evidence that should be presented?

What we find in the article is a lengthy series of anecdotes describing discrete events in which some instance of alleged incompetence occurs. It makes interesting reading, but it is also very misleading in relation to the situation the reporter wants us to see. We have no way of knowing how these instances of incompetence relate to the overall picture; they provide no basis for estimating the pervasiveness of incompetence within the boundaries. What is really needed to fill in such a picture is the kind of systematic survey approach described in Chapter 5, rather than an assorted collection of anecdotes. This would mean selecting a random sample of medical institutions and asking a standardized set of questions to observers within each institution.

In my own professional experience, I recall observational problems that I could have solved more easily if I had had a better way of analyzing them. As a member of a professional film-making team a few years ago, I dealt with the problem of putting together a film report that would show how man-made structures (for example, billboards, power lines, auto graveyards) interfered with enjoyment of the Wisconsin landscape. Our biggest problem in constructing this report hinged on observing the obstructions in a context that made evident the relations of "obstructing." Fortunately, we were able to spend over a year constructing our picture, so we could throw away all our false starts. We traveled over the state filming obstructions, but when we screened the raw film footage, we realized that something was missing. Somehow the obstructions that had looked so ugly and so obviously inappropriate to us when we filmed them did not look that way at all on the screen. Our film footage did not show unsightly obstructions at all, but rather an interesting sequence of patterns and colors.

In our next round of filming, we used telephoto lenses to squeeze several obstructions together into one picture, for example, a row of billboards or power poles. This, we were sure, would convey the impact of unsightliness. We were wrong again. The resulting film footage was even more interesting than the first footage. Now we had interesting geometric patterns with signs and power lines trailing off into the distance—every bit as appealing as those pictures of railroad tracks stretching to a vanishing point across the prairie.

Despite our uncomfortable feelings about the footage we had, we decided to continue with our portfolio of unsightly objects. Our next target was garbage dumps. The first dump was an old slough being filled in with garbage and debris. There was still water in the slough, some cattails around the edge, and even some ducks that landed while we were filming. At the second location, a smoldering dump had been gouged into a hillside set in rolling, pastoral countryside, and there was a small family cemetery right beside the dump.

It was hard to miss the point. Obstructions appeared unsightly only because of the context in which they appeared—because they obstructed something worth seeing. It was only when we found ourselves in two situations where the context was so thoroughly intertwined with the obstructions that we got the point. Focus or emphasis on obstruction could be accomplished by juxtaposing obstructions and scenic landscape both spatially and in sequence. The sequence juxtaposition allowed us to salvage some of our earlier footage by interspersing shots of unobstructed landscape with shots of the potential obstructions.

The Focus Concept

This experience illustrates some things about *focus* as a journalistic concept. First, it is important to distinguish focus from related journalistic concepts. When you manipulate the focus on a camera, some objects within the camera frame are brought into sharp relief and others become fuzzy.

Observing the obstructions in juxtaposition with a scenic landscape brought the relation of obstructing into sharp relief. The concept of focus applies equally well to other media. Newspaper reporters often use an inverted pyramid structure as a focus device, or they use the flashback in feature material. These are both manipulations of sequence used to obtain a particular focus.

Simple changes in grammatical structure can even be used as powerful focus devices. Take, for example, verb voice. Journalistic practice tends to emphasize the use of active voice. This practice is really asserting that in any situation the focus should be upon the object doing the acting. But this rule for writing does not always serve our observations very well.

To illustrate just a few of the focus possibilities available in journalistic observations, Figure 2 diagrams four news focuses described recently by communication scientist Richard Carter.[1] The use of these news focuses is then shown in Figure 3 for a series of story leads on an environmental controversy.

Consideration of these four focus options reveals two useful principles of observation:

---

[1] Richard F. Carter, "A Journalistic View of Communication." Paper presented to Communication Theory and Methodology Division, Association for Education in Journalism, 1972, Carbondale, Illinois.

FIGURE 2 *Schematic Description for Four News Focus Options*

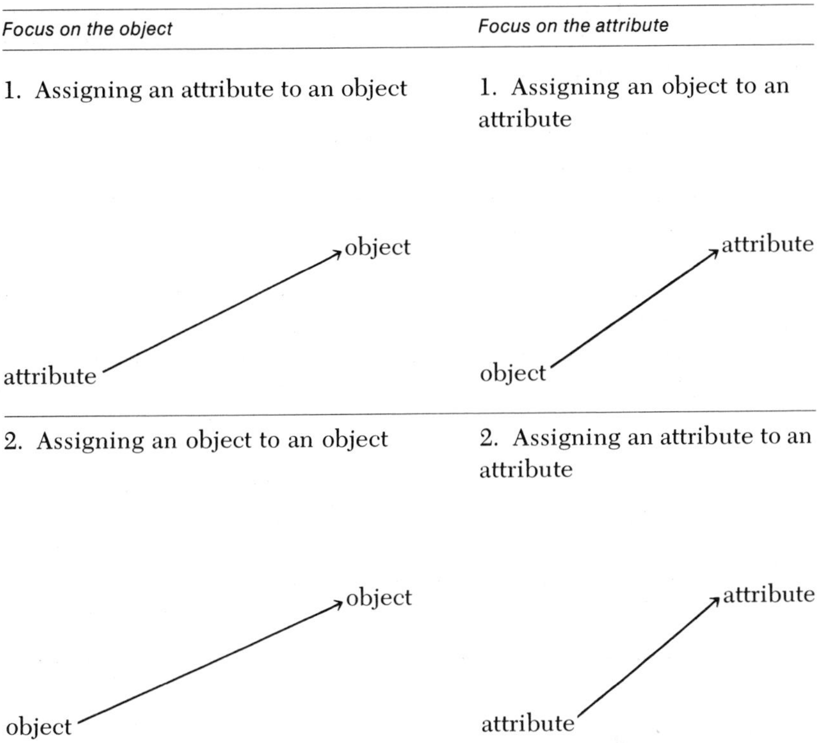

Focus on the object	Focus on the attribute
1. Assigning an attribute to an object	1. Assigning an object to an attribute

object

attribute

attribute

object

2. Assigning an object to an object	2. Assigning an attribute to an attribute

object

object

attribute

attribute

1. Object focuses lead to observations with human interest as the major news value.
2. Attribute focuses lead to observations with significance as the major news value.

Any of the four focuses, if pursued, will provide enough information for a news story. There would be differences, however, in the *observational techniques* used to implement each of these four focuses. An example is the environmental controversy referred to in Figure 3.

The story suggested by the first lead could be readily covered by using *participant observation*—for example, attending the

FIGURE 3   *Story Leads Illustrating Four Possible News Focuses*

"A spokesman for the Washington chapter of the Sierra Club, Robert E. Swan, made a point-by-point attack today on power company plans to raise the level of Diablo Dam."

"The leading critic today of power company plans to raise the level of Diablo Dam is a veteran environmentalist and spokesman for the Washington chapter of the Sierra Club. Robert Swan's many battles against 'progress' go all the way back to . . ."

"Today's testimony criticizing the proposed raising of the Diablo Dam typifies the long-standing opposition of 'environmentalism' to any plans to increase power production in the Northwest. The environmentalist view was exemplified in statements by Robert D. Swan, spokesman for the Washington chapter of the Sierra Club."

"Environmentalist sentiment expressed at yesterday's hearings on a proposal to raise Diablo Dam echoed a theme that has predominated at power company hearings in recent months. 'The environmentalist view is always present, and it is always critical of plans to increase electric power production,' said Albert Haas, vice president for Seattle City Light."

---

meeting and hearing Swan's criticisms. A *personal interview* with Swan would be appropriate for doing the personality sketch suggested by the second lead. The third story could be based in part on a *content analysis,* in which the statements made by Swan were analyzed for their manifestations of "environmentalism." Documentation that environmentalists are frequently critical of power company plans—as required by the fourth lead—could be derived from a *survey* or from a *content analysis.*

These focus options are not revolutionary journalistic practices. All the options have been utilized before, but object focuses have been used too often and attribute focuses have not been used often enough. And because the focus options have not been clearly defined, reporters have often become confused about which observational techniques would be most appropriate to document a given focus.

Conversely, journalists who have encountered techniques and data that do not fit an object focus have not been able to handle them. Take, for example, the tendency of journalists to use election poll data to fill in a picture of a horse race in a field of political candidates. The news media, despite themselves, give election coverage that focuses on candidates (objects) rather than on issues (the attributes).

An even better example of how the concept of focus can determine news coverage is the relative lack of news coverage on science. Scientists generally take an attribute focus, but journalists tend to force coverage of science into an object mold. The results are out-of-context announcements of "discoveries," that is, the "objects" produced by science, and personality sketches of scientists.

The Point-of-View Concept

The concept of *focus* is distinct from that of *point of view*. The two concepts often are confused and even treated identically, or lumped together. Point of view refers to the vantage point we take in relation to the situation we are observing.

A simple example of the distinction between the two concepts involves the camera. Point of view, or position, could simply refer to the physical location of the camera. Notice that the focus of the camera could be changed without changing the point of view. Notice, too, that changing the point of view without readjusting the focus would result in a focus change. This shows that in practice point of view and focus are interrelated, but they can be manipulated independently, providing you know something about the interrelationships.

The type of perspective built into the observers is a more complicated example of point of view. First, consider the point of view of the camera itself, which sees reality in terms of objects, with attributes like size and color as only properties of the objects. There is another possible view—that the objects are manifestations of underlying attributes—but the camera is not capable of taking that view.

To illustrate, suppose you were told to take a picture of sunshine. The only way that you could do it is by taking a picture of some consequence of sunshine. Any consequence of sunshine, as seen by a camera, invariably turns out to be an attribute or manifestation of an object—for example, a shadow or a reflection on the water. Thus, the only way that you can get a picture of sunshine is to photograph a shadow, a highlight on a leaf, a reflection, and so on.

Fortunately, you are not constrained to take the same point of view all the time. Sometimes you can develop a story better by combining two or more points of view. This is apparent in news reports where the written or oral report, which may use one or more points of view, is combined with news photos or film utilizing the camera's point of view.

Multiple points of view are very prevalent in film reports. In fact, they are imperative in television reporting if audio and pictoral tracks are not to be redundant. This point can be illustrated with another film-making experience. This time the object was a film series on wildflower communities. Community was the key word. We wanted people to see wildflowers from a community point of view. But that is an abstract point of view, so the camera by itself was incapable of handling it. To help people see more than the attributes of the individual flowers—as seen by the camera, of course—we used narrative and a series of abstracted drawings of community relationships.

Using Point of View

Manipulating point of view is yet another way to solve some common journalistic problems. The 1973 telecast of the tennis match between Billie Jean King and Bobby Riggs demonstrated that. From your recollection of the telecast, if you saw it, try analyzing the points of view yourself. My list turned up five points of view from which the match was being observed (and you may think of others). The strengths and weaknesses of that telecast reveal much about the general problem of managing point of view.

Howard Cosell pointed out early in the telecast that this event was more than another tennis match—it was *a happening*. The ABC program slug billed the match not as "King vs. Riggs" but as

"The Battle of the Sexes." There were points of view present that would not normally accompany a tennis match. The overriding points of view, if we take the "battle of the sexes" billing seriously, were male and female points of view.

A second encompassing point of view concerned the *game of tennis* itself. From the point of view of the game, what is the significance of using it as the vehicle for such a symbolic match? The possibility of increased popularity of the game beyond this particular event has many implications.

Neither of these points of view was directly concerned with the match. Many people who had never watched a tennis match before and knew nothing about the rules of the game found themselves watching because of these other points of view. King provided the focus for a *woman's point of view* and Riggs the focus for a *man's point of view*.

Finally, there is the *match* itself—the point of view from which the cameras observed what happened in time and space. What made it a "happening," however, was the presence of the other points of view.

That brings us to how ABC tried to cope with all of those points of view. First, there were numerous observers: several cameras providing several different physical points of view with instant replay, plus two tennis pros, one man and one woman, helping the sportscaster. The idea ostensibly was to report the event from all these points of view. But, as you may recall, ABC's observers did not all take the points of view they were assigned, and there were many difficulties in coordinating all the observers as well.

Conclusion

The thrust of this chapter has been to develop some ways of thinking about what *could* be observed in a news situation *before* observational techniques are selected. This amounts to a reversal of the generally prevailing practice in which techniques predetermine what is observed. By reversing this process, you can avoid being limited by the techniques that you know at a given time.

It must be kept in mind that any observational technique is a product of a desire to observe the world in a particular way. The invention of the microscope, for example, provided a technique for observing tiny organisms. It is not a useful instrument for observing a legislative hearing. If you learn more carefully the range of observations that are possible, you will be able to select appropriate techniques better, and even to identify the need for new ones. Selection of appropriate methods of observation is, after all, what reporting and this book is all about.

Author And Source Index

(See also Subject and Topic Index)

Subject and Topic Index

(See also Author Index)

real-estate discrimination, 244–245,
    256, 263–264
suburban life, 25
white man poses as, 218–219
Bly, Nellie, 212, 214
body language, 203–205, 302
Bosworth's Community Services scale,
    111–112
boundary concept, 315
Bow, Clara, 196
broadcasting, data presented on, 277
"buzz words," 277, 283
bystanders
    intervention by, 270
    theft report by, 267

Caldwell, Earl, 179
callbacks, 98, 131
Candid Camera, 252
capital punishment, 56
car
    inspection, 252, 254
    repair, 252–253, 265
    stopping to aid victim, 260
    vandalism, 49
Case, Herbert W., 56
causal analysis, 245–249
causal inference, 54–58, 72–75
causation, and correlation, 283–284
CBS Evening News, 292–293
censuses, 124
Chambers of Commerce, 170
chance fluctuations, 260
change
    across cultures, 146–147
    across time, 146–147
    technological, 231, 307–308
"checkbook journalism," 206
checklists, 224–227
Chicago Daily News, 91, 244–245, 256,
    263–264
Chicago Tribune, 49–50, 212, 240
Chicanos, coverage of, 179
Chinese, discrimination against,
    251–252
chi-square, 120–121, 261
city-block series, 239–240
city directories, 168–169
clarity, 304
classification of news, 293–295
cluster analysis, 150
cluster sampling, 131–132
coal-mining survey, 104–105
coding
    for content analysis, 154–157
    reliability of, 61–63, 145

cognitive dissonance, 182
columns and columnists
    interpretation by, 45–46
    lovelorn, 147–149, 150
    problem-solving, 152–163, 167
Committee to Re-elect the President,
    178, 206–207
communication, nonverbal, 202–205
communities
    assessing social programs of, 23–27
    content analysis of, 145–147
    data analysis of information on,
        273–291
    documents of, 139–173
    how to obtain information on, 139–
        173
    performance of, 23
    physical capital of, 20–21
    records, 139–173
    social capital of, 21–22
    structure of, 23
    systems theory for, 23
Community Services scale, 111–112
computer studies
    on crime information, 31
    on Philadelphia courts, 163–166
computerized record systems, 32–34
concentration of media ownership, 307
concepts
    new, 314–324
    quantitative, 277–284
    traditional, 292–313
conciseness, 304
confidence in press, 301
confidence interval, 136–137
constraints on reporter, 292–305
consumer-problems column, 152–163,
    167
consumption
    of news, 308
    of public goods, 22
content analysis, 139–173
    of a community, 145–147
    of community records, 167–172
    of court reporting, 34
    decision points in, 151–167
    defined, 140–145
    of documents, 132–133
    examples of, 151–167, 320
    hypothesis for, 144
    information collection for, 156–158
    of media bias, 167
    of media content, 147–151
    need for care in using, 172–173
    objective observation for, 144
    operational definitions for, 156
    and participant behavior, 232
    reliability coefficient for, 61–62

content analysis (*continued*)
   reporting findings, 163–167
   study objectives, 152–153
   systematic observation for, 145
   universe for, 153
controlled experiments, 73, 245–253
convergent validation, 176
copy editor, 306
correlation
   artifactual, 284
   and causation, 283–284
   coefficients, 61, 62
   spurious, 284
Cosell, Howard, 322
cost
   of polls, 97–99
   of prescriptions, 268
county clerk records, 169
court
   records, 171
   reporting, 34
courts, criminal, 163–166
credit bureaus, 170
crime
   citizen reaction to, 75–76
   computer information on, 31
   index of daily, 45–46
   journalist's vs. scientist's approach
     to, 44–46
   obscenity and pornography's effect
     on, 55–57
   Philadelphia courts' treatment of,
     163–166
   rates of NYC precincts, 32–33
   unreported, 172–173
   witnesses to, 252, 255, 262, 266–267
"Crime Count, The", 45–46
criterion variable, 158
Cronkite, Walter, 43, 292–293
cross-tabulation, 118–121
crowd size, estimation of, 67–68
cultural change, 146–147

daily city life, series on, 239–240
Daniel, Clifton, 67
Darwin, Charles, 248, 258
data
   analysis of, 116–121, 273–291
   on crime, 31
   presentation of, 273–291
   tables, 121–122
debates, political, 39–40
decade study, 15–17
deception in research, 75–76
decision makers for news presentation,
   306–307

decision points in content analysis,
   151–167
definitions
   of content analysis, 144
   of news, 308–309
   operational, coding of, 156–157
delayed reward, 294
demographic analysis, 117–118
dependent variables, 107–108, 110,
   120, 246–247, 254, 257
Detroit Free Press, 179
Detroit News, 240–241
Diablo Dam, 320
Diefenbaker, John, 198–199
directories, city, 168–169
discrimination, *see* racial discrimination
dissonance, 182
distortion, 217–218, 230–232
documents
   content analysis of, 139–173
   sampling of, 132–133
   what they don't tell, 172–173
   see also records
Dylan, Bob, 76
dynamite purchase, 251, 264–265

Eagleton, Thomas, 214
eavesdropping, 36–37
economics, 8–14, 24–25, 59
editors
   as gatekeepers of news, 305–308
   letters to, 149–151
elements, news, 295–305
empiricism, 47, 55, 120, 135, 261
environmental problems, 11–12, 240–
   241, 318–320
error in interviewing, 180–200
   reporter's, 180–193
   and respondent bias, 193–200
error in sampling, *see* sampling error
Esquire, 76
estimation
   of crowd size, 67–68
   numerical, 280–281
   and sampling error, 134–137
ethics
   of behavior research, 75–76
   of eavesdropping, 36–37
   of field experiments, 261–262
   of interviewing, 203–209
ethnic background, 179–180
evaluation
   of polls, 81–95
   research on, 25–26
events, news, 3–5

inferences (*continued*)
  defined, 47
  unjustified, 54–56
  use in content analysis, 141–144
informant, socially marginal, 229
information
  analysis of, 158–163
  from data, 273–291
  qualitative, 34
  quantitative, 34
  from surveys, 116–121
  validity of, 221
insanity-sanity study, 211–223 *passim*,
    234–237
internal validity, 69
inter-observer validity, 61
interpretation, *see* content analysis;
    data analysis
interval for sampling, 130
interviewing
  accuracy in, 298
  ethics of, 203–209
  examples of good, 196, 201–202,
    209–210, 320
  face-to-face, 97–103
  interviewers, 89, 91, 114–116
  man-in-the-street, 125–126
  modes of, 97–103
  and nonverbal communication, 202–
    205
  observation in, 201–203, 215
  off-the-record, 208
  personal vs. telephone, 298
  for polls, 97–103
  reporter error in, 189–193
  respondent bias in, 193–200
  sample for, 87
  self-serving, 198–199
  shortcomings of, 245, 250
  timing of, 92
  tips on question clarity, 187–190
  weakness as a reporting method, 245
  see also polls
invasion of privacy, 205–206

Jackson, Richard, 198–199
Johnson, Junior, 201–202
journalistic fallacies, 51–58
journalists
  compared with novelists, 304–305
  as content analysts, 144–145
  ethics of, 75–76
  role of, 43
  students, 185, 301–302
  use of scientific method by, 42–77
  see also reporters

judgment, definition of, 47
judges, of content, 61–63

Kennedy, John F.
  assassination of, 58
  debates with Nixon, 39–40
  and integration issue, 183
  quoted, 14
kinesics, 203, 204
King, Billie Jean, 322–323
King, Martin Luther, 179, 217
Kingdom and the Power, The, 67
Kuralt, Charles, 201, 294

language, nonverbal, 202–205, 302
letters to the editor, 149–150
libraries
  as news source, 106
  newsroom, 168
  public, 169
Lindsay, John, 126–127
Literary Digest, 127
lotteries, 128
Loud family, 229
Louisville studies, 15–16, 104–105
lovelorn columns, 147–149, 150

McCarthy, Joseph, 7, 209
McGovern-Nixon election, 134
McIntire, Carl, 67
magazines
  on behavioral science, 50
  change as affecting, 312
  letters to the editor in, 149
mail-delivery survey, 247, 249, 265–
    266
mail questionnaires, 91–92, 97–103
man-in-the-street interviews, 53–54,
    69, 96, 125–126
mapping, behavioral, 34
marginals, 120
Markel, Lester, 67
mean, 279–281, 288, 290
measurement, scientific, 60–61
media
  bias, 167
  as community indicators, 147–151
  concentrated ownership of, 307
  content analysis of, 147–151
  coverage of U.S. Senators, 147
  use by blacks, 39
  voters' use of, 118–120
  see also press

median, 279–281, 288, 290
mental hospitals, 211–223 *passim*, 234–237
methods of reporting, *see* reporting methods
Miami's WCKT-TV, 75–76, 252, 255, 262, 266–268
Michigan Survey Research Center, 39
Milwaukee Journal, 251–252, 264–265
Mind, Self and Society, 224
minority groups
  interviewing of, 179–180
  sampling of, 91
  at University of Texas, 66
  see also blacks
misquoting, 190–191
mode, 279–281, 288, 290
modeling, in field experiments, 260, 267
model of news, 315–316
Montreal factory worker series, 240, 242–243
morgue, newspaper, 106
Morton, Bruce, 43
mosaics, social, 8–11, 28
motivation, in interviewing, 197–200
Moyers, Bill, 48
multiple operationism, 34–41, 176
multi-stage sample, 129–132

National Opinion Research Center, 150
Negroes, *see* blacks
Negro Yearbook, 59
Neilson, Judith, 270
"new journalists," 66–67, 201–202, 238, 313
New York
  daily life on city block, 239–240
  precinct crime rates, 32–33
The New York Times
  Corry pieces on city block, 239–240
  slogan, 292–293
  syndicate, 311
  Talese study of, 67
  treatment of polls, 83–84
news
  accuracy in, 295–299
  "bad," 7–8, 14–15, 294
  classification of, 293–295
  as consumer product, 308
  data for, 273–291
  decisions on presentation of, 305–308
  definition of, 308–309
  elements of, 295–305
  events, 3–4, 6, 43, 275

feature, 293
functionally organized, 310–311
geographically organized, 310
"good," 7, 14–15, 294
hard, 293
model of, 315–316
nature of, 273–324
new concepts of, 314–324
new sources of, 30–34
objectivity of, 299–303
reporters' bias on, 185–186
soft, 293
straight, 293
timeliness of, 303–304
traditional concepts of, 292–313
news beat, 27–30, 309–313
news conferences, 188
news media, *see* media
news syndicates, 311
The News Twisters, 62–63
newspapers, *see* press
newsroom
  libraries, 168
  situation as determining news, 305–308
Nixon, Richard M.
  attack on press, 301
  debates with Kennedy, 39–40
  and integration issue, 183
  news conferences of, 188
  poll on 1972 election, 134
  tax problems, 38
  Watergate transcripts, 139–141
Nixon Administration, coverage on, 9–11
"no comment," 199
non-objectivity, 47–48. *See also* bias
non-probability, 124
non-response, 87, 99–100
nonverbal communication, 202–205
North Carolina Gazette, 84
note-taking
  during interviews, 192
  for participant observation, 229–234
novelists-journalist study, 304–305
numbers, use of, 274–275
nursing homes, 49–50

obedience studies, 75, 250, 256
obituaries, 151
objectivity
  and attribution, 63, 66
  of news, 299–303
  as not possible, 47–48
  of observation, 144–145
  see also bias

post hoc, ergo propter hoc, 56–58
postal survey, 247, 249, 265–266
precinct crime rate, 32–33
Precision Journalism, 83
prescription costs, 268
Presidential nomination acceptance speeches, 146–147
press
 confidence in, 136–137
 criticism of, 7–8
 focus of, 6–8
 Nixon's attack on, 301
 treatment of polls, 83–85
 watchdog role of, 18, 22, 24
 see also media; news
press conferences, 4, 188, 301
press releases, 298
pretesting a questionnaire, 113–114
priorities, social, 18–22
prison brutality, 49
privacy, invasion of, 205–206
probability
 estimate, 120–121
 sample, 84, 88, 125–132
problem-solving column, 152–163, 167
Procaccino, Mario, 126–127
prostitution story, 220–221
proxemics, 205
proximity, as news element, 303
pseudo-event, 4–5
psychiatric patients, 211–223 *passim*, 234–237
psychological distance, 303
Psychology Today, 50
public libraries, 169
public records
 content analysis of, 132–133, 139–173
 as news source, 30–34
 secondary analysis of, 38–41
 see also documents

quantification, 34, 60–61
quantitative data, 274–291
questionnaires
 design of, 106–108
 mail, 91–92, 97–103
 wording of, 92–93
 see also polls
questions
 focal, 314
 for interviews, 187–190
 for participant observation, 224–226
 for polls, 108–110
 for surveys, 100–101, 106–108
quota sampling, 127–128
quoting from interviews, 190, 302

race
 and consumer problems, 161–162
 and interviewing, 179–180
 manipulation in experiments, 257
 observations of white man, 218–219
race riots, 217, 232
racial discrimination
 against Chinese, 251–252
 in housing, 244–245, 256, 263–264
 in public accommodations, 268–269
 in suburbia, 25
Radical Chic, 67
Raleigh, N.C. community problems, 152–163, 167
Raleigh Star, 84
random number tables, 129
random sampling, 52–53, 69, 128–132
randomization in experiments, 258
ratio, 281–282
Raymond, Alan, 229
Raymond, Susan, 229
The Reach of Science, 43
real-estate discrimination, 244–245, 256, 263–264
recording, tape, 191–192, 208
records
 content analysis of, 139–173
 as news source, 30–34
 secondary analysis of, 38–41
 traditional community, 167–171
 see also documents
reliability
 check, 157–159
 coefficient, 61
 of content analysis information, 157–159
 of observation, 61–69
 of polls, 85
 of scientific data, 47
 see also validity
reporters
 anonymity of, 207–208, 227
 black, 179–180
 constraints on, 295–305
 danger to, 236–237
 distortions by, 217–218, 230–232
 interviewing by, 174–210
 methods of, 81–270
 as participant observers, 211–243
 predispositions about news, 185–186
 as processors of information, 277
 strategies for, 3–77
 use of scientific method by, 42–77
 use of social indicators by, 3–41
 see also journalist
reporting methods, 81–270
 behavioral vs. verbal, 250–252
 community records' use, 139–173

social priorities, 18–19, 21–22
social programs, assessment of, 23–27
social trends, 8–19
Society, 50
sociology, 50–51. *See also* behavioral
    science
soft news, 293
speeches, Presidential acceptance,
    146–147
"spitball" story, 175
sponsor of a poll, 86
spot coverage, 304
standard deviation, 136
standards for polls, 85–86, 94–95
standby research, 26–27
states of the union, 62–63
Statistical Services, 31
statistics
    data presentation by, 282–283
    of field experiments, 259–260
    interpretation of, 10–11
    of sampling error, 136
    for survey tabulation, 119–121
    use of, 10–14, 38, 61
stereotyping, 218
straight news, 293
strategies for reporting
    use of scientific method, 42–77
    use of social indicators, 3–41
stratification in sampling, 131
straw polls, 84, 125–127
strip-mining survey, 104–105
student directory, 70
suburbia
    pollution in, 240–241
    racial discrimination in, 25
    social trends in, 51
surveys, *see* polls; sampling
Swan, Robert D., 320
symbolic interaction, 224–225
Syracuse University School of Public
    Communications, 169
systems theory, 23

tables
    for cross-tabulation, 118–122
    of survey data, 117–121
    use of, 290
tape recorders, 191–192, 208
tax offices, 170
techniques of observation, 34–41
technological change, 231, 307–308
telephone
    book, 168
    interviews, 298
    surveys, 91–92, 97–103, 135, 192–193
    unlisted, 102

television
    data presentation on, 277
    sets, repair of, 268
ten-year city study, 15–17, 151
terminology, choice of, 284–286
Test, Mary Ann, 260, 267
test, statistical, 260–261
Texas, University of, *see* University of
    Texas
theory
    journalists' use of, 69–71
    in scientific method, 59
time, change across, 18, 147
Time magazine, 47–48
timeliness of news, 303–304
time-order evidence, 247, 284
timing of interviews, 92
Toronto Telegram, 198–199
traditional concepts of news, 292–313
Transaction, 50
transcripts, Watergate, 139–141
trend designs, 38–41
Truman, Margaret, 67

unemployment, ads as index to, 35
unit
    of analysis, 278
    for sampling, 130
United Press International, 5, 90, 299,
    306–307, 311
universe, in content analysis, 153
University of Texas
    minorities at, 66
    student directory, 70
unlisted telephones, 102
Unobtrusive Measures, 76, 230
unreported crime, 172–173
unrepresentative sample, 51–52, 126
UPI, *see* United Press International
urban
    crisis, 24–25, 32–33
    life in NYC, 239–240
U.S. Senators' news visibility, 147–149

validity
    convergent, 176
    external, 69, 102
    internal, 69
    of observation, 61–69
    of polls, 85
    of sample, 133–134
    of survey data, 116
    see also reliability
vandalism, 49
variables, presentation of, 277–279

verb voice, 318
verbal reports, 250–252
Vietnam
  demonstration coverage, 186
  participant observation study, 238
viewpoint, 321–322
violence
  coverage of, 55–58
  journalist's vs. scientist's approach
    to, 44–46
voter registration records, 160–161
voters' use of media, 118–122

W's and H technique
Washington, D.C. riots, 217, 232
Washington Post, 177, 179, 206, 299,
  311
Washington Post-Los Angeles Times
  syndicate, 311
Washington Star, 179
watchdog role of press, 18, 22, 24, 83
Watergate coverage, 51–52, 118–122,
  139–141, 177–178, 206–207, 299,
  311–313

WATS lines, 98
WCKT-TV, Miami, 75–76, 252, 255,
  262, 266–268
Weberman, A. J., 76
welfare hotel, 223
welfare mothers, 116
White, Theodore, 48
wire services
  accuracy of, 298–299
  competition among, 307
  hard news stressed by, 311
  national digests, 306
  see also Associated Press; United
    Press International
witnesses to crime, 252, 255, 262,
  266–267
Woodward, Bob, 177–178, 200, 206–
  207, 312–313
word
  choice, 284–286
  use and objectivity, 302
"The Worst American State," 62–63

zip code survey, 247, 249, 265–266